De-centering queer theory

Manchester University Press

THEORY FOR A GLOBAL AGE

Series Editor: Gurminder K. Bhambra, Professor of Postcolonial and Decolonial Studies in the School of Global Studies, University of Sussex

Globalization is widely viewed as a current condition of the world, but there is little engagement with how this changes the way we understand it. The Theory for a Global Age series addresses the impact of globalization on the social sciences and humanities. Each title will focus on a particular theoretical issue or topic of empirical controversy and debate, addressing theory in a more global and interconnected manner. With contributions from scholars across the globe, the series will explore different perspectives to examine globalization from a global viewpoint. True to its global character, the Theory for a Global Age series will be available for online access worldwide via Creative Commons licensing, aiming to stimulate wide debate within academia and beyond.

Previously published by Bloomsbury:

Connected sociologies   Gurminder K. Bhambra

Eurafrica: The untold history of European integration and colonialism   Peo Hansen and Stefan Jonsson

On sovereignty and other political delusions   Joan Cocks

Postcolonial piracy: Media distribution and cultural production in the global south   Edited by Lars Eckstein and Anja Schwarz

The Black Pacific: Anti-colonial struggles and oceanic connections   Robbie Shilliam

Democracy and revolutionary politics   Neera Chandhoke

Published by Manchester University Press:

Race and the Yugoslav region: Postsocialist, post-conflict, postcolonial?   Catherine Baker

Debt as power   Tim Di Muzio and Richard H. Robbins

Subjects of modernity: Time-space, disciplines, margins   Saurabh Dube

Frontiers of the Caribbean   Phillip Nanton

John Dewey: The global public and its problems   John Narayan

Bordering intimacy: Postcolonial governance and the policing of family   Joe Turner

Diaspora as translation and decolonisation   Ipek Demir

De-centering queer theory

Communist sexuality in the flow during and after the Cold War

Bogdan Popa

MANCHESTER UNIVERSITY PRESS

Copyright © Bogdan Popa 2021

The right of Bogdan Popa to be identified as the author
of this work has been asserted by him in accordance with the
Copyright, Designs and Patents Act 1988.

Published by Manchester University Press
Oxford Road, Manchester M13 9PL

www.manchesteruniversitypress.co.uk

British Library Cataloguing-in-Publication Data
A catalogue record for this book is available from the British Library

ISBN 978 1 5261 5695 2 hardback
ISBN 978 1 5261 7465 9 paperback

First published 2021

The publisher has no responsibility for the persistence or
accuracy of URLs for any external or third-party internet
websites referred to in this book, and does not guarantee
that any content on such websites is, or will remain, accurate
or appropriate.

Typeset by Newgen Publishing UK

Contents

List of figures	page vi
Series editor's foreword	vii
Acknowledgments	ix

Part I: Communist sexuality in the flow   1

1 A materialist conception of queer theory   3

Part II: Gender and the erasure of Soviet Marxist epistemology   37

2 Productive bodies in eastern European Marxism   43
3 The birth of gender epistemology during the Cold War   70
4 Marxism and queer theory at the end of the Cold War   97

Part III: De-contextualizing Marxism   131

5 Abolition   137
6 Counterfetish   157
7 The unconscious   178
8 Trans   200
9 The future of queer communism   219

Bibliography   226
Index   240

Figures

1 *Cultural Revolution*, by Ion Grigorescu.
  Photo courtesy of Maria Alina Asavei   *page* 102
2 *Masculine/Feminine*, by Ion Grigorescu.
  Photo courtesy of Maria Alina Asavei   103
3 *The 13th Congress: Politics with Sweets*, by
  Ion Panaitescu. Photo courtesy of PostModernism
  Museum, https://postmodernism.ro
  (accessed July 25, 2021).   104

Series editor's foreword

The Cold War occupied much attention in the social sciences, from modernization theory to civilizational analysis. In his exciting new book, *De-centering Queer theory: Communist sexuality in the flow during and after the Cold War*, Bogdan Popa examines the ways in which understandings of gender and queer theory were configured during this period. He expertly brings socialist theory into conversation with eastern European Marxist films in order to understand better the repertoires of contemporary queer theory, many of which have been lost to dominant understandings. The aim, in part, is to de-center the US grounding of much queer theory and resituate its categories and concepts within a more materialist understanding of history.

The innovative use of eastern European film as the focus of the analysis offers the possibility of thinking through alternative epistemological frameworks that enable a more critical understanding of capitalism and its intersections with the construction of ideas of gender and sexuality. The key themes at the heart of Popa's analysis are the ways in which particular understandings of the body and sexuality were configured during the Cold War period and, more specifically, the ways in which some understandings were erased. Popa also astutely explores the extent to which liberal queer theory might be considered complicit in the elimination of a communist sexuality, to its detriment.

The Theory for a Global Age series, of which this book is part, provides space to rethink the concepts and categories central to disciplinary understandings from the experiences of those who are rarely made central to such processes. Through its focus on the conjunctions between queer and socialist theory, and its attention to film materials and theoretical resources from an eastern European archive, *De-centering Queer Theory: Communist sexuality in the flow during and after the Cold War* constructs an alternative analytical framework to think through our contemporary times. It is a superb book that reorients our understandings of gender and sexuality by drawing attention to the erased archives of Soviet Marxism, and points to what there is to learn by bringing these aspects into conversation with each other.

Gurminder K. Bhambra
University of Sussex

Acknowledgments

I have presented material from drafts of this book to audiences at the Centre for Gender Studies and the "Queer Cultures" conference, University of Cambridge; the Association for Political Theory, University of Oxford; the London Conference in Critical Thought, Department of Sociology at Goldsmiths, University of London; the workshop on "Cinema & teoria critica," Pompeu Fabra University, Barcelona; the American Studies Association, Atlanta; the Greyzone Workshop, University of Edinburgh; the American Political Science Association (APSA), Boston, MA; the "Race at the Juncture" conference, Queen Mary University of London; and the Centre for Memory, Narrative and Histories [CMNH] Symposium, "Blackness and the Complex Temporalities of the Transatlantic Slave Trade," University of Brighton. I want to thank my hosts and interlocutors for their warm reception and insightful questions. The book would also have been less clear without the help of the editor at Manchester University Press, Tom Dark; the series editor, Gurminder Bhambra; and the three anonymous reviewers for the Press.

The time I spent teaching in England was instrumental in developing the core argument of the book. In particular I want to thank Mihaela Mihai, Lauren Wilcox, Julienne Obadia, Jude Browne, Lisa Baraister, Kerry Mackereth, and the organizers of both the Cambridge "Queer Cultures" conference and the CMNH Symposium at University of Brighton. In the United States I received important feedback from Danielle Skeehan, Erin McElroy, Shana Leodar Ye, Tiffany Willoughby Herard, Jasmine Yarish, Matthew Bowker, David McIvor and Yukari Yanagino. In Spain I benefited from the insights of Camil Ungureanu. Of course, the project could not have been possible without the conversations I had in Bucharest and Belgrade with Mihai Lukács, Erin McElroy, Ovidiu Pop, Veda Popovici, Crenguța Mihăilă-Podolan, Livia Pancu, Florin Bobu and Noah Treister. Portions of this work have appeared in previous publications, including *Law, Culture and Humanities* ("The Future of Stalinist Art," 2020 online publication); the *Journal of Psycho-Social Studies* ("Laplanche and the Antiracist Unconscious," 2020 online publication); and *The Undecidable Unconscious: A Journal of Deconstruction and Psychoanalysis*, 5 (2018), 27–53 ("Trans* and Legacies of Socialism: Reading Queer Postsocialism in *Tangerine*").

There would be no book without the vital support of my parents, Maria and Vali Popa. The socialist world that I lived in for my first twelve years constitutes the reason and justification for taking on this project.

Part I

Communist sexuality in the flow

The role of Part I is to introduce readers to the overall argument and offer them a map to navigate it in Parts II and III. This part explains why queer theory needs not only a deeper materialist understanding of its emergence and theoretical production, but also a novel approach to its epistemology. I call it "Communist sexuality in the flow" because I seek to anchor queer theory in a Marxist understanding of sexuality, which was articulated as part of a communist project in eastern Europe. In the first section of Part I, I explain that queer theory has to be infused with historical materialism, given its historical emergence at the end of the Cold War and its development in US academia. In the part's second section, I argue that my intervention is not only a historical account of queer studies, but also a theoretical contribution that revitalizes a field that has been shaped by anti-communism. Finally, I offer brief definitions of key conceptual terms and describe the organization of the book.

1

A materialist conception of queer theory

Queer studies has been recently called to interrogate more forcefully its history and genealogical production. In a 2020 special issue of *Social Text* titled "Left of Queer," David Eng and Jasbir Puar advance the argument that the cleaving of Marxism from queer studies has been a major inflection point that has as a consequence the return of right-wing nationalisms and call-out cultures across the political spectrum.[1] Previously, in a 2012 *GLQ* issue titled *Queer Studies and the Crisis of Capitalism*, Jordana Rosenberg and Amy Villarejo called for a methodology that was attuned to both sexuality and the specificities of capitalist crises.[2] To undo the deadlock between queer studies and Marxism, the queer left seeks to move away from its specialized object of research – sexuality –, break the impasse between queer and working-class politics, and unpack distinct and overlapping conceptions of social positionality and subjectivity.[3] Hearing to the invitation to think about Marxism and queer theory together, *De-centering queer theory* has a similar ambition to introduce historical materialism into queer theory, but its main strategy is to understand the theoretical impasses that derive from the emergence of the field's vocabulary. I begin from Marx's suggestion that historical materialism as a method needs to start from historicizing its objects of analysis or, as he put it, the birth of communism is the process of making sense of historical transformations.[4] To advance the movement to transform and shift queer studies from its conventional objects of analysis, I look at the Cold War as the driving social formation for understanding categories such as gender and queer. In so doing, I reorient queer theory to a different conception of bodies and sexuality that was based on a dialectical theory of human emancipation and was dominant in eastern European socialist countries during the Cold War. The main purpose of bringing the history of communist sexuality into queer theory is to expand the movement to abolish its current boundaries and demarcations, which hinder its theoretical force.

A materialist conception of queer theory has to take seriously the historical binaries that are constitutive to the field. The key contribution of the book is to articulate a contrast between the concept of a productive body, which draws its epistemology from Soviet theorists, and the notion of Cold War gender, which is defined as the social construction of the body. In Soviet Marxism, productive bodies were theorized against the idea of an individual identity and functioned as vehicles to achieve communism. According to an anti-capitalist philosophy that was at war with western capitalism, categories such as man and woman were articulated in a dialectical relationship to produce the emancipation of human beings. In turn, by Cold War gender, I understand a specific anti-communist ideology about bodies that is derived from the idea of personal identity and freedom. The concept of gender was articulated in the mid-1950s United States to distinguish between a biological body and its cultural/social understanding, and drew its logic from social constructivism. The theory that drew on social construction and identities as key analytical tools was a dominant anti-communist social science program, which was put forward explicitly as a competitor to Marxist-Leninist science.[5] By explaining the historical emergence of a Cold War epistemological rivalry, the book shows that a dialectical conception focusing on communist sexuality breaks the impasse between Marxism and queer studies. It does so by contributing to various queer intersections such as the abolition of gender, the materiality of queerness, the conceptualization of the unconscious and the historicity of trans studies.

Eng and Puar noticed that queer theory has become "its own particular form of US area studies – one that takes American exceptionalism, its political economy and popular culture, as its unspoken premise."[6] Building on this observation, the book's findings de-center queer theory in two ways. First, they offer not only a historical angle to understand the emergence of queer theory's vocabulary, but also an alternative epistemology that has at its core a communist theory of emancipation. Second, they introduce Marxist dialectics and film materials into queer studies, which often neglected to engage critically the capitalist underpinnings of liberal societies. Many studies showed that terms such as "gender" and "queer" were deployed in American cultural studies after the nominal end of the Cold War to interrogate the essentialized nature of sexual identities.[7] Queer theory, which is understood as an avant-garde political and aesthetic movement not unlike Dada and the Situationist International, has transformed their meanings and suggested a new theoretical deconstructivist approach to sexuality.[8] Judith Butler's "gender" was a term that challenged binaries such as nature vs. culture, while "queer" has increasingly been deployed as a concept to link various critical approaches to sexuality, nation, imperialism and race. The move to a post-identitarian and subjectless queer theory, however, has not been supplemented with analyses that investigated competing ideological understandings of sexuality. This study explores the rival model of communist sexuality with the goal of taking queer theory out of its American exceptionalist narrative and anchoring it in a materialist conception of history.

I focus on communism in eastern Europe because of the lingering anti-communist histories and legacies in queer studies. My main concern is that queer theorists have not directly confronted the ideological and historical problem of the power struggle between eastern European Marxism (also called Marxism-Leninism) and liberal capitalism. Although important studies such as Rosemary Hennessy's, Kevin Floyd's and Petrus Liu's have analyzed the relationship between Marxism and queer theory, the standpoint of the conflict between the eastern European Marxist world and western liberal capitalism has been rarely touched upon.[9] These authors called for an increased attention to Marxism in queer studies, and gestured to a historicized view of the emergence of US categories for sexual and gender identities. Petrus Liu, in particular, advanced a Chinese queer Marxism that offered a distinctive analysis of systemic workings of power, the project of decolonization in Asia and the study of capitalism in relation to modernity theories.[10] What *De-centering queer theory* adds to this literature is an analysis of the process by which eastern communist sexuality has been erased as an alternative epistemological and ideological formation during the Cold War. While Keti Chukhrov has investigated the theoretical contrast between Soviet models of sexuality and western theories of sexual liberation, an exploration of this conflict focusing on the historical changes during and after the Cold War is needed.[11] Also, this book provides a dialectical understanding of social transformation that has been missing from queer theory. I develop a theoretical hybrid that I call decontextualization, by juxtaposing socialist theory, an archive of Marxist films and queer anti-racist theory. In working with this method, I draw on arguments that show the common historical materialist and queer interest in concepts such as totality (which locates sexuality as part of a totality such as global capitalism) and the critique of reification (which criticizes the abstraction of labor from social categories).[12] Decontextualization is not unlike the tactics of the Situationist International in its intention to transcend the division between Marxism and cultural criticism.[13] Like détournement, the goal of my dialectical method is to set side by side two fields – socialist films and queer anti-racist theory – that have been designed to be antagonistic and generate a third analytic, which I call queer communism.[14]

The book derives its energy from a suspicion that queer theory's terminology is a device to universalize a US-led production of epistemic categories, which has elided other critical traditions that oppose the ideology of market economy. The material I work with is constituted primarily by socialist theory and eastern European Marxist films because they offer an alternative standpoint to understand the vocabulary of contemporary queer theory. This is why I ask: How was a specific Marxist understanding of bodies and sexuality erased during the Cold War? The second question follows the consequences of this erasure, but focuses on the post-Cold War period: If queer theory was a participant in the elimination of a communist sexuality, what alternative analytic can be forged to reinsert historical materialism into a queer anti-racist scholarship?

I answer these inquiries by following two routes. In Part II of the book, I turn to Soviet Marxism to reconstruct an alternative epistemology because it offered a communist model of how bodies interact and feel politically.[15] I coin the concept of productive body from Soviet Marxism, particularly from the work of the leading figures of the Proletarian Culture movement (Proletkult), Alexander Bogdanov and Boris Arvatov. As Emma Widdis argues, "the early revolutionary avant-garde envisaged the construction of the new Soviet subject as taking place first and foremost through the body."[16] For Arvatov, the new Soviet individual is a psycho-physiological project, which meant two things: "the dominance of the monistic vision of mind and body, and the proximity between cultural production and psychological/physiological science."[17] According to these theorists, a dialectical mode of production generates a new anti-capitalist Soviet person who has a higher affective and intellectual life than capitalist people.[18]

The anti-communist Cold War was an attack not only on the economy of socialists, but also on the type of sexed bodies and sexuality forged by Soviet Marxists.[19] The study traces the conflict of competing theories from early Soviet theory, to the birth of gender epistemology in the USA in the mid-1950s, to queer studies at the end of the 1980s. To differentiate between a pre-1980s version of gender in the USA and a post-1980 deconstructivist gender, I name the first "Cold War gender" and the second "post-Cold War gender." I choose the 1980s, and particularly the end of this period, as an indicator of a shift in the meaning of gender because the rise of cultural studies, queer liberalism and poststructuralism is located in this interval.[20] To explain the difference between the two historical genders, when I talk about pre-1980s gender, I mean specifically the thesis that social gender constructs biological sex. Unlike this concept, post-Cold War gender refuses the distinction between sex and culture and analyzes sexuality as a product of psychological and social processes. While, during the Cold War, gender was directly opposed to communist sexuality, Marxism was gradually eliminated as a generative epistemology in queer theory. Rosemary Hennessy and, more recently, Petrus Liu, have investigated the gradual process of the eradication of Marxism, with a particular focus on Gayle Rubin's queer theory.[21] To this previous scholarship, I add a comparative perspective looking at the elision of Marxism from both eastern Europe and North America at the end of the Cold War. While I argue that the theory of race, gender and class became a dominant analytic in US Left theory after the 1990s, I also illuminate the impulse in queer theory to produce a theoretical alternative to historical materialism.

In Part III, the book changes its goal and method. Rather than thinking about socialist and queer sexuality as disconnected, I use their shared history to build dialectically a queer communist analytic. My first objective is to add to queer anti-racist theory an explicit materialist dimension that shows how the abolition of gender was theoretically possible in eastern European socialism.

Queer anti-racist theory and socialism have a shared history of seeking to eliminate gender in capitalism and build a broader global anti-racist coalition. While the political claim to abolish gender roles is highly influential in US queer and cultural studies, communist history has the advantage of showing how such a radical goal was articulated. My second objective is to demonstrate that the materiality of communist history can reveal a different conception of queer resources. Needs-based socialist materiality points to a vast historical infrastructure that was produced by Marxist economies and circulates under new conditions of global capitalism. Also, eastern European Marxism infuses psychoanalytical theory with a materialist understanding of the unconscious, and adds to trans critiques of body normativity a historical investigation of anti-communism and anti-gender ideology.

Marxism and queer theory share not only a common history but also a current risky positionality. Defenders of alleged natural roles for man and woman have recently used the expression "gender ideology" to argue that the term "gender" is an ideological construction that derives from Soviet Marxism and studies of gender and non-normative sexuality. Given the post-Cold War anti-communism in the USA and eastern Europe, communist theory and material objects function not unlike queer bodies, namely as elements that do not have any value to the new liberal capitalist regimes.[22] In working with both queer and socialist theory, the book offers an alternative strategy to respond to the current anti-gender campaigns, primarily in eastern Europe.[23] The natural order of the family for the anti-gender advocates is a vision of the past projected as a desired future, not unlike how theorists of postsocialist transitions looked for a desired future in the past of western Europe.[24] A discursive attack on ideas such as queer and gender is not a historical novelty. During the Cold War, a liberal anti-communist discourse saw communists as challenging the natural norms of humanity. Like maligned atheists who destroyed churches and norms about proper human behavior, transgender and gender queer people are currently placed in the position of being the enemies of the biological order of sexes. In response to anti-gender campaigns, LGBT organizations have not only argued about their relevance and importance in terms of human rights, but have also associated their campaigns with an anti-communist rhetoric.²⁵ As such, in addition to passing laws that discriminate, the anti-gender movements create a deep rift between anti-capitalist histories and queer theory. A study of sexuality through a Cold War lens can bring in Marxist theory, which has historically served as a critical attack on natural gender roles. Instead of erasing this history, *De-centering queer theory* suggests an alternative strategy that underscores the shared and complicated history of communist projects and queer theory. This is why I argue that not only is the past of a progressive Anglo-American world is important for non-normative sexuality, but so also is an eastern European Marxist epistemology that has been ignored within a new global vocabulary. Instead of merely appealing to the concept of individual gender and its associated ideas of freedom and choice, an abolitionist gender politics needs to draw on the lessons of eastern socialism. A revolutionary past should not be lost to a new queer generation that seeks to transform current capitalist societies. The history of Marxist projects is important not only to minoritarian subjects who survive under capitalism, as queer of color theorists such as Jose Esteban Muñoz argue, but also to subjects who see themselves as revolutionary agents. To crack the Cold War door open means to see eastern European Marxism and liberated gender/sexuality not as adversaries, but as ideological allies in an effort to contest the politics of anti-gender activists.

What does the book want?

The book has two main goals. Its first goal is to put forward a historical argument about the erasure of a Soviet Marxist epistemology with regard to bodies and sexualities. After World War II and the critiques of the Soviet Union as a totalitarian country, Marxism-Leninism has become *the bête noire* of the Left in the West. Jennifer Delton has documented how the liberal left in the USA became anti-communist in the 1950s.²⁶ The opposition between a western liberal left and eastern European Marxism had critical consequences for the conceptualization of sexuality. *De-centering queer theory* investigates the consequences of this separation with regard to bodies and their sexual desires.²⁷

The perception that Marxism and sexuality are antagonistic was consolidated during the Cold War. While a leftist imagination currently recognizes the North American 1950s as repressive, the period gave rise to a winning liberal ideology that evolved around the idea of a third way between extremes such as Stalinism and Nazism. Not only have influential western left theorists framed state socialism as authoritarian, but Soviet Marxists also have rejected western theories and categories regarding gender and sexuality.[28] As David Hoffman argues, both communist Trotskyites and anti-communists saw Stalinism as a retreat from socialism, whereas Soviet Marxists saw their ideology as a fulfillment of communism.[29] While many studies have analyzed the relation between Soviet Marxism and sexuality, there are few works exploring how Cold War ideas have become the main reference for a vocabulary of sexual antinormativity. During the Cold War, two terms – namely liberated gender/sexuality and communism – have been placed in opposition, and this conflict has generated the perception that Marxism and sexual liberation are incompatible.[30] For instance, the Marxist historian Eric Hobsbawm declared that there is "a persistent affinity between revolution and puritanism."[31] In the same vein, Eric Naiman, a scholar of Soviet sexuality, argued in his groundbreaking study of the Soviet Union in the 1920s that "sex may act as symbolic shorthand for all forms of contamination" that come with communist utopias.[32]

This first part of the book undertakes a historical investigation to show that the Cold War was foundational to the emergence of gender- and queer theory. The Cold War represented a key moment that deeply shaped the theoretical imagination and epistemology of the West and the East. I concentrate on how the eastern European Marxist alternative to queer theory was gradually eliminated and made obsolete by an Anglo-American version of sexuality. Many studies in queer theory deploy a genealogical method, which emphasizes the discursive and material changes in society, but which rejects the teleological movement of history and the unique role of the proletariat.[33] This is why, unlike Karen Barad, who takes for granted a "multiplicity of times" and "a coexistence of time beings" in our historical life, I take the Cold War as the key frame that generated an Anglo-American discourse focused on gender- and individual freedom.[34] While my method embraces the Foucauldian emphasis on the contingent nature of social formations, it also draws from historical materialism the belief that history moves towards human emancipation. By historical materialism I understand a Marxist method that shows that the production of material life shapes our categories of thought.[35]

Cold War was not only a conflict of rival economies, but also shaped the attitudes about sexuality on each ideological side. Anti-normative sexuality and Soviet sexuality were intentionally contrasted to keep queer-oriented politics and socialist politics in opposition. Simply put, the west was sexually liberated while eastern comrades were sexually repressed and puritanical.[36] The idea that socialists were more repressed than their western counterparts has been challenged and nuanced in recent scholarship. Among other scholars, Josie McLellan has argued, for instance, that during socialism East Germany experienced a sexual revolution that, in some cases, was more radical than those that took place in West Germany and the rest of the West.[37] Among changes were the introduction of the abortion pill, the widespread distribution of the contraceptive pill, and the growing acceptance of single-parent households and cohabitation.[38] In a review of recent scholarship on gender and the Cold War, Marko Dumančić notes that the Cold War and anti-communism have been "formative for the queer community's sense of identity."[39] For example, queer visibility became an important theme, given the Cold War anxieties about infiltration and spying. Although this scholarly literature serves as a counterpoint to the dominance of anti-communism, an Anglo-American vocabulary and its assumptions have been deeply shaped by the rhetoric of the Cold War. Even when they critically challenge assumptions about the sexual inferiority and authoritarianism of the socialists, the categories that McLellan and Dumančić deploy, such as gender or gay politics, are deeply constituted by Anglo-American anti-communist histories. They are already interpreting Soviet Marxism with an analytic that functioned as a US Cold War political frame.

To offer an account of the gradual elimination of Soviet epistemologies with regard to bodies, I focus on three key historical moments: the productivist Marxist aesthetic in the early Soviet cinema of the 1920s (Chapter 2), the emergence of the competing analytic of gender in the 1950s USA (Chapter 3), and the relation between the new poststructuralist theories of sexuality in the USA and Marxism at the end of the Cold War (Chapter 4). By an eastern European Marxist epistemology, I understand an anti-capitalist project in the Soviet Union and eastern Europe that forged specific modes of knowing attached to an ideological language. After the 1917 Soviet Revolution and World War II, socialist states wanted to materialize Soviet Marxism as a political project that would surpass capitalism; because of this agenda, socialism had been used as a key term for articulating a State-oriented egalitarian program. In addition to creating new vocabularies, Soviet Marxism sought to remake the world by constructing new modes of feeling and acting.[40] Early Soviet Marxists conducted a vast program of destroying bourgeois institutions: church weddings were no longer required, divorce could be easily granted, doctors could perform legal abortions, cohabitation was recognized as a legal union, and campaigns of sexual education would focus on "contraception, hygiene and preventing venereal disease."[41] Later, Marxist Stalinism kept at its core an anti-capitalist political economy. Historical socialism not only created an epistemological anti-capitalism, but also changed the material factuality of existence to give rise to a communist ontology and ontic objects.[42]

The study not only offers an historical argument but also seeks to understand the effects of anti-communism on concepts such as gender and sexuality. The Cold War had a deep impact on constituting categories of knowledge. The specificity of the term "gender," as opposed to other earlier forms of denoting sexuality used by German sexologists, is that it mobilizes an individualist language of freedom and identity to suggest the possibility of changing social norms.[43] Gender is not a term that is unique in the Cold War language wars. American studies scholars have identified the construction of categories such as terror and empathy as part of anti-communist operations. Terror as a category of feeling that emerges during the Cold War has deeply shaped US counter-terrorism rhetoric.[44] Christina Klein showed that during the Cold War the US Government's rhetoric appealed to the value of empathy.[45] While North American Cold warriors constructed a global imaginary of containment that imagined the Cold War as a crusade against communists, a global imaginary of integration "represented the Cold War as an opportunity to forge intellectual and emotional bonds with people of Asia and Africa."[46] The "warm" capacity to feel the emotions of others became a tool for denouncing the cold ghetto of communism.[47] Yet, while the term "gender" has emerged as a Cold War category, it has been deployed according to various historical contexts after the 1990s. Terms that describe sexual and gender identities such as "gender," "gay," "queer" and "trans" have been circulated in the former socialist bloc by being separated from their North American activist context of origin. The risk in their circulation is that they become globally available according to a capitalist dynamic and, as such, have an orientation quietly to foreclose anti-racist and anti-capitalist work.

The second intention of *De-centering queer theory* is to investigate what the epistemology of Soviet Marxism can bring to a queer anti-racist analytic.[48] From a historical investigation, I shift to a dialectical method that introduces Marxist history into contemporary queer politics. In this regard, de-centering queer theory means to create new political linkages that can break the dichotomy between Marxism and queer theory. Research in sexuality studies has shown that the emergence of sexual sciences is deeply enmeshed in a global history of colonization and racialization, but there is little work critically to explore the anti-Marxist assumptions of counternormative sexuality.[49] Queer theory has not so far contributed in important ways to a critical literature about the role of the Cold War in the emergence of US-based gender theory.[50] Dan Healey has brilliantly shown that "the survival of male homosexual subculture" during Stalinism challenges the assumption that the Soviet State was more totalitarian than other western states, but the historical process of the development of competing sexual and political ideologies has been left uninterrogated.[51] In addition, the logic of linearity where an old version of sexuality (such as sodomy and homosexuality) is replaced by new categories (queer) falls into the trap of progress and a rising civilizational arch. While the term "queer" avoids the homophobic tones of a category such as homosexuality, it too often signals a superior Anglo-American vocabulary about sexuality. One of the problems with this narrative is that it disconnects sexual counter-normativity from a dialectical analysis of ideological and social conflicts. Another is that it abandons a historical understanding of the emergence and evolution of sexual categories.

My book draws on the possibility of creating a broader anti-racist, Marxist and queer coalition, which sees eastern European Marxism as a key resource for rethinking the future of queer theory. This analytic actively opposes the necropolitical move to turn communism and its people's sexuality into a project oriented towards death. Queer politics has invested a lot of energy in practices and theoretical strategies that undermine heteronormativity without paying attention to collective anti-capitalist politics. For instance, Eve Kosofsky Sedgwick's *Touching Feeling* proposed a distinction between paranoid and reparative reading that emphasizes the individual act of reading texts, rather than, let's say, collective anti-capitalist action.[52] As Keti Chukhrov argued, the epistemology of performativity is based on a model of anti-capitalist creativity that enhances rather than undermines alienation.[53] While Chukhrov's argument suggests a total rejection of a queer performativity, I seek to generate a new Marxist queer model that captures the progressive potential of a queer critique.

The book shows how a Marxist epistemology can bring new insights to various queer interdisciplinary intersections. In Chapter 5, I propose to take the ideal of abolition seriously as a common project of Marxism and queer theory. For Marx, only the abolition of private property can lead to a complete emancipation of human senses and qualities.[54] The socialist project in eastern Europe has generated not only the abolition of private property, but also that of capitalist social positions on gender and sexuality. The maligned history of Stalinism contains important moments of eradicating conventions that emphasized the ownership of women's bodies and their subordinate economic role. I argue not only that that the abolition of capitalist sex roles was at the heart of Soviet Marxism, but also that queer theorists such as Gayle Rubin and Marco Mieli situated the abolition of gender norms at the center of a theory of sexuality. In Chapter 6, I argue that socialist objects, which I call counterfetishes, can offer a new type of materiality to queer theory. The dis-connection of a commodity from labor and its material production has served as an important site for Marxist critique, particularly in the case of sexual identities. My claim is that Marxist counterfetishes, which are objects that are produced within a socialist system, point to a materiality based on needs that can reinfuse queer of color theories, in particular José Esteban Muñoz's and Fred Moten's work. In emphasizing a

Marxist materiality, I also describe its gradual loss in socialist films, with a focus on the 1980s Romanian film *The Cruise*. In Chapter 7, I draw on Soviet Marxist theorists such as N. Y. Marr to conceptualize the unconscious as having a class character. To reintroduce Soviet Marxism in queer psychoanalytic debates, I conceptualize unconscious productions such as dreams and sexual desires as guides and instigators of social revolts. The chapter reinterprets Jean Laplanche's concept of the unconscious with a Marxist lens to open new avenues for psychosocial theory. To flesh out this argument, I focus on Roma people's tactics against the practices and agents of slavery in eastern Europe, which were celebrated in Soviet Marxist films such as *The Fiddlers*. Last but not least, in Chapter 8 I show that the introduction of a Marxist historical method in transgender studies highlights the connections between trans people and postsocialist emigrants in the USA. As an example, I analyze films such as *Tangerine* that raise the question of potential alliances of trans subjects of color with racialized eastern European migrants. The argument of this chapter is that when trans bodies are conceptualized primarily in the liberal language of individual resistance, broader political connections and histories are lost in late capitalism.

Key terms

Here I offer to the reader brief working definitions of my conceptual apparatus. Since the concepts that I work with and interrogate circulate with a vast potential of connotations, I have a specific understanding of their meaning, which I clarify in this section. As I do not want to circumscribe such terms according to a definitional straitjacket, I offer a map of the terms to trace their scope, emergence, and circulation.

Gender and queer

By queer theory, I designate a critical orientation to challenge not only heteronormative sexuality and gender, but also an investigation that interrogates the historical role of nations, empires, colonialism and capitalism. By gender theory, I understand a theory that challenges the naturalized distinction between men and women. Currently, "gender" means bodily presentation, while "queer" is a broad term for sexual desire and queer-designated people who have non-normative body presentations and sexual desires.

Historically, gender and queer have been defined according to multiple criteria that have evolved and transformed. For instance, the term "invert," which was associated with homosexuality around the 1900s, was initially designed around the 1850s to name a broad category of transgender and sexually non-normative people.[55] Also, if "queer" designated an anti-corporate LGBT politics in the 1990s, around 2010 it became an identity – queer identity – that serves as an umbrella term for many non-normative identities, including gay and lesbian. To address the problem of the historicity of terms, here is how I use them in this study. For the interval between 1920 and 1990, I use the term "sexuality" to name not only gender presentation but also sexual desire when I talk about the communist world. My choice corresponds to a legal designation in the socialist world that used "sex" to name both gender and sexuality. To mark the difference between people in terms of gender presentation, I use categories such as male-bodied and women-bodied people. For both the Anglo-American world and the postsocialist world after the end of the Cold War, I use terms such as "gender," "queer" and "trans" to talk about the sexuality and categories for bodies. I use the term "Cold War gender" to designate the influential idea that bodies are constructed by culture. By "post-Cold War gender" and "queer," I designate two conceptual terms that challenged the distinction between sex and culture. They are theoretical terms that allow for multiple identifications, both in terms of bodies and of sexual desires.

Communist sexuality in the flow

Whereas Katherine Verdery sees gender as "a symbol system by which bodies enter into sociality," I see communism as a mode of production by which bodies become material.[56] Marxism-Leninism was the ideology of socialist states in eastern Europe and had at its core the abolition of capitalism. By Soviet Marxism, I understand not only Lenin's interpretation of Marxism, but other rival theories such as that developed by the Proletkult theorists, who by the 1960s became in the Soviet Union a left-wing deviation.[57]

I use the term "sexuality in the flow" to show how communist sexuality was articulated at different historical periods. Socialism needs to be historicized in order to grasp the connections and the interactions between the West and the East.[58] After 1917, the new modes of being a socialist person were at odds with a program that naturalized capitalist sex roles.[59] The wider project urged the destruction of the old world and the forging of a new system of production that would create not only new people, but also an anti-capitalist gender and sexuality.[60] Lenin used the word "abolish" to show the commitment of the new republic to a broad program of social change. In Lenin's project, a special place was reserved for categories such as capitalist womanhood and youth.[61] This political interest in fighting capitalism was translated into a new conception of art and its productions.[62] During the Cold War, communism and free gender/sexuality were part of a playing field that was constituted by two rival universalisms, Soviet Marxism and Anglo-American liberal capitalism, which produced their own epistemologies.[63] While socialism was a theory of existing societies, communism was the designated goal of a socialist world.

The Cold War

By the Cold War scholars designate a historically bounded period from 1946 to 1991, which constituted a specific and distinctive set of geopolitical and cultural circumstances. The Cold War in the USA has defined itself by its opposition to communism (communism was defined as "a fanatical force committed to the destruction of the West, or freedom").[64] Communist people were described as prone to dogmatic thinking and collectivism, and incapable of creativity.[65] Within the USA, people of color and Soviet bodies were racialized in different ways, yet new political and geographical connections can be drawn between eastern communism and queer anti-racist theory.[66]

Gender and American studies scholars, as well as historians and critical theorists, have been interested in showing the formation of terms and disciplines according to a Cold War anti-communist rhetoric. They have demonstrated not only the constitutive role of the Cold War in the dominance of analytic philosophy in North American philosophy departments, but also the role of rational choice vocabulary in shaping the social sciences.[67] The Cold War imaginary made anti-racism in the USA both a liability and an imperative, because anti-racism politics was a mark of "lingering leftist commitments" and "an integral program of winning the support of the decolonizing world."[68] While some scholars have focused on North American constructions of sexual deviance,[69] others have studied the role of gender and sexuality in shaping politics outside the USA in relation to the Cold War.[70] There is a lack of substantial scholarship that investigates how the Cold War has produced binaries in the relation between gender/sexuality and communism.

Queer theory

"Queer" emerged in US academia in the 1990s as a critical term aimed at challenging the normativity of the white nuclear middle-class couple. As a critical term, "queer" has a history that, like the history of terms such as "transgender" and "black abolitionism," offers a critique of heteronormativity in Anglo-America. I focus on the term "queer" because I seek to speak to queer theorists, who would be interested in the argument of the book. The queer project was primarily rooted in a US academic setting, and queer studies articulated histories that were conceptually and historically anchored in Anglo-American politics. The term "queer" was used academically to reject a politics of white middle-class sexual normativity, but it gradually became an analytic term deployed to interrogate the intersections amongst sexuality, race, empire and the nation. By queer theory, I am referring specifically to a politics that embraces sexual and gender disorder, given that a politics of normalization seeks to reify, stabilize and strengthen both hetero- and homonormativity.[71] "Trans" emerged as part of the term "transsexual," which was a mode of marking the transition from one sex to another, but like "queer" and "gender" it became "anything that disrupts or denaturalises normative gender."[72] In queer and trans scholarship, discussions about whether terms such as "queer" and "transgender" could signify a broader opposition to current liberal biopolitics are ongoing.[73]

Queer theory covers a vast range of academic and political interventions that span from early queer theory, such as Eve

Kosofsky Sedgwick's and Judith Butler's, to recent critiques of white gay theory that have erased non-Anglo-American histories of sexuality and gender.[74] Queer theory has challenged gay and second-wave feminist studies, so that queer became an alternative project that sought to move beyond the homo–hetero binary and expand the range of sexual counter-normativity. Starting in the 1990s, queer studies has become a lively field of rebel theoretical contestation in global academia, particularly in gender and sexuality studies, American studies, ethnic studies, and critical race studies.[75] It initially articulated itself as a critical project that aimed to challenge professional and disciplinary boundaries in US academia, as well as its underlining heteronormativity. In its early actualization, queer thinking deployed by Michel Foucault, Eve Kosofsky Sedgwick and David Halperin has operated with an unacknowledged binary between the East and the West, which, as Liu argues, drew on a Cold War liberal imagination.[76] Given the problems that are raised by the current politics of queer liberalism, which is the organization of anti-normative sexualities to privilege certain subjects, standards and political engagements, as well as by the increased role of US academia in a global production of knowledge, queer studies has developed into a broader critique of contesting entrenched relations of power in articulations of empire, nationalism, disciplinarity, racial hierarchies and the commodification of gender.

Eastern European Marxism vs. western Marxism

By eastern European Marxism, I am referring to a project of building a revolutionary communist society that was put into practice in the Soviet Union and the eastern socialist bloc. The term overlaps in many ways with Soviet Marxism, although eastern European Marxist regimes claimed their own version of Marxism. Romanian Marxism was, for instance, very different from the Yugoslav project of self-management.[77] Although the many versions of Marxism are very different in their historical actualization, I keep "eastern European Marxism" as an umbrella term that designates the ideology of State socialism, which has deep roots in Marxism-Leninism. In addition to official ideology, I name eastern European Marxist theories such as Lenin's, Arvatov's, and Bogdanov's, alongside Agnes Heller's *The Theory of Need in Marx*.[78] While it is a given that the term communism has many meanings, I understand it as a State-socialist project of achieving an egalitarian and anti-capitalist society. As part of the intersection between socialism and communism, the latter was the never-achieved anti-capitalist horizon of socialist states and societies.

By western Marxism I refer primarily to a project of critical theory that broke with Marxism-Leninism and intended to create a Marxism that was different from Soviet theory. It emerged from the defeats of the working-class movements before World War II, the discussions about Stalinist trials and the Soviet Union's pact with Hitler, and the various theoretical attempts to create a critical theory that distanced itself from class struggle and theories of revolution.[79] Western Marxists have drawn on the idea that Soviet Marxism was a project of authoritarian control. A theory of sexual repression was not only a generative frame for anti-communist critics, but also a central analytic for New Left movements equally to denounce national socialism and Soviet socialism.[80] For Herbert Marcuse, who, in *Soviet Marxism*, makes several references to a "totalitarian administration," Soviet society is "an unfree society" that is supported by "terroristic conformity."[81] An important critique of western theorists argued that Soviet Marxist politics is as repressive as the authoritarian politics of the West. As part of this political attitude, Stalinist art started to be perceived as lacking any esthetic value. Clement Greenberg's 1939 statement that socialist realism is kitsch already drew a stark opposition between Leftist modernism and Stalinist art.[82] After World War II, an entire field of Left theorists from situationists such as Guy Debord to Gilles Deleuze argued that Marxist-Leninist and socialist art have become reactionary.[83] Soviet Marxism has been deemed an authoritarian project of the past, as opposed to a New Left that imagined non-dogmatic strategies and vocabularies.

Postsocialist studies

After 1989, postsocialist and post-Soviet studies emerged as an exciting field of research that critically interrogated the victory of liberal democracy and its undergirding language in countries where Marxism was the official ideology.[84] In breaking with the

A materialist conception of queer theory

normalization of the language of Cold War liberalism, such as modernization theory, transition, and democratization, postsocialist studies has critically analyzed the conditions of US-Euro dominance and its ideological operations. In response to the erasure of a communist-oriented project, postsocialist thinkers have adopted various strategies. They argued that the epistemology of State socialism, and primarily of Soviet socialism, has been misunderstood or elided by western scholars.[85] Also, they replaced the term "postcommunist" – which was often used in political science and history to advance the view that liberal democracy is the endpoint of the transition of formerly Soviet Union and eastern European countries – with "postsocialist."[86]

Scholars such as Boris Groys, Keti Chukhrov, Boris Buden and Serguei Oushakine have taken important routes to distinguish between the epistemologies of western capitalism and eastern European Marxism, but a critique focused on the Cold War is very much needed. Soviet Marxism saw itself as a different body of theory from the theoretical analyses produced by Marxist-influenced theorists in the West and, as such, it contributed to this historical split. To an important extent, Soviet Marxism has lost its internationalist dimension by focusing on defending its State-focused ideology.

Counterfetishes

By counterfetishes, I understand either objects that are produced in an anti-capitalist economy (socialist objects) or objects rerouted from a capitalist economy to an anti-capitalist existence (queer counterfetishes). What Marxism and queer thought have in common is that counterfetishes function as *a key site* of revolutionary potential. While these two theoretical orientations have a shared interest in anti-capitalist materiality, they part ways when they theorize what kind of *objects* a revolutionary imagination produces. Unlike queer objects, historical counterfetishes were made in a political economy that functioned in opposition to Anglo-American capitalism.[87] In queer studies, counterfetishes are defined as subversive anti-commodities that undermine the economy of market exchanges.

Decontextualization

By decontextualization I understand a method of dialectically juxtaposing socialist theory and film with queer theory. Groys used the term "decontextualization" to argue that art archives need to preserve an impulse to take artworks from their historical context and provide them with a revolutionary goal by introducing them in a new context.[88] What I share with Groys is the emphasis on a dialectical move to take a material object, which has its own history, and give it a transformative mission. Decontextualization is not unlike Lev Kuleshov's montage, which sought to create a new visual language from the juxtaposition of two elements. Drawing on montage, détournement functioned for Situationists as "a powerful cultural weapon in the service of a real class struggle."[89] For Debord, détournement was where "the mutual interference of two worlds of feeling, or the bringing together of two independent expressions, supersedes the original elements and produces a synthetic organization of greater efficacy."[90] If, for Debord, anything can be used, the method gains a historical angle with artistic groups such as Irwin-NSK and soc art, which worked with socialist realism and the history of eastern European Marxism.[91] Like Situationists, eastern artists juxtapose socialist realism against a different context to create a new artistic relationship to communist art. For instance, soc artists who emigrated to the United States inserted Leninist art elements into American pop art.[92] After the 1990s, as the Moscow declaration shows, this eastern art sought to theorize the experience of historical materialism that was erased in new liberal democracies.[93] They juxtaposed historical Marxist objects with the new capitalist logic that defined eastern European countries.

The organization of the book

The book is structured in two main parts. In Part II, "Gender and the erasure of Soviet Marxist epistemology," I offer a historical view of the elimination of Soviet Marxism simultaneously with an analysis of the rise of terms such as "gender" and "queer." In Chapter 2, I look at early Soviet Marxism as an epistemological framework that produced a productivist understanding of bodies and sexual attraction. Communist figures in socialism were neither individual territories of freedom, nor subjectivities who fought against the conformism of an established ideology. Early Marxist films emphasized a productivist body that is not individualistic, but the unfinished product of a collective and dialectical process to achieve communism. To begin the process of analyzing the erasure of eastern European Marxism, I explore the gradual disappearance of the productivist Soviet body during "the thaw," with a focus on socialist Romania.[94] While, in the 1950s, Romanian socialism followed a Soviet politics of sexuality, I show that during the 1960s Romanian socialism reflected a western European trend to naturalize conservative norms about marriage and abortion. I analyze the 1964 Romanian film *The District of Gaiety* and argue that conservative tropes about sexuality altered the project of Marxist sexuality.[95]

In Chapter 3, I suggest that Cold War gender is part of a broader social constructivist program in US social science. Unlike scholars such as Jemima Repo and Susan Stryker, who criticized the use of gender as an analytic, I focus on its epistemology's emergence as part of an anti-communist ideology. To flesh out my claim, I analyze how gender emerged in the work of sexologist John Money as a term with anti-communist and racialized assumptions. While Money understood gender as an imprimatur given by society, his term was undergirded by an ideal of white Anglo-American masculinity. I also continue to explore how Cold War gender was theoretically at odds with Soviet Marxism, particularly in its racial epistemology.

In Chapter 4, I investigate the formation of a deconstructivist gender and trace it to the 1980s and the end of the Cold War. First, I historicize the elision of Soviet Marxism from the avant-garde art and theory of 1970s critics of socialism to the beginning of the 1990s in queer theory.[96] Second, I offer a close reading of queer theory texts to show that the fall of State socialism at the end of the 1980s has taken Marxism out of queer theory. In the refusal of the narrative that gender is only gender identity, gender became a vehicle to deconstruct categories such as man and woman (Judith Butler), historicize them (Joan Scott), or analyze how they are part of larger processes of racialization (Hortense Spillers). Unlike a

Soviet Marxist epistemology, queer theorists such as Butler did not produce an aesthetic and vocabulary that was explicitly anti-capitalist. In response to this problem, I argue that the epistemology of Soviet Marxism can transform queer theory and point to novel historical possibilities for sexed bodies.

In Part III, my intention is to show that Marxist theory and film can insert new theoretical routes into queer studies. I discuss in particular the project of abolishing gender norms (Chapter 5), the role of counterfetishes in films (Chapter 6), a Marxist understanding of the unconscious (Chapter 7), and the relationship between trans and post-Soviet immigrant bodies (Chapter 8). My analytic draws its theoretical resources from queer theory, but it critically interrogates this theory's translation to an eastern European context. In Chapter 5, I argue that abolitionist ideas are key to both Stalinist art and a queer of color analytic. I claim that Stalinist art is a refusal of capitalist codes about gender and sexuality according to a global Anglo-American imagination. In rearticulating an abolitionist imagination of capitalism, socialist films can generate a new imagination of the future. I identify common themes between Boris Groys and José Esteban Muñoz's theories: if socialist realist artworks function like a contemporary avant-garde, not unlike queer performances of color, they can help de-naturalize the normative performances of the body. I show that the Romanian realist socialist film *The Valley Resounds* offers a surprising archive regarding the meaning of sexuality that has been buried under the umbrella of Stalinism.

In Chapter 6, I claim that sensuous material objects from socialism constitute important starting points for rearticulating the notion of materiality in queer theory. I read Marxist films in conversation with the work of José Esteban Muñoz and Fred Moten, and the role of this conversation is to investigate the role of objects that were imagined to abolish the domination of private property. In a queer of color analysis, practices such as counterfetishes are "potentialities" that have the goal to generate a new utopian imagination.[97] To underscore a historical process of abandoning a Marxist materialist epistemology, I concentrate my analysis on the role of counterfetishes in the Romanian socialist film *The Cruise*. In Chapter 7, I suggest that a Marxist conception of the unconscious can offer new insights into racial dynamics about class exploitation.

I ask: How did the Cold War shape the concept of the unconscious, so that Marxist ideology and New Left psychoanalytic theory were kept at odds? I insert Soviet Marxism into conversations regarding the epistemology of psychoanalysis. I put Jean Laplanche's psychoanalytic theory in dialogue not only with queer theory but also with a socialist film made in the Soviet Union about Romanian Roma, *The Fiddlers*.

The last chapter of Part III has the role of displacing the narrative that Soviet Marxism is relevant only to those parts of the world who have lived behind the so-called Iron Curtain. I develop the term "queer communism" by discussing the work of Susan Stryker, Jacques Rancière and postsocialist theorists. Because an anti-communist tradition in the United States has deeply shaped a right-wing rhetoric with roots in the Cold War, part of that rhetoric is a refusal not only of labor resistance, but also of gender antinormativity. In drawing on Cold war sci-fi – Jack Arnold's *It Came from Outer Space* and Sean Baker's *Tangerine* – I argue that queer liberalism in the USA has elided this alliance between trans and working-class politics. A Marxist dialectical method illuminates the trajectories of bodies socialized in eastern Europe, who have later become migrants under global capitalism. The final section, Chapter 9, offers a short conclusion about the future of queer communism. By comparing and contrasting my study with previous scholarship, I argue that queer communism offers not only a distinct Marxist archive but also a dialectical vision of history. Rather than looking at queer studies as an interruption in the history of human emancipation, I see it as an important part of this process.

Archive

My interest in this book is to work primarily with socialist theory and Marxist films to tell a different story from the one told by a victorious Anglo-American queer theory. While exciting theoretical projects draw on Jacques Derrida's warning that communism is "a specter to come," this investigation is not merely a project of conjuring ghosts that have been dematerialized by global capitalism.[98] The material bodies of communism are not just spectral forces, but people with material histories that are present in film archives.[99] The book draws not only on canonical studies in sexuality and cultural studies, but also on important films that are key to the development of Marxist cinema. I analyze texts that have become part of the history of US queer, feminist and sexology scholarship, such as John Money's sexology scholarship, Muñoz's *Cruising Utopia*, critical race theory and Laplanche's psychoanalytical theory. Also, I focus on a cinematic archive produced in eastern Europe and the Soviet Union as well as the United States between the 1950s and 2018. Film was a privileged site for the exploration of a new Soviet and socialist person because it encapsulated a novel philosophy of perception.[100]

Notes

1 David L. Eng and Jasbir K. Puar, "Introduction: Left of Queer," *Social Text*, 38:4 (2020), p. 6.
2 Jordana Rosenberg and Amy Villarejo, "Queerness, Norms, Utopia," *GLQ*, 18:1 (2011), 1–18.
3 *Ibid*.
4 "The entire movement of history, just as its [communism's] *actual* act of genesis – the birth act of its empirical existence – is, therefore, for its thinking consciousness the *comprehended* and *known* process of its *becoming*." Karl Marx, *Economic and Philosophic Manuscripts of 1844*, www.marxists.org/archive/marx/works/1844/manuscripts/comm.htm (accessed April 18, 2020) (italics in original).
5 Peter Berger and Thomas Luckmann, *The Social Construction of Reality: A Treatise in the Sociology of Knowledge* (London: Penguin, 1966), p. 66. Their argument was based on the idea that human beings shape the biological setting that they are part of: "While it is possible to say that man has a nature, it is more significant to say that man constructs his own nature, or more simply, that man produces himself" (p. 66).
6 Eng and Puar, "Introduction," p. 4.
7 From this literature, see Rosemary Hennessy, *Profit and Pleasure: Sexual Identities in Late Capitalism* (New York: Routledge, 2000), pp. 111–143.
8 For the argument that queer theory can be seen as part of traditional avant-gardes, see *ibid.*, pp. 130–133.
9 See *ibid.*, but also Petrus Liu, *Queer Marxism in Two Chinas* (Durham, NC: Duke University Press, 2015); and Kevin Floyd, *The Reification of Desire: Toward a Queer Marxism* (Minneapolis: University of Minnesota Press, 2009).

10 Liu, *Queer Marxism*, p. 7.
11 Keti Chukhrov, *Practicing the Good: Desire and Boredom in Soviet Socialism* (Minneapolis: University of Minnesota Press, 2020), pp. 121–179.
12 Floyd, *The Reification of Desire*, pp. 4–26.
13 Hennessy, *Profit and Pleasure*, p. 131.
14 *Ibid*.
15 For the productivist nature of socialism, see Evgeny Dobrenko, *Stalinist Cinema and the Production of History: Museum of the Revolution* (Edinburgh: Edinburgh University Press, 2008). Dobrenko argued that the function of an aesthetic such as socialist realism was "to produce socialism" (p. xii). See also Serguei Alex Oushakine, "'Against the Cult of Things': On Soviet Productivism, Storage Economy, and Commodities with No Destination," *Russian Review*, 73 (April 2014), pp. 200–202, for the claim that productivism defined the political economy of State socialism in the Soviet Union. Productivism in Soviet film was analyzed by Gal Kirn, "Between Socialist Modernization and Cinematic Modernism: The Revolutionary Politics of Aesthetics of Medvedkin's Cinema-Train," in Lars Kristensen and Eva Mazierska (eds), *Marxism and Film Activism: Screening Alternative Worlds* (New York: Berghahn, 2015), pp. 32–38. For productivism in Soviet theory, see Alexander Bogdanov, "What Is Organization Science?" ("Ocherki organizatsionnoi nauki"), *Proletarskaya kul'tura*, 7/8 (April–May 1919), https://en.wikipedia.org/wiki/Alexander_Bogdanov (accessed April 2, 2020). In Bogdanov's view, the Soviet subject emerges from the changing of a capitalist mode of production to a productivist model. The term "productivism" is central to communism: "Engels, the founding father of scientific socialism, created the formula: the production of people, the production of things and the production of ideas. The term 'production' contains hidden within it the concept of organizing activities" (Bogdanov, "What Is Organization Science?").
16 Emma Widdis, *Socialist Senses: Film, Feeling and the Soviet Subject, 1917–1939* (Bloomington: Indiana University Press, 2017), p. 28.
17 Arvatov quoted in *ibid.*, p. 33.
18 See *ibid*.
19 See Leerom Medevoi, *Rebels: Youth and the Cold War Origins of Identity* (Durham, NC: Duke University Press, 2005), p. 47, and his argument that the war on communism has led to a specific organization of the vocabulary of the New Left: "By casting 'woman,' 'black,' 'Chicano,' 'gay' or 'queer' as their protagonist in the Cold War metanarrative of identity narrative, postwar social movements embraced and deployed the rebel figure as a new subject of history: an

emergent self establishes its psychopolitical autonomy in a struggle against an authoritarian world of 'role expectations.'"
20 See Liu, *Queer Marxism*, p. 1, for the new homonormativity in China after Deng's 1978 marker reforms. Also, see Hennessy, *Profit and Pleasure*, p. 28, for the rise of cultural studies and demise of Marxism at the end of the 1980s.
21 Hennessy, *Profit and Pleasure*, pp. 179–189; and Petrus Liu, "Queer Theory and the Specter of Materialism," *Social Text*, 38:4 (2020), pp. 28–29.
22 For the term "sexomarxist" as an anti-gender campaign slur, see Oana Mateescu, "The Romanian Family Referendum; or, How I Became a Sexo-Marxist," *Focaalblog*, October 23, 2018, www.focaalblog.com/2018/10/23/oana-mateescu-the-romanian-family-referendum-or-how-i-became-a-sexo-marxist/ (accessed February 24, 2020).
23 For gender ideology, see Roman Kuhar and David Paternotte (eds), *Anti-Gender Campaigns in Europe: Mobilizing against Equality* (London: Rowman & Littlefield, 2017), p. 5: "'gender ideology' does not designate gender studies, but is a term initially created to oppose women's and LGBT rights activism as well as the scholarship deconstructing essentialist and naturalistic assumptions about gender and sexuality." For Kuhar and Paternotte, gender is "the ideological matrix of a set of abhorred ethical and social reforms, namely sexual and reproductive rights, same-sex marriage and adoption, new reproductive technologies, sex education, gender mainstreaming, protection against gender violence and others" (p. 5).
24 See Boris Buden, "Children of Postcommunism," *Radical Philosophy*, January–February 2010, www.radicalphilosophy.com/article/children-of-postcommunism (accessed February 24, 2021).
25 See one of the logos of the Romanian LGBT organization Accept, "I am human, not an ideology," which suggests that they reject any attempt to associate LGBT rights with communism. See www.facebook.com/asociatia.accept (accessed February 24, 2021).
26 Jennifer Delton, *Rethinking the 1950s: How Anticommunism and the Cold War Made America Liberal* (Cambridge: Cambridge University Press, 2013), pp. 1–13.
27 For the Cold War as a US project, see Anders Stephanson, "Cold War Degree Zero," in Joel Isaac and Duncan Bell (eds), *Uncertain Empire: American History and the Idea of Cold War* (Oxford: Oxford University Press, 2012), pp. 24–25. In the US version of the Cold War, the USA is opposed to the imperial project of the Soviet Union (see Medevoi, *Rebels*, p. 12: "One principal way the United States validated itself as the proper model for developing third world nations was by mobilizing its claim to a history of colonial revolt"). For a

history of debates between western and Soviet Marxism, see Marcel Van der Linden, *Western Marxism and the Soviet Union: A Survey of Critical Theories and Debates since 1917* (Leiden: Brill, 2007).

28 For a history of the debates about sexuality and Marxism in the Soviet Union, see Eric Naiman, *Sex in Public: The Incarnation of Early Soviet Ideology* (Princeton: Princeton University Press, 1997); and Gregory Carleton, *Sexual Revolution in Bolshevik Russia* (Pittsburgh, PA: University of Pittsburgh Press, 2005). In these scholarly accounts, the circulation of categories for gender/sex between the Soviet Union and the West is scarcely discussed. For a history of the relationship between psychoanalysis and Soviet Marxism in the 1920s, see Martin Miller, "Freudian Theory under Bolshevik Rule: The Theoretical Controversy during the 1920s." *Slavic Review*, 44:4 (Winter 1985), 625–646. For a discussion about how the KGB used the issue of AIDS during the 1980s, see Douglas Selvage, "Operation 'Denver': The East German Ministry of State Security and the KGB's AIDS Disinformation Campaign, 1985–1986 (Part 1)," *Journal of Cold War Studies*, 21:4 (Fall 2019), 71–123.

29 David L. Hoffman, *Stalinist Values: The Cultural Norms of Soviet Modernity, 1917–1941* (Ithaca: Cornell University Press. 2018), pp. 1–3.

30 For a serious exposition of the view that the Cold War is not over, see Stephanson, "Cold War Degree Zero," pp. 25–26.

31 See Eric Hobsbawm, quoted in Carleton, *Sexual Revolution*, p. 1, who offers an account of the western perception of the Soviet Union as puritanical.

32 Naiman, *Sex in Public*, p. 16.

33 Mark Olssen, "Foucault and Marxism: Rewriting the Theory of Historical Materialism," *Policy Futures in Education*, 2:3–4 (2004), p. 454.

34 Karen Barad, "Troubling Time/s and Ecologies of Nothingness: Re-Turning, Re-Membering, and Facing the Incalculable," *New Formations*, 92 (2017), pp. 61, 74.

35 Karl Marx, "Preface," in *A Contribution to the Critique of Political Economy*, trans. S. W. Ryazanskaya (Moscow: Progress, 1993), www.marxists.org/archive/marx/works/1859/critique-pol-economy/preface.htm (accessed February 22, 2021).

36 In this vein, Gail Kligman, *Politica duplicității: Controlul reproducerii în România lui Ceaușescu* (Bucharest: Humanitas, 2000), writes that under Ceaușescu's politics Romanians' sexuality was a privileged site for the State's totalitarian intervention (p. 14). In Kligman's Cold War interpretation, communists generated Romanians' disregard for individual rights. Also, in Kligman's view, because Anglo-Saxon individual

rights are superior to Marxist social rights, people coming out of socialism did not have the language to resist the State's dictatorship.

37 See Josie McLellan, *Love in the Time of Communism: Love and Intimacy in the GDR* (Cambridge: Cambridge University Press, 2011), p. 9. For an argument that East German socialism produced conditions that encouraged sexual intimacy, see Dagmar Herzog, *Sex after Fascism: Memory and Morality in Twentieth-Century Germany* (Princeton: Princeton University Press, 2005), 216–219.
38 McLellan, *Love in the Time of Communism*, p. 53.
39 Marko Dumančić, "Spectrums of Oppression: Gender and Sexuality during the Cold War," *Journal of Cold War Studies*, 16:3 (2014), pp. 193–194.
40 Widdis, *Socialist Senses*, p. 337, has shown that film was at the heart of a project for the sensory remaking of a new Soviet self.
41 Carleton, *Sexual Revolution*, p. 3.
42 Chukhrov, *Practicing the Good*, pp. 22, 308.
43 For the language of German sexologists, see Robert D. Tobin, *Peripheral Desires: The German Discovery of Sex* (Philadelphia: University of Pennsylvania Press, 2015), pp. 1–27.
44 For a detailed argument about the role of ruins and terror in the early stages of the Cold War, see Joseph Masco, "Engineering the Future as Nuclear Ruin," in Ann Laura Stoler (ed.), *Imperial Debris: On Ruins and Ruination* (Durham, NC: Duke University Press, 2013), pp. 254–262.
45 The rhetoric of the US Cold War did so not only by deploying "a strategy of containment" but also by producing "a global imaginary of integration"; see Christina Klein, *Cold War Orientalism: Asia in the Middlebrow Imagination* (Berkeley: University of California Press, 2003), p. 23.
46 The imaginary of integration drew on and appropriated tactics that were historically part of Left-oriented politics such as those of the Popular Front and the Soviet Union. See *ibid*., p. 50, on the role of Eisenhower's "People-to-People" program during the Cold War: "Perhaps more surprising, the People-to-People program also perpetuated elements of left-liberal internationalism. The program seems to have been part of Washington's effort to emulate Soviet cultural strategies. At the level of institutional organization, People-to-People echoed the Popular Front's structure of a loosely affiliated network of groups that promoted participation in international affairs."
47 See Klein, *Cold War Orientalism*, p. 53: "Eisenhower made sympathy – the ability to feel what another person feels, to share in his or her conditions and experiences – the defining feature of American

globalism, and he commended those Americans who engaged in international communication that entailed 'talking from the heart to the heart.'"
48 Boris Groys, *The Communist Hypothesis*, trans. Thomas H. Ford (London: Verso, 2009), pp. 76, 80–81, argued that the English language is a unique commodified medium and that the Cold War in the USA has decisively contributed to this transformation. While Groys has intimated that English is a language shaped by anti-communism, the commodification of Anglo-American theoretical terms has been less investigated.
49 For racialization and sexuality, see for instance Angela Willey, "Monogamy's Nature: Global Sexual Science and the Secularization of Christian Marriage," in Veronika Fuechtner, Douglas E. Haynes and Ryan M. Jones (eds), *A Global History of Sexual Science 1880–1960* (Berkeley: University of California Press, 2018), p. 99: "the history of sexuality is also the history of colonization – and indeed sexual sciences are deeply enmeshed with a process of racialization." For the relation between race and Foucault's *The History of Sexuality*, see Ann Laura Stoler, *Race and the Education of Desire: Foucault's History of Sexuality and the Colonial Order of Things* (Durham, NC: Duke University Press, 1995), pp. 19–55.
50 There are important exceptions to this lack of engagement between the two fields. See Liu, *Queer Marxism*; Robert Kulpa and Joanna Mizielińska, *De-Centering Western Sexualities* (Farnham: Ashgate, 2011); and Robert Kulpa, "Western Leveraged Pedagogy of Central and Eastern Europe: Discourses of Homophobia, Tolerance and Nationhood," *Gender, Place and Culture: A Journal of Feminist Geography*, 21:4 (2014), 431–448.
51 Dan Healey, *Sexual and Gender Dissent: Homosexuality as Resistance in Stalin's Russia* (Ithaca: Cornell University Press, 2002), p. 368.
52 Eve Kosofsky Sedgwick, *Touching Feeling: Affect, Performativity and Pedagogy* (Durham, NC: Duke University Press, 2003) 123–153.
53 Chukhrov, *Practicing the Good*, p. 30.
54 "The abolition [Aufhebung] of private property is therefore the complete *emancipation* of all human senses and qualities"; Marx, *Economic and Philosophic Manuscripts*.
55 Hennessy, *Profit and Pleasure*, pp. 100–101.
56 Katherine Verdery, *What Was Socialism and What Comes Next?* (Princeton: Princeton University Press, 1996), p. 62.
57 See Zenovia Sochor, *Revolution and Culture: The Bogdanov–Lenin Controversy* (Ithaca: Cornell University Press, 2018), p. 10, for the observation that the Soviets considered the Chinese Cultural Revolution a left-wing deviation and a form of Bogdanovism.

58 See Shana Ye, "Red Father, Pink Son: Queer Socialism and Post-Socialist Queer Critiques," Ph.D. dissertation (University of Minnesota, Minneapolis, 2017), for this project of historicizing queer socialism.
59 See Hoffman, *Stalinist Values*, 59–62, 88–117. For tensions between abolishing and preserving sex roles in the Soviet Union of the 1920s, see Naiman, *Sex in Public*, 81–91.
60 "It is this break with obsolete tradition that is one of the substantial conditions which have created the possibility and evoked the necessity of regulating production and of public control over it. In particular, speaking of the transformation brought about by the factory in the conditions of life of the population, it must be stated that the drawing of women and juveniles into production is, at bottom, progressive." Quoted from Vladimir Ilyich Lenin, *The Emancipation of Women: From the Writings of V. I. Lenin* (New York: International Publishers, 1966), at www.marxists.org/archive/lenin/works/subject/women/abstract/99_dcr7.htm (accessed February 24, 2021).
61 See Lenin's statement "One of the primary tasks of the Soviet Republic is to abolish all restrictions on women's rights," in Alice Schuster, "Women's Role in the Soviet Union: Ideology and Reality," *Russian Review*, 30:3 (1971), p. 261.
62 In early sci-fi scenarios such as *Red Star* (Alexander Bogdanov, 1908), a human cosmonaut visits a communist alien utopia where its inhabitants are not only transgender but also have multiple lovers and sexual relationships. In the first Soviet sci-fi film, *Aelita: The Queen of Mars* (Yakov Protazanov, 1924), the Martians are imagined according to a Constructivist aesthetic, which hinders an easy recognition of their gender.
63 Medovoi, *Rebels*, p. 10.
64 Stephanson, "Cold War Degree Zero," p. 29. The term "totalitarian" became the main anchor of Cold War discourses because all its incarnations hold the equation of Stalin with Hitler and the Soviet Union with Nazi Germany. For the observation about totalitarianism as a key Cold War metaphor, see Medevoi, *Rebels*, p. 164. See also Anders Stephanson, "The Cold War Considered as a US Project," in Silvio Pons and Federico Romero (eds), *Reinterpreting the End of the Cold War* (London: Routledge, 2004), p. 58: the term "totalitarianism" "became available to Truman after the war as a way of making sense of what was read as Soviet intransigence and impositions: crude power moves, subversion and conspiracy, and unilateral takeovers, all in flagrant contravention of agreements honestly concluded. Tyrants, in the end, were tyrants, and tyrants recognized only the language of force, etc., etc. 'Totalitarianism,' thus, served to

A materialist conception of queer theory 33

collapse the differences between fascism and communism and, in the larger scheme of things, to render morally and politically suspect any argument in favor of defined limitations on US commitments."

65 Socialists in the East were racialized as "the enslaved" who were in need of US white abolitionism. From Roosevelt's "gangsters," the enemies of the free world became, in the rhetoric of the Truman administration, "slave owners" who denied freedom to their citizens (Stephanson, "The Cold War Considered as a US Project," p. 57). The Cold War was a product of a discursive shift from policing, pacification and order to abolition and freedom; the war against communism became another version of the civil war and the abolition of slavery (Stephanson, "The Cold War Considered as a US Project," pp. 56–58). As a frame of representation, the Cold War constructed communism as a totalitarian space, which was an occupied space and unreal (Stephanson, "Cold War Degree Zero," p. 31).

66 Marxist countries were states that were officially fighting racial discrimination, both nationally and internationally. Given this political situation, communist bodies experienced a specific racialization during the Cold War in the US imagination. In Tony Shaw, *Hollywood's Cold War* (Edinburgh: Edinburgh University Press, 2007), pp. 13–14, racialization through anti-Semitism is analyzed in early US anti-communist propaganda in films of the 1920s.

67 A Cold War mode of govermentality shaped academic philosophy as a practice with an emphasis on the rationality and preferences of voters, but devoid of an analysis of its historical production. For the role of the Cold War in creating the dominance of analytic philosophy in North American philosophy, see John McCumber, *Time in the Ditch: American Philosophy and the McCarthy Era* (Evanston: Northwestern University Press, 2001). For the relation between the Cold War and rational choice theory, see S. M. Amadae, *Rationalizing Capitalist Democracy: The Cold War Origins of Rational Choice Liberalism* (Chicago: University of Chicago Press, 2003).

68 See Klein, *Cold War Orientalism*, p. 41. An emphasis on anti-racism during the US Cold War led the centrality of the civil rights movement in the imaginary of Left politics. See Roderick Ferguson, *The Reordering of Things: The University and Its Pedagogy of Minority Differences* (Minneapolis: University of Minnesota Press, 2012), pp. 25, 33.

69 See Paul Preciado, *Pornotopia: Arquitectura y sexualidad en "Playboy" durante la Guerra Fria* (Barcelona: Anagrama, 2010), p. 29. In his argument, the magazine *Playboy* has constructed an architecture of intimacy around a heterosexual indoor masculinity

that emerged from a racialized and anti-communist production of white suburban spaces.

70 For instance, the famous fraternal kiss between Erich Honecker and Leonid Brezhnev has become "a key part of a distorted Cold War memorabilia, making the communist systems seem even more depraved and feeble in retrospect." See Dumančić, "Spectrums of Oppression," p. 2.

71 For a critique of homonormativity outside an Anglo-European context, see Liu, *Queer Marxism*, p. 2: "queer critics point out that liberalism has spawned a homonormative desire to dissociate from culturally undesirable practices and experiences such as AIDS, promiscuity, drag, prostitution and drug use."

72 Susan Stryker, "Transgender Feminism: Queering the Woman Question," in Stacy Gillis, Gillian Howie and Rebecca Munford (eds), *Third Wave Feminism: A Critical Exploration*, 2nd edn. (Basingstoke: Palgrave Macmillan, 2007), p. 64.

73 See an influential definition of queer liberalism: "Mechanisms of normalization have endeavored to organize not only gay and lesbian politics but also the internal workings of the field itself, attempting to constitute its governing logic around certain privileged subjects, standards of sexual conduct, and political and intellectual engagements," in David Eng, José Muñoz and Jack Halberstam, "What Is Queer about Queer Studies Now?," *Social Text*, 23:3–4 (2005), p. 4. For trans liberalism, see Nat Raha, "The Limits of Trans Liberalism," *Verso Books* (2015), www.versobooks.com/blogs/2245-the-limits-of-trans-liberalism-by-nat-raha (accessed April 5, 2020).

74 See the problem with using "queer" outside Anglo-European histories of sexuality in Elisabeth L. Engebretsen, *Queer Women in Urban China: An Ethnography* (London: Routledge, 2013), p. 9: "['queer'] tends to oversimplify what is after all complex social processes and experiences, culturally specific adaptations and paradoxes, and leave the specifically Euro-American underpinnings of such processes largely unexamined in a way that often serves to universalize and re-essentialize them."

75 For an insightful genealogy of queer studies, see William Turner, *A Genealogy of Queer Theory* (Philadelphia: Temple University Press, 2000). For a critique of US domination in global academia, see Robyn Wiegman, *Object Lessons* (Durham, NC: Duke University Press, 2012), pp. 197–239.

76 Liu, *Queer Marxism*, p. 30. For binary thinking as a product of Cold War politics in relation to Soviet socialism, see Alexei Yurchak, *Everything was Forever, until It Was No More: The Last Soviet Generation* (Princeton: Princeton University Press, 2005), p. 6.

77 For the link between the Cold War and self-management in Yugoslavia, see Branislav Jakovljevic, *Alienation Effects: Performance and Self-Management in Yugoslavia, 1945–91* (Ann Arbor: University of Michigan Press, 2016). For Romanian Marxism, see Alex Cistelecan and Andrei State, *Plante exotice: Teoria și practica marxiștilor români* (Cluj-Napoca: Tact, 2015).
78 Agnes Heller, *The Theory of Need in Marx* (London: Verso, 2018).
79 Douglas Kellner, *Herbert Marcuse and the Crisis of Marxism* (London: Macmillan, 1984), p. 126.
80 See Herzog, *Sex after Fascism*, pp. 2–3.
81 Kellner, *Herbert Marcuse*, p. 227.
82 See Boris Groys, "The Cold War between the Medium and the Message: Western Modernism vs. Socialist Realism," *eflux*, 104 (2019), www.e-flux.com/journal/104/297103/the-cold-war-between-the-medium-and-the-message-western-modernism-vs-socialist-realism/ (accessed April 18, 2020).
83 For Deleuze's attitude towards Soviet Marxism, see his rejection of communism as a term of identification in Nicholas Thoburn, *Deleuze, Marx and Politics* (London: Routledge, 2003), 9–10. For Debord's anti-Stalinist politics, see Guy Debord, "Report on the Construction of Situations and on the International Situationist Tendency's Conditions of Organization and Action," *Situationist International Online* (1957), www.cddc.vt.edu/sionline/si/report.html (accessed April 18, 2020).
84 See a concise definition of postsocialism: "a category that marks the post-Cold War reconfiguration of power relations and the ideological and geopolitical fault lines that continue to shape the present," in Dace Dzenovska and Larisa Kurtović, "Introduction: Lessons for Liberalism for the 'Illiberal East,'" *Cultural Anthropology*, April 25, 2018, https://culanth.org/fieldsights/series/lessons-for-liberalism-from-the-illiberal-east (accessed April 4, 2020).
85 Yurchak, *Everything Was Forever*, p. 6. See also Groys, *The Communist Hypothesis*, who deployed dialectical materialism to argue that the defeat of the Soviet Union represented the success of communist ideology, given that the Soviet decision to abolish communism of its own free will "makes the realization, the embodiment, the incarnation of communism complete" (pp. xix–xx).
86 Groys, *The Communist Hypothesis*, argued that since the Soviet Union was a socialist society also on the path of communism, the distinction between socialism and communism might not be entirely useful (pp. 92–93).
87 Oushakine, "Against the Cult of Things," pp. 200–202.
88 Boris Groys, *In the Flow* (London: Verso, 2016), pp. 187–188.

89 Guy Debord and Gil Wolman, "A User's Guide to Détournement," *Les lèvres nues*, 8 (1956), www.cddc.vt.edu/sionline/presitu/usersguide.html (accessed August 14, 2020).
90 *Ibid.*
91 For Irwin and soc art, see Marina Gržinić, *Fiction Reconstructed: Eastern Europe, Post-Socialism, and the Retro-Avant-Garde* (Vienna: Edition Selene, 2000), pp. 120–129.
92 *Ibid.*, p. 128.
93 *Ibid.*, p. 129.
94 By "the thaw" I mean the period that starts with the death of Stalin (1953) and continues until the end of the 1960s, when the Soviet Union and Soviet-influenced countries became economically closer to the West.
95 Vance Kepley, Jr., "*Intolerance* and the Soviets: A Historical Investigation," in Richard Taylor and Ian Christie (eds), *Inside the Film Factory: New Approaches to Russian and Soviet Cinema* (London: Routledge, 1991), p. 57, analyzed how the Soviet institutions detoured the US film *Intolerance* according to their ideological goals: "By insisting that the stories of *Intolerance* represent some dreadful past, the Soviets could fit the film into a Marxist schema which promises a glorious future."
96 See Herzog, *Sex after Fascism*, pp. 2–3.
97 José Esteban Muñoz, *Cruising Utopia: The Then and There of Queer Futurity* (New York: New York University Press, 2009), p. 9.
98 Jacques Derrida, *Specters of Marx: The State of the Debt, the Work of Mourning, and the New International* (New York: Routledge, 2011), p. 46.
99 For Groys, *The Communist Hypothesis*, pp. 80–82, communism as a specter to come encapsulates the same Cold War trope of Soviet communism as not-real communism.
100 Widdis, *Socialist Senses*, p. 2. In her argument, if capitalist senses were impoverished, a socialist revolution sought to create a new sensorium that remade objects according to new ideological priorities.

Part II

Gender and the erasure of Soviet Marxist epistemology

Part II advances the argument that queer North American studies needs to be de-centered from its position of authority over the socialist past. To show why this theoretical move is necessary, I concentrated in the first part of the book on the disappearance of the Marxist epistemology of bodies and sexuality during the Cold War. My effort is to underscore the consequences of the loss of Marxism for queer theory. Part II's first goal is to show that a communist epistemology in eastern Europe had different assumptions from social constructivism in the USA. In a global struggle for ideological supremacy, communist sex and bodies were designated as the opposite of the sexual freedom in capitalism. The second goal of this part is to unpack how liberal capitalism and eastern European Marxism functioned historically according to competitive epistemological ideas. Specifically, I analyze the trajectory of the conflict from the conceptualization of productivist bodies in 1920s, to the emergence of gender in the 1950s, to the rise of queer theory at the end of the 1980s.

Two main obstacles arise against a project of reconstructing a Marxist epistemology during the Cold War. First, the current language of bodies and sexuality is permeated by the values of a post-1989 liberal ideology that centered on freedom and individual sexual liberation. After the fall of State socialism, the analytic of gender identity, for instance, was widely deployed to analyze the relationship between the categories of man and woman.[1] Anglo-American critical scholars have begun to use gender not only to evaluate the past of socialism, but also to create normative judgments about the future of eastern European countries. Gender was a main criterion to measure the state of social equality across the globe, provided that the ideology of liberal democracy defined such measurement.[2] Neither was the dominance of an Anglo-American language of sexuality an abrupt temporal break that took place after the fall of State socialism, nor was it deterministically inscribed in the course of the ideological conflict. The erasure of Marxist epistemology happened as a gradual process during the Cold War.

Marxist political regimes not only allowed western ideas to circulate to a certain degree, but also incorporated them as part of their ideological program. The official politics of eastern socialism was to authorize many western aesthetic and cinematic genres, such as high modernist productions, as long as they were subsumed under official communism.[3] Yet the contrast between western aesthetic categories and socialist politics became harder to manage towards the mid-1980s, when State socialist countries were exposed to increased financial pressures from institutions such as the International Monetary Fund and the World Bank. In contrast to this artistic incorporation of western genres into eastern European Marxism, socialist realism was hardly, if at all, deployed as a program in US cinema after World War II. This brief comparison illustrates the dominance of western aesthetic categories that gradually sidelined Marxist-Leninist categories of art and knowledge.

The politics of bringing gender in after 1989 to analyze socialism was part of a broader narrative about the authoritarian nature of communism. Gender is not a value-free concept. It locates individual freedom at the core of a liberal narrative that distinguishes between free and unfree countries. As opposed to a perceived lack of political freedom in socialism, the epistemology of gender described its rival system with terms such as "paternalism" and "puritanism." Within eastern European socialism, the Romanian case is unique because it was perceived as a special instance of unreformed Marxism-Leninism. In following the logic of describing gender as a social construction, Katherine Verdery claims that, as opposed to the agency of liberal citizenship, Romanian socialism functioned as "socialist paternalism" and produced dependency for its subjects.[4] For Verdery, socialism has not been exclusively detrimental to its citizens: it also increased gender equality between them by providing maternal leave, child-care, access to abortion

The erasure of Soviet Marxist epistemology 39

(except in Romania) and women's participation in the labor force.[5] Verdery defined gender as the social construction of man and woman, or "the joint product of prevailing cultural understandings and people's social situations."[6] Not only gender but also sexuality served as a criterion to assess State socialism as deficient in relation to liberal democratic countries. In 1978, Daniel Chirot saw Romania as a unique case of sexual puritanism in the eastern bloc.[7] Chirot wrote about the rule of "official puritanism" before socialist Romania entered in the 1980s, a period that has started to be seen as defined not only by economic austerity and extreme poverty, but also by intense sexual repression.[8] Ironically, he offered his assessment without taking into account that the Soviet Union and eastern European states had important histories of pro-abortion laws.[9] Chirot's argument shows that at the end of the 1970s sexuality has become an important category to describe socialism as a repressive ideology.

A second obstacle complicates this project of reconstructing eastern European Marxism. Soviet Marxism was neither simply an alternative ideology to liberal capitalism, nor one of the many ideologies that was in competition on a free market of ideas. The war involving two political systems was a conflict that saw its adversary as a rival that had to be eliminated. In the famous report to the National Security Council in 1950 (NSC 68), it is stated that "the ever-present possibility of annihilation" is part of a new condition where Americans are threatened "by a new fanatical faith, antithetical to our own."[10] This necessity to fight against enemies is articulated as a process of fighting slavery. As slavery disappeared and was eradicated, freedom had to win against Marxist ideology: "There is a basic conflict between the idea of freedom under a government of laws, and the idea of slavery under the grim oligarchy of the Kremlin ... The idea of freedom is peculiarly and intolerably subversive of the idea of slavery."[11] Not just at the beginning of the Cold War, but also at its end, the war on socialist bodies was one with a world that was condemned to disappear. A politics of feeling nearly dead, or nearly annihilated, is powerfully described by Madina Tlostanova's observation that socialism "was a condition of a dinosaur that somehow did not die in due time and had to languish in the backyards of history."[12]

The socialist body was one taken out of history, since communism in the East was an archaic, dinosaur-like formation.

On its side, eastern European Marxist politics affirmed that the logic of human emancipation would lead to the elimination of western capitalism. As a CIA 1962 report relays Nikita Khrushchev's statements in 1956, he asserted that "We Leninists are convinced that our social order, socialism, will in the long run conquer capitalism. Such is the logic of the historical development of mankind."[13] Interestingly, the remarks of the the First Secretary of the Communist Party of the Soviet Union were translated into the direct threat of the US vernacular "We will bury you."[14] Like many translations of terms from one side to another, the threat of annihilation was embedded in the ideological background of the conflict. While the US press inserted the statement as the declaration of a slave owner who fights against the freedom of the American Republic, the statement was part of an anti-capitalist fight against exploitation and the free market.

To conclude, the naturalization of post-Cold War ideology and the perceived lethal nature of the conflict serve as key epistemological obstacles to my project. To address these obstructions, I focus on the emergence of productivism in early eastern European Marxism and trace the beginning of the erasure of Marxism in socialist countries. The limited goal of the next chapter is to reveal rather than challenge the necropolitical logic behind the Cold War. While the concept of necropolitics describes primarily a dominant global politics towards black and brown bodies, I briefly explore the implication that the Cold War was also a politics of death oriented against Soviet Marxist ideology.[15] Racialized necropolitics was defined as a politics that decides which categories of people are worthy to live and which worthy to die.[16] I suggest that necropolitics is also a politics that was conducted to certify that only given forms of life (such as an Anglo-American vocabulary) can be considered legitimate categories of human sexuality. The politics of death has shaped not only the people's experiences of the conflict, as Tlostanova's observation makes explicit; it also shaped the categories that allow our current memory access to the socialist past.

Notes

1 See Katherine Verdery, *What Was Socialism and What Comes Next?* (Princeton: Princeton University Press, 1996); and Gail Kligman, *Politica duplicității: Controlul reproducerii in România lui Ceaușescu* (Bucharest: Humanitas, 2000).
2 See Kligman, *Politica duplicității*, p. 35, where "gender" is translated from its original English as "sexual equality" ("egalitatea între sexe").
3 The prevailing Marxist politics was that nationalist politics was promoted as long as its content was ideologically socialist.
4 Verdery, *What Was Socialism?*, p. 63.
5 *Ibid.*, pp. 64–65.
6 *Ibid.*, p. 62.
7 See Daniel Chirot, "Social Change in Communist Romania," *Social Forces*, 57:2 (1978), pp. 484–485: "The morality imposed on the daily social behavior of the population, though it has a great deal in common with the puritanism, even prudery, so common in Communist societies, is less logically connected to Marxism; and in Romania it has been pushed to an extreme unique in the European Communist world in at least one respect, demographic policy."
8 Chirot, "Social Change," p. 487, uses neither "gender" nor "sexuality" in his account of Romania's "official puritanism." In Chirot's argument, Romania was constructed as an anomaly within the socialist bloc. For a history of pro-abortion legislation in western Europe (in Italy, abortion was decriminalized by law in 1978; in the UK the law to legalize first- and second-trimester abortions was passed in 1967), see Dagmar Herzog, *Sexuality in Europe: A Twentieth-Century History* (Cambridge: Cambridge University Press, 2011), pp. 155–159.
9 For various laws on abortion in socialist eastern Europe, see Herzog, *Sexuality in Europe*, p. 101.
10 See "National Security Council Report, NSC 68, 'United States Objectives and Programs for National Security,'" Wilson Center Digital Archive, https://digitalarchive.wilsoncenter.org/document/116191.pdf?v=2699956db534c1821edefa61b8c13ffe (accessed May 8, 2020).
11 *Ibid.*
12 Madina Tlostanova, *What Does It Mean to Be Post-Soviet? Decolonial Art on the Ruins of the Soviet Empire* (Durham, NC: Duke University Press, 2018), p. 9.
13 The CIA report, titled "Khrushchev's 'We will bury you,'" is online at the CIA Library, www.cia.gov/library/readingroom/docs/CIA-RDP73B00296R000200040087-1.pdf (accessed May 8, 2020).

14 *Ibid.*
15 See, for instance, Achille Mbembe, "Necropolitics," in Timothy Campbell and Adam Sitze (eds), *Biopolitics: A Reader* (Durham, NC: Duke University Press, 2013), pp. 2–5.
16 See the relationship between what Jasbir K. Puar, *The Right to Maim: Debility, Capacity, Disability* (Durham, NC: Duke University Press), p. 128, calls "the right to maim" and necropolitics in the conflict between Israel and Palestine.

2

Productive bodies in eastern European Marxism

The role of this chapter is to begin to show why an analytic such as gender identity obscures, rather than helps illuminate, the logic of the communist project. I will demonstrate that communist and socially constructed bodies functioned according to contrasting ideological programs. In opposition to the Cold War articulation of gender identity, which sees people's sexed bodies on a path to becoming free, communist bodies were primarily vehicles to promote a Marxist ideal of human emancipation. A communist person is a producer of a new system of human organization, unlike the gendered person in the US imagination who represents the potential of a territory of independence and freedom. A communist became a productive body on the basis that socialism had been achieved in eastern Europe.[1] A productive body was not only a material realization of a socialist society, but also its ongoing task. To articulate this apparent paradox differently, communist bodies mattered only as a vehicle for advancing a communist ideal that was already present. In the Soviet dialectical conception, men and women were not given as a material embodiment that was fixed and unchanging. According to a Marxist logic, they were elements in a mode of production that had to abolish capitalism continuously.

Rather than taking for granted the power of given cultural ideas, eastern European Marxists were fascinated by the possibility that they could produce new social norms. Unlike Cold War gender, which seeks to explain the world and hide its normative assumptions, for Marxists the communist artists and bodies were transforming and producing a new society.[2] Productivism in Soviet Marxism created not only an important theoretical and industrial infrastructure, but also a wealth of artistic creations that were actively shaping a communist horizon. As Dobrenko argued, socialist realism's basic function was not propaganda but "to produce reality," and "was a radical aesthetic effort" to represent the future as the present.[3] If Boris Groys is right, then communism was a project of creating an autonomous world in relation to market economy by generating a new conceptual apparatus.[4] This vocabulary functioned according to an explicit abolitionist ideology, which aimed to surpass the backward ideas of liberal societies. It also created, as I will show, a specific theory about bodies and sexuality that was defined as a step forwards in the emancipation of humanity.

During the Cold War, the stakes were high in the struggle for ideological domination. As I will argue in detail in the next chapter, the term "gender" drew its logic from an anti-communist program in the USA. The term grew as part of the rise of social constructivism in US social science. To comment on one of the most influential books of this program, Peter Berger and Thomas Luckmann's 1966 *The Social Construction of Reality* forged a strong alternative to Marxist explanations of social life. In opposition to Soviet Marxism, it argued that it has a better grasp of the objective nature of reality, and differentiated between a cultural representation of the body and a biological body. Berger and Luckmann's argument was based on the idea that human beings shape the biological setting that they are part of: "While it is possible to say that man has a nature, it is more significant to say that man constructs his own nature, or more simply, that man produces himself."[5] Berger and Luckmann's use of the term production, while it gestures to Marxist epistemology, is part of a program of making a social and culturalist program palatable to an audience of US liberal scientists. It does so by taking from social explanation a theory of revolutionary goals. More than that, social constructivism was based on a deeply anti-communist program. As Manfred Prisching argues, it derives from a research plan that led to Rudolf Carnap's logical positivism, Karl Popper's falsificationism, and Friedrich Hayek and Ludwig von Mises's theory of economics and human nature.[6] While it insisted on a productive capacity of the human being, it excluded any possibility that social science can be deployed to produce a new revolutionary man. Unlike the goal of Marxism to generate a total change of society, it asserted that social scientists can neutrally understand the world.

Soviet Marxism was based on a theory of new human beings who seek to destroy capitalism. Its revolutionary imagination was concerned not only with types of interaction among socialist people, but also with the affective processes by which a new society can be put in place. Yet, in its historical development, the productivist aesthetic in communism gradually incorporated various tropes about bodily and sexual interactions that moved away from an initial focus on the abolition of capitalism. Gradually, the call to uproot private property and exchange value had lost its salience. This transformation has multiple historical sources, and as I will show, the socialists' incorporation of conservative norms of sexuality is an important cause of this evolution. The following chapter is organized in two different historical sections. First, I argue that Soviet Marxism conceived a productivist body that was not individualistic, but a device that generated a collective and dialectical process to achieve communism. To demonstrate this argument, I focus on how bodies function as anti-capitalist elements in eastern European cinematography. Second, I show that the productivist body was gradually elided with the rise of new tropes about sexuality during the thaw. In reading a 1964 Romanian film, *The District of Gaiety*, I suggest that Romanian socialists incorporated western European conservative norms to justify their politics on abortion.

My claim is not that all people in socialism were or behaved like productivists. I do not speculate about how most socialist people felt and acted; instead, my analysis is primarily an exploration of a discursive field that focused on the creation of the communist person with a focus on cinematography.

The productive body: beyond individual gender

> Art is not a mirror to hold up to the world, but a hammer with which to shape it.
> (famous Soviet saying attributed to Vladimir Mayakovski)

The main contrast that I develop in this book is between a productivist economy of human beings and gender as a social construction of individual bodies.[7] To restate my argument, my analyses of Marxist films do not look for gender in the character development of narrative plots, but focus on a communist epistemology that underpins how bodies and their sexual interest are made visible. I theorize socialism as an epistemological framework that generated a dialectical understanding of human nature. I take the conception of a productivist epistemology of bodies from early theorists of eastern European Marxism such as Alexander Bogdanov and Boris Arvatov.

In Soviet Marxism, various Bolshevik theories such as those of Lenin, Georgi Plekhanov and Alexander Bogdanov were engaged in a struggle to be at the center of Soviet cultural and sexual politics.[8] Out of these debates, productivism emerged as key theoretical component of Soviet Marxism. In developing a productivist theory, Bogdanov and Arvatov assumed that a socialist mode of production would generate new Soviet people who would be different from western capitalists. A very influential Marxist theorist in the 1920s, Bogdanov wrote about the possibility of achieving a better communist person under the new conditions of the Bolshevik State. He founded the Moscow branch of the Proletarian Culture movement (Proletkult), which had between 400,000 and 500,000 members by the end of the 1920s.[9] His ideas were based on a Marxist understanding of the material world, which argued that it needed to transgress false oppositions, such as the individual vs. the collective or material vs. spiritual. Because he understood the world as a totality, he suggested the overcoming of the division between mental and physical labor and the separation between a ruling party and a proletarian class.[10] Like Bogdanov, Arvatov was a key theorist of Proletkult, and his 1926 book *Art and Production* argued that a revolutionary attitude requires a reorientation of the meaning of art. Art had to shift its meaning from a capitalist withdrawal from the world to a change in its material conditions. The artist, like the proletarian and the engineer, had to tackle directly the transformation of the world. In drawing on Bogdanov's work, Arvatov argued that "proletarian monism" has to erase the boundary between art and the production of the social (what he calls "a general social technique").[11] For him, artists should enter the factory to transform the production for profit to a production for need.[12] In a theory of productivism, a dialectical transformation of old capitalist categories will lead to the suppression of capitalism.

Productivism was an important theoretical thread in Soviet Marxism, particularly in its emphasis on destroying an old capitalist system by abolishing its epistemological ideas. Instead of merely living in the world, productive bodies were designed to be political and artistic devices to achieve communism. Productivism was powerfully challenged by Lenin's distrust of a proletarian Cultural Revolution. He was concerned that Proletkult saw the direction of cultural change from proletarians to the upper political echelons, rather than the product of the Communist Party.[13] Moreover, Stalin's cultural imperatives had an ambivalent relationship to the first Cultural Revolution and experiments of early avant-garde theorists.[14] Leaving aside heated debates in Soviet Marxism, my argument builds on the centrality of productivism to eastern European societies. In highlighting its prominence, Serguei Oushakine argued that "Soviet productivism was also a particular cultural practice, a particular regime of materiality."[15] Bogdanov and Arvatov were not only theorists of ideology but were also considered influential to the development of a socialist realist aesthetic. The artistic programs of socialist realism and the Proletkult movement were deeply interconnected. By socialist realism I understand a dominant artistic and political method with a basis in Lenin and Marx's ideas that focuses on themes such as the relation between art and the people, the class underpinnings of art, and the role of the artist to support the mission of the Communist Party.[16] In art, socialist realism generated a Marxist epistemology of bodies, because the basic function of socialist realism was "to create socialism – Soviet reality, and not an artifact."[17] The goal of socialist realism was that every object and human person in socialist countries would become a product of a communist and collective artistic production.[18] In a revolutionary society, the meaning of art was to engender new material relations to escape the fetishization of commodities.

The difference between the theories of productivism and social constructivism points to important ideological contrasts during the Cold War. Unlike the US understanding of identity, political bodies in socialism were neither individual territories of freedom, nor subjectivities that fought the conformism of an established ideology.[19] They were bodies that produced a future communist society by acting in line with the Communist Party.[20] Also, for Marxists, socialism *produces* human subjectivities for their social value, as opposed to US social science's emphasis on the social that *constructs* a given body and personality.[21] If the body is a social construction, it does not produce, but merely reflects a social situation that is already given.[22] In turn, productive bodies were imagined as ideological devices to forge better anti-capitalist bodies and sexualities. Given that individualism was the tactic and philosophy of capitalism, Alexandra Kollontai wanted, for instance, a communist sexuality was that was aimed at leaving aside the ideals of the bourgeois couple: "The old ideal was 'all for the loved one'; communist morality demands all for the collective."[23] In contrast to a theory that sees gender as process by which bodies "enter into sociality," socialism situated human beings in the process of material transformation.[24]

Socialist sexed bodies were not only created by communism, but were elements that sought to lead to this transformation. For Soviet Marxists who worked with a dialectical understanding of the future, the process of achieving communism was more important than the idea of a final stage where communism was fully actualized. One of the main innovations of socialism was the emphasis on production itself rather than on a product of labor:

> The product of labor is dissolved in the grandeur of the project: the Soviet Union did not produce footwear, clothing, dwellings, or food produce, but rather made "cast iron and steel" and "factories and blast furnaces," and "waged a harvest battle" ... The product itself ceases to be self-sufficient, the process of producing it becoming self-sufficient instead. This is without a doubt the very thing that socialism introduced as new.[25]

The idea that communism was a process of production is key to understanding the new reconceptualizations in Soviet socialism. This theoretical novelty has extraordinary consequences regarding the production of sexed bodies. Rather than products in themselves, which were understood as individual bodies, socialist bodies were a collective entity that accelerated the movement to a higher phase of historical consciousness. Instead of having a gender waiting to be discovered, productive bodies were organized around an epistemology that aimed to realize fully the potential of humanity as a whole.

In Soviet-inspired socialism, the communist body was inserted into dialectical movement with other bodies. According to socialist thinking, and in the light of the rejection of capitalist individualism, an individualist-focused construction of a sexed body was considered a bourgeois aim. The process of producing communists was more important than the achievement of freedom for a male and female body. The function of the Party was to lead the process of realizing communism. In this socialist imagination, if the body felt more intensely and had a stronger connection to the material world, then it would be able to produce a more highly educated social consciousness.[26] For Soviet Marxists, productive labor was to be "the foundation of the educational process" and the development of the communist child.[27] In the words of Anton Makarenko, one of the most influential theorists of pedagogy in the Soviet Union, education was primarily a collective task.[28] As he also argued, a productivist approach to becoming communist was an anti-capitalist program that could lead to world revolution: "The Soviet collective defends the issue of world unity of the working humanity as a matter of principle. It is not merely a biotic unification of people, but a part of the humanity's battle front in the era of the world revolution."[29]

To clearly distinguish between Cold War gender and the communist body, I argue that Marxist film characters were theorized *against* the idea of an individual identity. Since a communist ideal did not primarily describe the role of an individual body, it was rather invested in the achievements of collective organizations. Productivism was not only a strong approach in education, but also a key philosophy of organizing the political economy of the State. A vital goal for socialists was the refusal of individualist bourgeois ideology, and Lenin made that task very clear.[30] As Serguei Oushakine showed, the political economy of socialists functioned according to a productivist system that rejected the principles of the market economy.[31] Oushakine extracts his theory from Boris Arvatov's ideas, who formulated the idea of a thing-system that offer an alternative to the market-dominated economy. Before becoming a commodity on the market, the product of labor was still a "thing," and was imagined as serving the necessary needs of the population. For Arvatov, a "thing" was not a commodity in two main aspects.[32] First, commodities were designed for the market and did not fit the needs of the people. In reversing this relationship, a thing was a product that was aimed to correspond to its social value and not to its alleged market value. Second, a commodity relied on a profit-driven marketization that deprived it of its connection to labor production. In turn, a thing was aimed at showing its connection to a socialist mode of production and its labor, rather than to its exchange value. In socialism, not only were commodities transformed but also bodies. Communist production emphasized not just objects but "forms of being" as well.[33] Communist bodies, like things produced in socialism, had rather a use-value instead of an exchange value. Through this lens, bodies were, like things that had not become yet commodities, entities that were not separated from their conditions of production.[34] This emphasis on a production process of material bodies, rather than on the finished product, is consistent with socialists' rejection of individualism. As I will show in this section, socialist realist strategies, such as dialectical conflicts between activists and workers, were designed to generate a new type of a human being who had a superior consciousness and education.

How do bodies function as anti-capitalist things in socialist cinematography? *Alone* is considered to be a prototype for master plots in a later Soviet aesthetic.[35] It is one of the first Soviet films situated at the point of transition from silent films to audio socialist realism. In the film's plot, bodies are shown to become communist when they seek to abolish capitalism. Kuz'mina, a female-bodied city resident in Moscow, has graduated as a teacher and wants to remain and work in a city. She is sent to a post in Altai. The film critiques the residues of the market economy in the Soviet Union, which were part of Leninist politics in the first years after the October Revolution. In doing so, it focuses on Kuzmina's attraction to the world of commodities. We are introduced to the heroine according to an ideological setting that socialists denounced: she lives alone in a single room in Moscow; sleeps in a laced nightdress; and is enchanted by symbols of comfort, such as shop windows with glittering commodities. At the beginning of the story, she and her lover visit a kitchenware shop and she is seduced by the materiality of objects. As Widdis notes, like in *New Babylon*, luxury signifies the exchange economy, but in this film, the main character, Kuz'mina, is kept outside the world of commodities.[36] While the store display is "an orgy of patterned textiles, compelling the spectator into an awareness of suffocating texture and materiality," Kuz'mina can see the objects in the shop, but cannot touch them.[37] Like her, the viewer is placed in a position of "refusing the sensory pleasure of a haptic encounter with the material" because they are encouraged to live in a different economy of affects.[38]

What *Alone* does is to show us an interruption in Kuz'mina's desired trajectory, because, although she wants commodities, she is not yet a commodified subject. Her transformation into a potential Soviet body is realized in an encounter with the sensuous world of the people in Altai. In the Soviet imagination, the indigenous people are shown to be closer to labor production and the material world of objects. They grasp, cut and rub wool, and live in world where they are part of natural life. Widdis argues that Kuz'mina develops a different sensory relationship to objects when she moves to Altai, which is the springboard for her becoming a communist.[39] The film captures the move from a desire to possess commodities to a socialist experiential world, which is deeply connected to the materiality of objects. This new material register is articulated particularly in its relation to their use-value. In Altai, Kuz'mina is redeemed because she becomes a producer of things. Like the thing-system into which she is absorbed, she becomes a body-thing whose value is given by her rejection of a profit-oriented world.

A Soviet film epistemology was very influential in newly socialist countries in eastern Europe. For instance, Romania's cinematography after 1948 was shaped by the idea that communism was an actualized ideal in the new republic.[40] Soviet epistemology led to the development of socialist realism in Romanian cinematography, from the 1949 *The Valley Resounds* to late Marxist-inspired films such as *Love and Revolution* and *Impossible Love*.[41] The idea of a body as a non-capitalist thing is present in early socialist films, such as the 1961 *The Man Next to You*. Like Kuz'mina, Corina is a city girl, a lawyer accustomed to city attractions such as high-end restaurants and museums. But when she falls in love with Ticu, an engineer who works on the construction site for dam in Bicaz in the northern part of the country, she renounces the city life for that of a married women in a small town. Corina's desire for the world of commodities is shown by her fashionable white shoes, skirt and blouse, which fit with the urban landscape that they are designed for. Yet, this style of dressing becomes an impediment when she visits her husband on the construction site. Her fashionable silhouette, similar to Kuz'mina's body in front of the kitchen shop, shows the lure of the world of exchange value. Corina changes fundamentally when she becomes a piece of a larger assemblage that produces State socialism. After she abandons her passive role of a wife, she contributes not only to the building of the dam, but also to the building of a communist person. The white shoes disappear, and Corina, like Kuz'mina, becomes part of the production of things. Her subjective self is less of a commodity and more of a piece in a socialist assemblage that is deeply connected to the conditions of producing her own existence.

This socialist epistemology of bodies was deeply entrenched in Romanian socialist productions. In *The Valley Resounds*, the boundaries between masculinity and femininity were subsumed by Marxist goals of revolutionary activity. Put differently, gender does not exist in this film outside the call to abolish a bourgeois distinction between masculinity and femininity. I focus briefly on a cinematic moment in the film to show that bodies in socialism have to be read according to a productivist labor politics and its rejection of individual identity. Radu, a miner from Lupeni, returns to a construction site (*șantier*) to bury his brother, who was accidently killed in a sabotage attack by capitalist enemies. As he walks on a dirt road close to the site of the *șantier* he is surrounded by his comrades who cheer him up: "Courage, Radule" ("Curaj, Radule"). Radu decides to speak to his comrades and honor his dead brother. What does he say to praise his brother to an audience of workers who mourn the death of their comrade? Radu tells them that "[Petre] was a good, trustworthy kid. He was like a diligent girl. They did not care enough for his life."[42]

In this funeral oration, a socialist masculine hero is described as a diligent girl. What is striking here, particularly in the context of what scholarly accounts of everyday socialism describe as fully "patriarchal," is that a communist, male-looking martyr is praised as a girl, a diligent girl.[43] Verdery was right to argue that socialism also functioned according to a process of devaluing feminine bodies and jobs, so that, for instance, women were brought into political office at a lower level and in areas considered "appropriately female."[44] In the context of the film, Radu deploys the categories of childhood and womanhood in contrast to the ideal of a rugged and experienced working man who knows the dangers of capitalism.[45] In the film, the desire for the rugged and experienced male Party activist functions as *the* referent for 1950s Romanian socialists. Since neither the Party nor responsible activists could save his brother, the working-class man has to take power back from his class enemies. In this hierarchy of the socialist world, Radu is neither child-like nor woman-like – the way his little brother was. At the end of the 1940s, before the coming of a new post-Fordist regime of labor when masculinity became more fluid, the male-bodied experienced worker was the ruling ideal for Romanian socialists.[46]

Yet socialism sought to abolish the capitalist life of men and women who acted according to their social positions. In *The Valley Resounds*, abolitionist politics rests on the possibility of reversals of bodily identifications, so that man and woman can lose their anchor in capitalism. Socialists took the abolition of capitalist sexed identifications as seriously as the production of communist people. Unlike in a theoretical model of gender performativity, Radu's speech act is not one of disidentification from heteronormative socialism. He upholds the political establishment and does not criticize it. His statement is not an act of freedom where one heroic character fights against a system of injustice that he/she denounces publicly. The moment of praising a male-bodied character as a girl is an act of disidentifying from capitalist norms about strictly male and female roles. To praise Petre as a "diligent girl" shows that in the socialist world one could move away from a single sexed identification. In Romanian socialism, the State project had at its core an attempt to educate a new generation of young activists.[47] Discipline children, indeed, but keep an eye on their process of moving beyond capitalist ideas of men and women.

In relation to Soviet Marxism, the current analytic of gender erases the communist ideal of abolishing capitalist sex roles. Verdery insightfully noted that categories of gender were politically deployed by socialist leaders in Romania as categories of political education.[48] For instance, even when he described motherhood as a woman's supreme mission, the socialist president Nicolae Ceaușescu presented "motherhood" as a profession, which helped equalize "male" and "female" forms of work.[49] Yet the question is whether the category of gender, along with its assumptions about freedom and individuality, can give us an account of what socialism was. While male-bodied workers were overwhelmingly idealized as part of the future of socialism, they also showed the path to human emancipation. While gender identity can reveal a structure of inequality that was present at the heart of State socialism, the problem with this theory is that it eliminates the Marxist epistemological assumptions about communist bodies. In turn, to rehistoricize socialist histories, I draw on the concept of productive bodies to excavate a rival theoretical view of sexuality. Rather than acquiring a gender identity, be that male or female, communist bodies were seen by socialists as unfinished and seeking to destroy a capitalist system.

A second important component of socialists' refusal of individual gender was the dialectical relationship that involved two or more individuals.[50] To build communism involved a historical process with struggles and failures that could nevertheless follow the direction of human emancipation. In socialist realism, communism emerges from a relationship between two kinds of heroes, the Party activist, who is sometimes depicted as intellectually brilliant but removed from real problems, and the working-class hero, who is uneducated but can act effectively to promote socialist goals. In many accounts, dialectics functions when a Party activist and a worker guide each other on the path to communism. This process was theorized at the level not only of method but also of a cinematic aesthetic. The technique of montage was considered key to a new Soviet understanding of art- and film production.[51] It served as a principle of producing a new society, as well as art objects, by placing two elements in a formative relationship. Unlike the historical strategy of the bourgeoisie, which was focused on representing reality in art (or what Arvatov calls depictive art), productivism calls for a dialectical production of facts. In Arvatov's words, art should create a new society by uniting an objective gaze with "a montage of actual facts."[52] When discussing the montage of facts, Arvatov was interested, like the Soviet film director Lev Kuleshov, in the capacity of art to produce a new element from two juxtaposed images.

The classic example of a dialectical relationship in the socialist realist archive is *Chapaev*. In this film, a Party activist and a Red Army commander have a tense but productive working relationship. As in *Chapaev*, in *The Valley Resounds* the Party activist has to work with ordinary workers such as Petre and Radu to fight against capitalist saboteurs. When one of the brothers dies, the other becomes the person who embodies revolutionary hope. Such dialectical conflict is important to the realization that communism is primarily a productive and collective activity of bodies, in contrast to a liberal model concentrated on the transformation of an individual identity. In socialist narratives, characters in films are helped by other participants in the same struggle to become productive. Individual transformation has to be oriented towards the transformation of the collective. In *The Man Next to You*, Ticu and Corina change roles with regard to their work on the construction site. When Ticu works as an engineer, Corina is a housewife, but they swap roles when Ticu loses his job and Corina becomes involved in the construction of the dam. The film suggests that they need to help each other in the construction of socialism, while the Party secretary, Muică, and other committed comrades are also deeply part of this process. The film shows that producing socialism cannot be done without laboring with others to produce goods that fulfill people's needs. Like *The Man Next to You*, *The Valley Resounds* focuses on the collective nature of producing a new society but seeks to show how Party activists and workers strive towards the same goals.

The communisim of *The Valley Resounds* is not unlike that of *The Parisian Cobbler*, a classic of Soviet avant-garde cinema. In both films, communists work to abolish capitalism and traditional sex roles. *The Parisian Cobbler*'s intention is to illustrate the various perils and possibilities of ideological education. Fridrikh Ermler's film warns the viewer that communism is in danger of becoming disconnected from its relationship to labor production and the materiality of the world. As such, a communist society cannot be separated from the process of becoming a productive body. In the Soviet film, the meaning of communism is a process that is negotiated among two key characters: Kirik Rudenko, a shoemaker who is both deaf and mute, and Grisha Kolobov, the Komsomol leader who wears spectacles and is always surrounded by books.[53] Unlike the Grisha, Kirik works with his hands to recraft matter. Kirik is an "intriguing hero" who is engaged in traditional craft amid the emerging industrial economy.[54] His world of instinct, sensation and feeling is much closer to an ideal communist body than Grisha's actions. Kirik, like other socialist realist characters such as Corina and Kuz'mina, is located in close proximity to the materiality of the labor process. Also, like Petre in *The Valley Resounds*, he is shown as having a sensitive and "feminine" disposition. He displays his emotions and acts without overthinking them. In turn, the Komsomol leader gets involved in communist life by acting primarily at the intellectual level. For instance, he offers to Andrei, a young man who left his lover, Katia, pregnant, a book about sexual roles titled *The Problems of Gender in Russian Literature*. Grisha educates others ideologically by telling them how to behave. Unlike Grisha, Kirik intervenes directly and successfully in the lives of the people he cares about. When Katia is in danger, he fights with those who threaten her life. Kirik understands that communism can be achieved more through struggle and less by converting people to a new world.

By deploying Kirik's body as heroic, the film suggests that socialism should not entail the preaching of dogmas to the working class. Kirik is not an individualized hero in a process of instructing others on how to achieve an ideological higher consciousness. On the contrary, he serves as an unfinished element in a program where he becomes a communist by struggling with the material world. His body is a special type of communist body, highly expressive in its relation to his surroundings. He uses neither words nor traditional modes of interacting with others, which serves well the conventions of silent cinema. His face and gestures, rather than portraying an individual self, speak to a fascinating human type that lives communism not only intellectually, but intuitively as well. He also shows that bodies are vehicles for producing a world that abolishes binaries such as masculinity and femininity. Kirik is highly feminized in his affective and intuitive approach to engaging with other characters. Through his acts, he undermines a world where his affective gestures would be regarded as unfit for a masculine body. The film tells us that the separation between the intellectual and the affective is a trap, and socialism needs to follow the path of abolition that is produced by characters such as Kirik, the Parisian cobbler.

Unlike the gender epistemology that emphasizes individual transformations, in this section I have discussed socialist films that function according to a productivist and dialectical epistemology. While it is based on the model of an individual striving to contest the norms of conformist America, gender is antagonistic to the world of dialectical emancipation that communists advanced. In a productivist theory, categories of man and woman consolidate the norms of Soviet communism and do not function as potentially subversive identities that are discriminated against under capitalism.[55] More than that, categories such as masculinity and femininity were not praised in themselves as valuable, but were part of a process of building a new communist person. They were devices utilized to achieve the goal of human emancipation, rather than achieved individualities that aimed to improve a capitalist world.

The gradual disappearance of the productive body

In this second section, my argument moves from early productivism in the Soviet Union to the politics of sexuality in Romanian State socialism in the mid-1960s. As I will show by focusing on a Marxist Romanian film, *The District of Gaiety*, the increased role of anti-abortion trends during the Cold War led to an important shift in the epistemology of productive bodies in Romanian socialism. During the opening of economic and cultural exchanges with the West, or the so-called "thaw," the defense lines of socialism, which were organized around realist socialism and productive bodies, started to be seriously transgressed. The influence of western tropes in Romanian cinema is not an exception for the socialist East, since the USA had an important impact on the Soviet Union's cinema and television during the Cold War.[56] The key to inserting capitalist tropes into State socialism's art and cinematography was to integrate them into a Marxist ideology.[57] If, in *The Valley Resounds*, the film is centered on the fight for the abolition of capitalist gender roles, the 1964 socialist film suggests a change to new goals, such as an increased population to fight the Cold War. The anti-abortion themes in the film indicate a gradual withdrawal from the epistemology of Marxist productivism.

Rather than looking at the Romanian politics of limiting abortion as derived primarily from the ideology of State socialism, as Gail Kligman claims, I introduce the abortion politics of Romanian socialists within the broader context of the Cold War.[58] While the Soviet Union and most eastern European countries had pro-abortion laws, Ceaușescu's Romania chose to limit abortion drastically after 1966. It was legal for the first time in the history of the Romanian State between 1957 and 1966. My claim is that the Romanian politics of severely restricting abortion were shaped by an international trend to naturalize conservative sex roles, which unfolded at the end of the 1950s in Europe around the theme of Nazism and its aftermath.[59] The conflict between eastern socialism and western capitalism was a war about biopolitical weapons such as demographics. As part of this conflict, the idea of natality became a key element in defining the role of women in socialism. Romanian Marxists thought that natality politics would offer them a competitive edge in their fight against capitalism, particularly given the growth in birth rates in the USA after World War II. Both the West and the East wanted to show an increase in population as an argument that their politics was better than that of the competing system.

This ideological fight had a direct impact on Soviet-style communism in Romania, which had previously depicted the socialist body as a tool to abolish capitalist sex roles. In *The Valley Resounds*, Radu and Sanda were two characters who were mobilized to show how to destroy the ideological norms of capitalism. In the State socialist Romania of the mid-1960s, the politics of sexuality shifted from showing communists destroying capitalist sex roles to showing communists helping the State to produce more children.[60] How did the socialist politics of natality change? Dagmar Herzog offers a potential answer in focusing on the changes brought about by attitudes towards Nazism after World War II.[61] Nazism was used as a term and ideological formation to explain everything related to sex, from the alleged marital crisis, to sexual crises, to the disappearance of eroticism. In Germany, for instance, Nazi politics has constituted the main referent for public debates about sexuality.[62] While the figure of the Nazi had a particular role in Germany, it was also deployed in State socialism to support its demographic politics. Herzog traces an important transformation at the beginning of the 1950s in Germany, when conservative politics had intensified its rhetoric: "Many of the sexually conservative attitudes now customarily associated with the 1950s, and particularly with the especially stuffy West German version of them" only became consolidated "gradually in the course of the early 1950s."[63] The Catholic Church had an important role to play in arguing that sexual restraint had to be introduced in Germany. It utilized and solidified the perception that there had been a close connection between Nazi criminality and sexual pleasure.[64] To mobilize opposition to abortion and contraception, Catholics attacked Nazi politics as one of unrestricted sexuality. For instance, Walter Dirks, a postwar Catholic intellectual, bluntly argued that abortions emerged from the ideology of Nazim.[65] The conservative movement in Germany deployed the legacy of National Socialism to underscore why some issues had to be addressed while others had to be kept undiscussed. For instance, the National Socialists' emphasis on pleasure and sex outside marriage was completely discarded, since it was a key element that contradicted the narrative of Germans as victims of National Socialism. The conservative movement gained many supporters because it was able to portray itself as an answer to the evil of National Socialism, provided that it presented itself as a victim of Nazism rather than as being among "its supporters and beneficiaries."[66] The legacy of Nazism deeply affected not only right-wing politics, but also the politics of the Left. Unlike what the student movement believed at the end of the 1960s – namely, that the Third Reich was sex-hostile and pro-family – conservative postwar politics was a new invention in reaction to Nazism.[67] Both the Left and the Right in Europe put at the core of their political proposals a refusal of Nazi legacy, yet they chose different elements to emphasize as key to their programs.

In *The District of Gaiety*, anti-abortion politics derives from the same aversion to Nazism that Herzog describes in her study. The socialist epistemology of productive bodies incorporates conservative ideas, given that the problem of natality takes center stage. In the film, Lia (Maria Clara Sebök) and Dima (Adrian Moraru) are two young people who are fighting on the side of the Romanian Communist Party. The action takes place sometime in 1938, when the right-wing parties are in power in Romania. The main theme of the film – that true love between comrades leads to marriage and children – is foregrounded from the opening shot. The film starts not only with a wedding in "the district of gaiety" (the Rahova neighborhood in Bucharest), but also with Lia and Dima's first meeting at the cinema. The initial shots combine a bride dressed in white and the march of a wedding party with Lia and Dima flirting and walking side by side. The conflict in the film derives from Lia and

Dima's efforts to overcome various obstacles to their relationship. Lia's older brother, Gheorghe II (Ilarion Ciobanu) does not like the budding flirtation between his sister and Dima. In addition, the police try to arrest Dima and blackmail Lia to denounce her lover. In comparison with *The Valley Resounds*, the emphasis in *The District of Gaiety* is on the romantic interest between the two young communists. Alexandra Kollontai's desire that communism should not be about the individual love of two individuals, but about a collective process of forging a new society, has disappeared from the concerns of Romanian socialists. While Radu and Sanda in *The Valley Resounds* fight for the abolition of capitalist gender roles, Lia and Dima share conservative assumptions about marriage and the politics of reproduction. Whereas Radu and Sanda's relationship is a product of the fight against capitalism, Lia and Dima end up in conflict with the fascist police by accident.

The District of Gaiety justifies anti-abortion politics as an effect of opposition to National Socialism. The plot in the second part of the film revolves around a political murder. Dima witnesses the assassination of a socialist journalist who denounced the exploitative politics of the Rahova factory, and he runs away and hides while the police try to find him. Lia is threatened by police agents, but she manages to warn Dima that the police are looking for him. The scene that follows Lia's intervention takes place in the office of a gynecologist. The head of the police (Commissar Buhăneanu), who is portrayed as a Nazi, enters the room and asks Lia if she wants to have an abortion. Lia says "no," and leaves the room. The head of the police then asks "the other" people to come in. Female-bodied people, who we learn are sex workers dressed in a sexually provocative manner, enter and take off their clothes. The camera follows the gaze of the commissar, who stares intently at the half-naked bodies. We are watching the sense of satisfaction that he derives from the scene. He takes off his glasses and his gaze alternates between sexual arousal and childish innocence. To portray Buhăneanu as a voyeur, the film connects the comissar's sexual curiosity to his threating behavior towards Lia.

A conservative politics of sexuality begins to inform the socialist narrative of the future of a Marxist society. Sexual pleasure and Nazism are indistinguishable, almost as if they cannot be thought of separately. In the following scene, Lia is beaten by a police officer, who informs the commissar that she does not want to denounce her lover. In response, the commissar tells Lia that she will be released from detention if she betrays Dima. When she refuses, Buhăneanu threatens her with abortion. Lia begs the doctor to let her keep the baby. The commissar calls the doctor and asks him to perform the abortion. The doctor refuses because, he argues, his professional ethic will not contravene the explicit interdiction of a patient. The commissar uses Nazi language to argue that the hysterical communist, "Lia," will give birth to a criminal and a degenerate, who will be a product of inferior races. As a final argument, the commissar claims that in the Third Reich abortion politics with regard to communists is the official law. The doctor tells Lia that she needs to keep a secret and asks her to pretend that she had an abortion. To show how generous the doctor is, his final line is "God bless you" ("Dumnezeu să te ajute"), which contrasts the doctor's religiosity with the commissar's fascism. To underscore the message of the increasing danger of National Socialism, the following shot is an excerpt from a newsreel showing Hitler and the goose-stepping SS.

The District of Gaiety marks an important shift in how productive bodies are deployed in Romanian socialism. A politics of reproduction becomes a key site for justifying the politics of the Romanian Communist Party. As in Germany, when Catholic intellectuals deployed images of Nazi sadists to buttress support, Nazism served as a reason for Romanian socialists to increase the pressure to regulate sexuality. Abortion was an issue that simplified a broader range of topics touching on bodily control and desire.[68] To prepare the ground for justifying the decisions of the Party severely to limit abortions, the film deploys women's bodies to promote a rhetoric of natality. The choice of a woman to keep her child is counterposed to a Nazi who wants to deny her choice. Women's choice to have babies, as a measure to fight Nazism, is an important element in the rhetoric of anti-abortion in the mid-1960s. Nazism was not the only vehicle for strengthening normative ideas about sexual behavior. In the 1966 *Virgo*, sex outside marriage leads to the deaths of two young people who take their own lives. The vehicle for criticizing non-normative sexuality is not the figure of the Nazi, but the Greek mythology that cautioned that unrestricted sex can lead to incestuous relations. Unlike free love, which can be tied to multiple stories about corrupted sexual behavior, abortion politics had to be politically connected to the legacy of Nazism.[69]

If we compare *The District of Gaiety* with earlier Soviet productions, the contrast in abortion politics is significant. In the 1927 *Bed and Sofa*, Liuda chooses to keep her baby despite the opposition of her two lovers. In the film, Liuda and her husband Kolia live in a single basement room in Moscow and have marital problems. When Volodia, Kolia's friend, arrives, he starts a relationship with Liuda, but he reveals himself to be even more dictatorial and insensitive than Kolia. In the end, Liuda decides to leave town and, like Lia, she seems to embody the figure of the emancipated communist. In the Soviet film, abortion is the strategy of controlling men deployed against women's desires. Like Lia, Liuda refuses to abort, but this time her lovers, Volodia and Kolia, ask her to go see a doctor at a private clinic. Rather than fascism, an abusive and non-communist masculinity seems to be the target of the director's anger. In both the socialism of the Soviet Union and middle-period socialism in Romania, pro-natalist policies function to portray women's choices as liberated, but only when they desire to become mothers. After thirty years, however, Romanian socialists needed the figure of the Nazi to underscore the necessity of an increased demographics to fight the Cold War. The productive body, which represented a key anti-capitalist epistemology for eastern European Marxists, was beginning gradually to incorporate elements of a conservative sexuality from western Europe.

Conclusion

The first chapter of Part II opens the project of de-centering queer theory by focusing on the epistemology of sexuality in Soviet Marxism. While some studies have concentrated on comparing different countries during the Cold War with regard to specific gender policies (e.g., reproduction and abortion), my strategy is to interrogate Cold War epistemologies of bodies. By interpreting theoretical and visual Marxist materials from the Soviet Union and Romania, the role of the chapter was twofold. First, it introduced the argument that the conceptualization of gender identity is in conflict with eastern European socialism. Bodies and sexuality in early Soviet Marxism gesture to an abolitionist politics that has been ignored as a theoretical resource by critics of queer liberalism. Second, my analysis revealed not only that corporal productivism constituted an important thread in Marxist cinema, but also that it was gradually transformed by Cold War dynamics. In historicizing the epistemology of productive bodies, I analyzed a Romanian Marxist film from the mid-1960s, which incorporated conservative western tropes of abortion.

This chapter has offered only a brief introduction to the question of conflict in the political contrast between two epistemologies, however. More research is required to understand the various evolutions of different socialist cinemas in their relation to sexuality during the Cold War. This investigation is needed, given that, at least in Anglo-American theory, the archive of Marxist cinema does not have an important role in queer studies. In bypassing this resource, the danger is that queer theorists can replicate the liberal anti-communist discourse that saw eastern European Marxism as a historical void.

Two consequences emerge from this chapter. First, the epistemology of productivist bodies offer a powerful challenge to theoretical accounts that work with the analytic of gender. Katherine Verdery's deployment of gender consolidated the perception that eastern European Marxism was an authoritarian regime, unlike those in the free countries of the Anglo-American world. In opposition to this argument, I have provided an account that sees productivist bodies as part of an emancipatory and dialectical project to abolish capitalist sex roles. Soviet Marxism offers a counternarrative to the contemporary assumption that bodies have to be theorized in alignment with values such as freedom and individuality. Similarly, I contested Kligman's idea that Romanian anti-abortion politics is a direct result of communist ideology. Studies such as Kligman's that trace in a causal argumentation abortion bans to communism miss not only the history of abortion laws in State socialism, but also historical developments that were part of the Cold War. In turn, I suggested that the ideological underpinnings of Marxism offer a strong progressive epistemology that was directly affected by the rise of conservative ideas on sexual reproduction.

Second, the epistemology of a productivist body offers a window onto not only eastern European Marxism, but also its rival developments in the West. Eastern European epistemology is not the only body of analysis that is affected by this theoretical account, given that the Cold War shaped the politics of decolonization in Africa, Asia and Latin America. To rephrase Verdery's formulation that gender is "a symbol system by which bodies enter into sociality," gender appears to be a symbol system by which bodies entered in the Cold War.[70] Yet, while gender became a dominant theory in social sciences, particularly after the 1990s, political dynamics during the Cold War are not perfectly aligned to the binary between communism and liberal capitalism. As I have shown, Romanian socialists have integrated a conservative rhetoric to justify anti-abortion restrictions. Also, I suggested that future detailed historical work can identify different turns and trajectories for Marxist sexuality in an eastern European context.

This chapter introduces the possibility that the analytic of gender needs to transform its epistemological assumptions. The danger is that its emphasis on individualism and freedom can block projects designed to lead to collective emancipation. I resume my historical analysis by looking at the emergence of gender in North America, concentrating on the sexology literature. I focus on John Money's texts between the 1950s and the 1970s, given his prominence in the rise of sexuality studies. The chapter continues the work of tracing the difference between productivist bodies and gender identity, but this time it provides a historical reading of Money's logic as part of US anti-communism during the Cold War.

Notes

1 See Evgeny Dobrenko, *Stalinist Cinema and the Production of History: Museum of the Revolution* (Edinburgh: Edinburgh University Press, 2008). His definition of socialist realism emphasizes the concrete presence of communist reality: socialist realism is in fact "reality given to us" (p. 14).
2 See *ibid.*, p. xix.
3 *Ibid.*, pp. 4–5.
4 See Boris Groys, *The Communist Hypothesis*, trans. Thomas H. Ford (London: Verso, 2009), pp. x–xi.
5 See Peter Berger and Thomas Luckmann, *The Social Construction of Reality: A Treatise in the Sociology of Knowledge* (London: Penguin, 1966), p. 66.

6 For this argument see Manfred Prisching, "Why Are Peter L. Berger and Thomas Luckmann Austrians?," in Michaela Pfadenhaue and Hubert Knoblauch (eds), *Social Constructivism as Paradigm? The Legacy of the Social Construction of Reality* (London: Routledge, 2018), pp. 21–44.
7 See Dobrenko, *Stalinist Cinema*, p. 19: "it is methodologically important not to search for, so to speak, political economy in Socialist Realism (how it 'reflects' or 'falsifies' reality), but rather to understand Socialist Realism itself as a political economy."
8 See Zenovia Sochor, *Revolution and Culture: The Bogdanov–Lenin Controversy* (Ithaca: Cornell University Press, 2018), pp. 3–21, for a history of debates between Leninism and Bogdanovism.
9 See Arran Gare, "Aleksandr Bogdanov: Proletkult and Conservation," *Capitalism, Nature, Socialism*, 5:2 (1994), 65–94.
10 *Ibid.*
11 See Boris Arvatov, *Art and Production*, ed. John Roberts and Alexei Penzin, trans. Shushan Avagyan (London: Pluto Press, 2017), pp. 95–96.
12 See *ibid.*, p. 111: "To the extent that the proletariat will master its own activities, to the extent that its organizational actions will spread across all the realms of life – the proletariat will have to move from spontaneity to a normalized change of everyday life. And that is possible only in one case: if artists desist from decorating or depicting everyday life and start *building* it" (italics in the original).
13 See Sochor, *Revolution and Culture*, pp. 17, 203–222.
14 See *ibid.*, pp. 203–221, for an analysis of the relationship between Stalin's Cultural Revolution and Proletkult.
15 Serguei Alex Oushakine, "'Against the Cult of Things': On Soviet Productivism, Storage Economy, and Commodities with No Destination," *Russian Review*, 73 (2014), p. 203.
16 For this definition of socialist realism, see C. Vaughan James, *Soviet Socialist Realism: Origins and Theory* (London: Palgrave Macmillan, 1973), p. 1. For political differences between Lenin and the Proletkult movement, see Sochor, *Revolution and Culture*, pp. 125–158.
17 Dobrenko, *Stalinist Cinema*, p. xii.
18 Arvatov, *Art and Production*, pp. 107–108: "To achieve the full sensation of reality, to become fully aware not only of the purpose of activity and the technique of its achievement, but also the form, the concrete realization of reality – all of this means reaching such a state of socio-aesthetic monism, where every phenomenon, every object is both constructed and perceived as a live, practicable organism ('construction,' as opposed to bourgeois 'composition'), i.e., is built and perceived collectively."

19 For the abandonment of iconoclasm and radical artistic gestures in Soviet Marxism after the 1930s, see David L. Hoffman, *Stalinist Values: The Cultural Norms of Soviet Modernity, 1917–1941* (Ithaca: Cornell University Press, 2018), p. 6: "No longer was it necessary to use iconoclasm to attack bourgeois culture, now that the economic basis and social classes that had spawned that culture had been eliminated in the Soviet Union. This is why the Soviet state in the mid-1930s tilted away from iconoclasm and radicalism in a range of fields, from art and architecture to education and history writing."
20 For "the new man" in Romanian socialist realism, see Alex Goldiș, "The Ideology of Semiosis in Romanian Prose under Communism," *Primerjalna književnost*, 39:2 (2016), p. 90.
21 See Dobrenko, *Stalinist Cinema*, p. 14, for a definition of socialist realism that emphasizes the concrete presence of communist reality: "socialist realism" is in fact "reality given to us."
22 In the Cold War debates about economies, a crucial ideological difference was Marx's distinction between use-value and exchange value. According to the former, commodities have value because of their capacity to fulfill people's needs, while in the latter, value is given by capitalism. The idea of use-value was key to socialism's fight against capitalist ideologies. In direct relation to the idea of building a Soviet person, it constituted socialist subjectivities as people who created use-value, as opposed to people who operated according to the market economy.
23 See Alexandra Kollontai quoted in Gregory Carleton, *Sexual Revolution in Bolshevik Russia* (Pittsburgh, PA: University of Pittsburgh Press, 2005), p. 41. For debates in the Soviet Union about Kollontai's position, see Carleton, *Sexual Revolution*, pp. 45–47.
24 See Verdery, *What Was Socialism?*, p. 62.
25 Dobrenko, *Stalinist Cinema*, p. xviii.
26 Emma Widdis, *Socialist Senses: Film, Feeling and the Soviet Subject, 1917–1939* (Bloomington: Indiana University Press, 2017), p. 33, shows that the Soviet person cannot be understood without the techniques that Soviet scientists deployed to create the communist person. An applied psychology that took the shape of "psychotechnics" describes the transformation of the psyche by transforming the body (Widdis, *Socialist Senses*, pp. 33–34).
27 Periklis Pavlidis, "Socialism, Labour and Education: From Marx to Makarenko," *International Journal of Educational Policies*, 11:1 (2017), pp. 1, 7.
28 See Anton Makarenko quoted in *ibid.*, p. 8: "Correct Soviet education must be organised by forming united, strong and influential collectives. The school must be a single collective where all the

educative processes are properly organised. Every separate member of the collective should feel his dependence on the collective, he should be devoted to the interests of the collective, he should uphold these interests and value them above all else."
29 Makarenko quoted in *ibid.*, p. 9.
30 Lenin is cited by C. Vaughan James, *Soviet Socialist Realism*, p. 12: "We want to establish, and we will establish, a free press, free not simply from the police, but also from capital, from careerism, and what is more, free from bourgeois-anarchist individualism."
31 Oushakine, "Against the Cult of Things," p. 203.
32 *Ibid.*
33 Arvatov, *Art and Production*, p. 111.
34 Against the idea that the Soviet system led to economic scarcity, Oushakine, "Against the Cult of Things," p. 202, showed that the Soviet system of productivism led to *storage* as a main economic outcome and not, as previously understood, to the production of commodities for the market.
35 Widdis, *Socialist Senses*, p. 238.
36 *Ibid.*, p. 240.
37 *Ibid.*, p. 238.
38 *Ibid.*
39 *Ibid.*, p. 240.
40 For socialism as a product of what "already existed," see Dobrenko, *Stalinist Cinema*, p. 5.
41 For the thaw in Soviet Cinema, see Josephine Woll, *Real Images: Soviet Cinema and the Thaw* (London: I.B. Tauris, 2000).
42 In the original Romanian: "era ca un copil bun, încrezător. Era ca o fată vrednică. N-au avut grija de viața lui" (my translation).
43 See Gail Kligman, *Politica duplicității: Controlul reproducerii in România lui Ceaușescu* (Bucharest: Humanitas, 2000), p. 37, for whom the notion of gender equality was foreign to socialism because Romanian socialism was a patriarchal society.
44 Verdery, *What Was Socialism?*, p. 67.
45 See Marko Dumančić, "Hidden in Plain Sight: The Histories of Gender and Sexuality during the Cold War," in Philip E. Muehlenbeck (ed.), *Gender, Sexuality and the Cold War: A Global Perspective* (Nashville: Vanderbilt University Press, 2017), p. 5, for the argument that a warrior-male rhetoric was a key tactic during the Cold War: "In 1962 Khrushchev memorably reflected on Berlin's limbo status: 'Berlin is the testicle of the West. When I want the West to scream, I squeeze on Berlin.'"
46 For a shift in ideologies of manhood in the USA from 1960s working-class masculinity to a countercultural embrace of androgyny and the

sensitive man, see Eric Lott, *Black Mirror: The Cultural Contradictions of American Racism* (Cambridge, MA: Harvard University Press, 2017), pp. 160–161.
47 Young people's sexuality was defined as a positive site for constructing a new socialist society. For this argument about youth in East Germany's socialism, see Josie McLellan, *Love in the Time of Communism: Love and Intimacy in the GDR* (Cambridge: Cambridge University Press, 2011), p. 26.
48 Verdery, *What Was Socialism?*, p. 66.
49 *Ibid.*
50 While I focus on the relationship between two individuals, Sergei Eisenstein's *Battleship Potemkin* shows that large collectives can become revolutionary agents.
51 See the key role of montage theory in the debate between Sergei Eisenstein and Bela Balázs (Widdis, *Socialist Senses*, p. 40). For Eisenstein, the power of Soviet cinema was the juxtaposition of shots, rather than the celebration of material as a description of reality.
52 See Arvatov, *Art and Production*, p. 118.
53 Komsomol is the abbreviation for Kommunisticheskiy Soyuz Molodyozhi, the political youth organization of the Soviet Union.
54 Widdis, *Socialist Senses*, p. 133.
55 See Leerom Medevoi, *Rebels: Youth and the Cold War Origins of Identity* (Durham, NC: Duke University Press, 2005), p. 320.
56 See Sergei Zhuk, "Hollywood's Insidious Charms: The Impact of American Cinema and Television on the Soviet Union during the Cold War," *Cold War History*, 14 (2014), 593–617.
57 See Vance Kepley, Jr., "*Intolerance* and the Soviets: A Historical Investigation," in Richard Taylor and Ian Christie (eds), *Inside the Film Factory: New Approaches to Russian and Soviet Cinema* (London: Routledge, 1991), p. 57, and his analysis of how the Soviet institutions detoured the US film *Intolerance* according to their ideological goals: "By insisting that the stories of *Intolerance* represent some dreadful past, the Soviets could fit the film into a Marxist schema which promises a glorious future."
58 Kligman, *Politica duplicității*, pp. 12, 15.
59 Dagmar Herzog, *Sex after Fascism: Memory and Morality in Twentieth-Century Germany* (Princeton: Princeton University Press, 2005), p. 96.
60 Radu and Sanda are discussed in further detail in Chapter 5. See pp. 000–000.
61 *Ibid.*, p. 64.
62 *Ibid.*, p. 72.
63 *Ibid.*

64 *Ibid.*, p. 75.
65 As Dirks argued, "The path of least resistance, the easy solution, the capitulation – the perfect solution, if one has managed to shut one's eyes before the single uncomfortable fact that the killing of human life is murder – all one has to do is walk in the footsteps of the SS doctors" (quoted in *ibid.*, p. 76).
66 *Ibid.*, p. 104.
67 *Ibid.*, p. 98: "the conservative sexual mores of the mid- to late 1950s and early 1960s were not a direct inheritance from Nazism, but rather a new postwar invention, developed also in complex reaction against Nazis."
68 *Ibid.*, p. 76: the image of abortion "functioned to condense a whole cluster of negative feelings about Nazism and to fuse distress over its genocidal policies with revulsion at its encouragement of popular libertinism."
69 In Romanian films addressing abortion, the Nazi figure was replaced in the mid-1970s with the corrupted abortionist. See, for instance, the character played by Draga Olteanu-Matei (Moașa) in the 1975 *Postcards with Wild Flowers* (*Ilustrate cu flori de câmp*, Andrei Blaier).
70 Verdery, *What Was Socialism?*, p. 62.

3

The birth of gender epistemology during the Cold War

The third chapter shifts from an investigation of eastern European Marxist materials to analyze the emergence of the concept of gender in US studies of sexuality. I show that the birth of gender is deeply entrenched in the anti-communist epistemology of the USA during the Cold War. I start from the premise that the birth of gender is historically connected to the erasure of eastern European Marxism as an analytic, and is a major development in the conceptualization of bodies and sexuality. John Money was a Cold War psychologist and sexologist who not only coined the term "gender," but also became a household name in studies of gender reassignment after the 1950s. As I will demonstrate, his epistemological assumptions are inspired by a liberal ideology that saw Soviet Marxism as a fundamental political threat. In contrast to a Marxist ideology that sought to create a new communist person, the analytic of gender reinserted the priority of individual consciousness and its freedom to transform social norms.[1] In the US Cold War model, white Anglo-American masculinity was not only the adequate response to the Soviet threat, but also the normative ideal underlying the racialized meaning of gender. In Money's conception of gender, blackness, indigeneity and racialized others are subsumed under the category of a defective gender in need of corrections. A hierarchically superior gender was acquired when one was able to internalize the conventions of white Anglo-America, provided that this achievement was the embodiment of a racially superior social norm.

My argument about gender challenges studies that locate its controversial nature in its deployment as a scientific and political theory. Unlike this scholarship, I show that the epistemology of Cold War gender was conceptually shaped by anti-communism. Influential scholars argued that the term "gender" has deep roots in Cold War politics, but they refrained from asking the broader

The birth of gender epistemology   71

implication in relation to its anti-communist epistemology. By historicizing the term "gender," Jemima Repo and Susan Stryker have opened new avenues for thinking about Cold War gender.[2] In her critique of the European Union's policy framework, Repo identifies a neoliberal deployment of gender rhetoric, which she traces back to its earlier use by US sexologists.[3] In locating the rise of the term "gender" to the Cold War political conflicts, she offers an important genealogical tool to think about the later usage of the term by feminist theorists in the 1970s. For her, "although it is often mistakenly taken to be so, gender is in fact not the brainchild of feminism, but a biopolitical apparatus whose deployment precedes its use in feminist theory."[4] As she argues, the birth of gender theory can be traced back to John Money and his colleagues Joan and John Hampton at Johns Hopkins University.[5] Money and his team showed that what was understood by psychosocial sex, which became gender in their vocabulary, was learned after birth. According to Repo's argument, the term "gender" functioned as a weapon of biopolitics to instill values about family, the necessity of reproduction, and maleness and femaleness in the post-World War II USA.[6] The problem with gender lies in its context of emergence, since Anglo-American feminists borrowed "this conceptual apparatus directly from that context so as to contest biologically determinist accounts of sex while failing to recognize the disciplinary uses for which it was originally created and applied in the clinic."[7] However, she identifies a critical feminist appropriation of the term "gender" that can operate as a powerful method, at least theoretically, outside the biopolitical context that she indicts.[8]

While Susan Stryker locates the birth of transgender in a Cold War and colonial context, she is optimistic about the term's possibilities for queer theory.[9] Instead of abandoning transgender because of its colonial genealogy, she argues that transgender "is not only a Eurocentric export" because "the colonized are not bereft of agency in their uptake of introduced forms."[10] In short, as both a term and analytic transgender can function as an anti-colonial tool. This argument is part of Stryker's analysis of the transsexuality of Christine Jorgensen, one of the first world-famous transgender people, which served as a spectacle to instill white colonial values in the Philippines in the context of post-World War II independence movements. For Stryker, Jorgensen's gender presentation and her transsexuality are part of a biopolitical deployment of colonial discipline.[11] More importantly, the role of Jorgensen was to erase the presence of other gender- and sexual non-normative subjectivities that do not correspond with a white US transsexual normativity:

> Jorgensen embodies the white, fashionably self-fashioning, glamorous ethos associated with the post-World War II US material culture that the film figures as ultimately desirable, and, on the other hand, she represents a prospect that the film forecloses for its protagonists.[12]

Both Repo and Stryker are interested in separating the history of the neoliberal and colonial use of gender from other progressive projects that deployed the term to generate anti-heteronormative and anti-colonial politics. Yet, in this chapter I show that a critical approach to gender focuses not only on attacks on the reappropriation of the term, but also on revisiting its rival epistemology during the Cold War. This revision also has consequences for the critical race- and indigenous scholarship exploring the racial history of the term "gender." Hortense Spillers and Mark Rifkin argue that an investigation of processes of racialization, slave economies and settler colonialism shows that gender politics advances white Anglo-American norms of masculinity and femininity under the assumption that they are universal.[13] In a landmark 1987 article, "Mama's Baby, Papa's Maybe," Spillers focused on gender's deployment by racial capitalism, and the subsequent abjection associated with black bodies. She showed that gender emerged from the imposition of capitalistic relations of property on a slave economy during the Middle Passage.[14] In her view, the term "gender" should not be dissociated from colonial violence because the enslaved "diasporic plight" marked "a theft of the body – a willful and violent (and unimaginable from this distance) severing of the captive body from its motive will, its active desire."[15] On a similar line of inquiry, but with a focus on indigeneity and sexuality, Rifkin shows that heteronormativity (which implies gendered understandings of man and woman, as well as their sexuality) is the result of an ongoing imperial project to reproduce the settler state against indigenous formations.[16] He gestures towards the possibility that "the coordinated assault on native social formations that has characterized US policy since its inception" can be "understood as an effort to make heterosexuality compulsory."[17]

In building on these scholars' work, I explore the epistemological consequences that generated the success of the term "gender." The use of white masculinity and white womanhood to exploit the enslaved, Native Americans and the immigrant working class is a historical dynamic that is a feature of what Cedric Robinson calls "racial capitalism."[18] The Cold War was a period when racial capitalism acquired specific dynamics by deploying a new vocabulary in relation to the communist threat. The following sections aim to unpack, on the one hand, some of the transformations in political language that are distinct to this period, with a focus on the rise of social constructivism. On the other, I trace how the productivist body of eastern European Marxism has become gradually irrelevant and replaced by a rival ideology of identity and its epistemology.

Gender and Cold War liberalism

Gender became a mode of indicating a person's identity as part of a strong wave of anti-communist politics at the beginning of the Cold War. After 1948, a conceptual transformation led to an important change in the Anglo-American vocabulary. Repo notices that "before the 1950s, gender could be used to refer to various types, varieties, kinds and models of any sort of phenomena, sometimes sex, but not necessarily."[19] Gender became what sex had been before World War II. As Repo argues in *The Biopolitics of Gender*, it transformed into a biopolitical weapon of control: "Gender, understood as the social, psychological and cultural dimension of sex, was forged by psychiatrists in order to discipline and normalize the minds, bodies, and selves of intersex children and trans-people as well as their families."[20] The problem with the science of psychology was that the sex of the body no longer provided "adequate explanation of either 'sex roles' or 'sexual behavior.'"[21] Gender emerged gradually as a dominant concept, but in the 1950s and 1960s it served mostly as a stand-in for identity, the leading category in the language of social scientists.

"Identity talk" permeated US culture and drew its relevance from the opposition between US liberalism and communism.[22] During the 1950s and 1960s the discovery of the self was associated with the rise of personal identity against the domination of a collectivist society.[23] Identity and its correlate, gender, were deployed to name personal autonomy and sovereignty under Fordist capitalism, and contrasted Soviet collectivism to anti-communist freedom-loving politics. Identity and gender fused as a theoretical method of analysis in social sciences only after the 1970s. The theory of identity construction was based on the premise of a liberated self that was in the process of finding its freedom. The term "identity" was coined by Erik Erikson in the *Childhood and Society* (1950), which was the first account to define identity as a normative goal of the self.[24] It soon became a hegemonic term and became associated with one's refusal of conservative and war-oriented politics.[25]

When it emerged, "identity" was a term of the liberal contestation of the USA's imperial politics. This contestation defined US citizens as people who seek to live as free individuals against the collectivist, slave-like politics of Soviet Marxism.[26] Given the power struggles between the western and eastern blocs, personal identity has become associated with Cold War liberalism. Within the context of Cold War politics, identity had a powerful role of supporting constitutional and democratic rights such as free speech by attacking the premises of Soviet Marxism.[27] In doing so, it deployed the communist threat to limit the demands of minorities such as women, people of color and queer people.[28] Liberals "used hysteria over the possibility that the federal government had been infiltrated by Communists, homosexuals and lesbians to prevent competing constructions of social reality from mobilizing popular support."[29] According to its historical narrative, liberalism has become the vantage point to describe communist projects as infringing on people's freedom. Identity was a core epistemological assumption that showed the possibility of Americans becoming free individuals.

As part of the emergence of a new anti-communist vocabulary, "identity" became an important term to articulate the conventions of Cold War liberalism. It was conceptualized in direct relation with the dynamic between repression, which was associated with the conservatives, and the liberation of the self, which was the goal of the liberals.[30] Seeking to contain communism, postwar US ideology articulated "far reaching forms of social regulations" that were undergirded by suburbia's nuclear family living arrangements.[31] The suburbs were defined as the space of capitalist freedom, "a utopian space of national abundance in which people could at last fully realize their individuality by making consumer choices that expressed and satisfied their inner wants."[32] As a response to the rhetoric of suburbia, liberals embraced the idea that one's freedom can be achieved by uncovering a hidden part of oneself, which is repressed by social norms. The fear of mass consumption in the US suburbs was translated into a critical discourse with regard to social conformity. White suburbs, which were supposed to protect their citizens from communism and the danger of inner cities, became prisons.[33] In reaction to the ideology of the suburbs, the young generation revolted against the conformism of their families. As a result, "identity" became a term to name this rebellion.[34] Along with other figures such as the rebel teenager (the "bad boy" of Cold War American culture), the concept of identity offered a critical tool to respond to "the red scare" and the growing concern about conformism.[35]

Identity in the United States became a "normative psychopolitical principle," "the idealization of youth rebellion" and a grounding conflict between "America" and Fordist suburbia.[36] In the social sciences, the concept of identity was taken on as one with a vital critical potential. It served a double role. It derived from a positivist thinking that sought behavioral changes, but these transformations were also understood as a path to freedom. Yet, while bodies and their behavior seem easier to modify, the self is harder to change. Scientists faced the question of the difference between a sexed body and a personal self, which was harder to transform than the body itself.[37] While social scientists sought to modify behaviors, the discourses of the revolt against suburbia emphasized the modification of the whole self. Against a widespread behavioralist theory, countercultural politics in the 1960s focused on the assumption that people's identities can be remodeled. As part of that discourse, the legacy of uncovering a hidden identity claimed that the discovery and the ownership of a better self leads to a critical resistance to social inequality. Like the rebel, the transexual acquired a hidden self that can be liberated.

At the beginning of the ideological war against communism, gender and its correlative terms had multiple political functions. The coinage of terms such as "transsexual" and "gender" had the role of protecting the USA from the threat of Soviet collectivism. As Joanne Meyerowitz argues about Christine Jorgensen, the anti-communist element is key to transgender identity transformation:

Her story, as she told it in *American Weekly*, offered the public an unusual twist on a tried-and-true tale of individual striving, success, and upward mobility. This tale had special resonance in the postwar years. In the popular discourse of the Cold War, a mythic version of American individualism stood in contrast to an equally mythic version of conformist imperatives in "totalitarian" societies.[38]

Communist theory can be challenged, as the story of gender shows, with American stories of transformative individual changes. Unlike Soviet people, who are stuck in a rigid communist role, free people can change their gender. More than that, to be free meant to fight against imperialism and colonialism. The story of transgender was also part of a liberal narrative about liberation from old imperial domination. As Medevoi argued, among the most influential of ideological US ideas was Erikson's identity concept, which explicitly shared this Cold War fantasy of a postcolonial revolutionary American character.[39] Social constructivism and the concept of identity challenged the claim that the USA lacks a capacity to generate social change. They were promoted in response to decolonial politics and the claims to postcolonial independence of many African nations.[40] The USA and the Soviet Union were struggling for political influence in the newly decolonized countries in Africa, Asia and Latin America. The USA rebranded itself as a postrevolutionary society and forged a narrative about its anti-colonial roots.[41] The term "transgender" became a concept in the new ideological offensive to show the USA's progressive history.

Freedom and individuality were not accidental terms in the deployment of the analytic of gender, but central to its formation. Cold War gender proposed a mode of thinking about bodies that derives from a culturalist assumption that one's culture shapes one's sex. Social constructivism defined that cultural and social liberation can be achieved when one can have a gender. According to John Money, liberation is possible when one moves through different stages of development. He coined the term "gender" in a 1955 paper where he sought to correct the presentation of intersex people. As he describes his own thinking process, Money felt that a single word can better incapsulate sexual anomalies: that is, gender.[42] The term was conceptualized as a step forward from looking at sexual identities as natural. Money's goal was to give gender the role of an overarching concept that will settle debates about the diversity

The birth of gender epistemology 77

of sexual presentation. It became a tool for correcting behaviors and enforcing norms about the nuclear family and proper sexual roles.[43] Gender corrected bad behavior and was encapsulated by Money in the idea of "imprimatur."[44] The metaphor of the imprimatur defined gender as a printing design for children to acquire either normative maleness or normative femaleness.[45]

For Money, gender functioned as imprimatur when it fulfilled a double function. It was designed not only to stop a multiplication of meanings but also to offer a flexible enough concept to encompass a wider diversity of non-normative bodies:

> the first step was to abandon the unitary definition of sex as male or female, and to formulate a list of five prenatally determined variables of sex that hermaphroditic data had shown could be independent of one another, namely, chromosomal sex, gonadal sex, internal and external morphologic sex, and hormonal sex (prenatal and pubertal), to which was added a sixth postnatal determinant, the sex of assignment and rearing ... The seventh place at the end of this list was an unnamed blank that craved a name. After several burnings of the midnight oil I arrived at the term, gender role, conceptualized jointly as private in imagery and ideation, and public in manifestation and expression.[46]

Money describes his process as working through a problem, which was provoked by "an unnamed blank that craved a name."[47] He wanted to eliminate the potential offensive character of sex disalignment, which was supposed to be a neutral medical operation desired by everyone. To ensure that intersex bodies are liberated, the process has to be guided by scientists and parents. Not only Money knows the right gender, but like him, parents can know it in relation to their child's sexual abnormalities. They, like scientists, can be Pygmalion, so that they can use clay to fashion a god or a goddess.[48] They need to know the gender of their child, approve corrective surgery early, and have hormones administered at the right age under the condition that the children will be informed about their treatments.[49]

By looking with the lens of anti-communism, gender appears not only to be a technology of medicalized control in the 1950s, as D. A. Rubin argues, but also a technology for creating the fantasy of political rebellion.[50] In Money's Cold War imagination, gender has become a territory of independent freedom that gave intersex people the possibility of becoming sovereign entities. In their new territories, designated as transsexual bodies, intersex people were free to choose their own destinies. Like decolonized countries, gender was a term for non-normative people to acquire their successful transition to modernity. Intersex people can become modern once they acquire the right gender. This model of development would allow intersex people to express their repressed inner needs, which were hidden under an old model of medicalization.

Money's epistemology of gender is part of the emergence of social constructivism, a dominant epistemological framework in the US social sciences in the 1960s. In the epistemology of social constructivism, personal identity has a similar role to the idea of gender in Money's work. Social constructivism shows not only that human beings acquire a sense of self, but also that identity explains the possibility of acquiring a better personality. In the arguments of sociologists such as Berger and Luckmann, the formation of one's identity is related to the consolidation of a functional sense of self, which represents the true self.[51] In Money's theory, gender allows intersex people to have a better self if they adjust to the norms of their society.[52] Gender roles were acquired by a process of censoring a body in the manner of a book.[53] This censorship would lead to the acquisition of a right sense of self as either male or female. The direct implication of Money's argument was that bodies that did not fit into a clear category of either male or female were located at the beginning of a process of acquiring the language of gender. As a result, these bodies were adjusted through new standardized medical, surgical and psychological sex reassignment. To have a functional body is to construct the gender of intersex people so that they will move to the top of the psychological and cultural ladder.

Social constructivism was not unlike other forms of Cold War liberalisms that asserted their theoretical superiority to Soviet Marxism. At the beginning of *The Social Construction of Reality*, the term "freedom" appears as a criterion to judge whether a society has a good grasp of reality and whether some countries have lost their sense of freedom.[54] In doing so, the book signals its political position in the Cold War. Berger and Luckmann continue their argument by insisting that Soviet Marxists misunderstood Marx's dialectics. Rather than understanding the revolutionary aspects of Soviet Marxism, Berger and Luckmann argue that Lenin had a mechanical view of dialectics when he looked at economics as the basis of human life.⁵⁵ In response, social constructivism offers a scientific theorization that will correct the mistakes of the eastern European Marxists and lead to a better human life. Their concept of identity was designed to show the flaws in Soviet Marxism's idea of dialectics.⁵⁶ Identity needs to replace the core ideas of Soviet Marxism, such as class conflict and the vanguard role of the proletariat, because it accurately explains social life. In their language, both economics and social life are produced by human activity, given that human activity is understood as labor in "the widest sense of the word."⁵⁷ Identity theory, unlike Soviet Marxism, "reflects the psychological reality that they purport to reflect."⁵⁸ From a method of realizing communism, as it was formulated by Soviet Marxists, in social constructivism dialectics became a method by which identity explains social change.⁵⁹ It was reduced to the idea that people shape social life, as social life shapes people. In Soviet Marxism, communists produce a new world in transforming its materiality and relations of inequality. In the Cold War rival theory of social constructivism, the struggle against exploitation and inequality makes room for a universal theory of identity construction. For social constructivists, any people can transform social life, in the same way that social life transforms them.

By centering on a theory of identity, Berger and Luckmann designed social constructivism as a racialized and heteronormative theory of the social life. They argue that norms of social behavior emerge from institutions, which are conceptualized as epistemological structures dominated by colonialism and imperialism. In their example, an institution arises when "a Man Friday" joins "a matchstick-canoe builder on a desert island."⁶⁰ Two fictional characters who were key to a colonial British imagination became an example of how identity produces social norms.⁶¹ From a one-time action, the interaction of Man Friday and the white builder will become routine. In acquiring their identities, Man Friday and the white builder build an objective world. The two social scientists also present some potential objections to their narrative. There are cases when the common shared world cannot be achieved. They imagine a situation when three people such as "a male A, a bisexual female B and a Lesbian C" seek to establish a social routine.⁶² In their example, different sexual identities will lead to a failure to construct a predictable world because a lesbian and a heterosexual male will not develop a "sexual relevance."[63] Like Soviet Marxists who did not understand dialectics, and unlike the fictional racist character of the white builder, the lesbian cannot make a common world with the American heterosexual. The social constructivist program of identity not only fought communist ideas of emancipation, but also produced racialized and heteronormative assumptions as explanations of the social world.

The role of this introductory section has been to show that, during the Cold War, the search for a gender identity was deeply connected to an anti-communist agenda. In the social sciences, the epistemology of social constructivism criticized eastern European Marxism for abandoning a scientific effort to explain reality. Identity became the reason why Marxist-Leninists lost the competition over science. People's personal identities explain how the world functions, whereas Soviet Marxists have an ideology that is distanced from reality. Berger and Luckmann have developed a theory that justifies the imposition of racialized and heteronormative values on others as the basis for explaining social change. Social constructivism justified the norms of white America under the pretense that it describes people's experiences and their diverse identities. In the next section, I go on to discuss how the epistemology of gender emerges from anti-communism in the USA. Specifically, I show how Money's ideas were part of a Cold War anxiety about sexual deviancy and hidden identities.

Deviancy and the Cold War

The politics of uncovering one's identity was a basic concern for countries fighting against communism. Scientists were given a privileged place in this struggle because they were producing the cutting-edge technology that had the role of winning the Cold War. In the USA, a technology that revealed the true identity of people was considered an important weapon in the survival against the Soviet threat. Given the fear of spies, the duplicity of one's identity was at the core of anxiety about communism and sexual deviance. As a sexologist, Money imagined himself as a scientist who eliminated confusion about gender roles and revealed the hidden structure of the human psyche. In his explanation of a gender role, the implication is that *not knowing* the psychological mindset of deviants is a major threat for science. His position of fighting deviancy and abnormalities is consistent with an increased anti-communist rhetoric.

In the 1950s, a discourse of deviancy and "passing" became dominant as part of the US anti-communist scare. Cold War liberals considered "homosexuality and lesbianism" to be developmental disorders. These defective behaviors were allied to communism because they undermined the foundations of a free society.[64] In this context, scientific explanations such as Money's "imprimatur" and the famous Alan Turing "imitation game" were concepts inflected by the threat of communism, blackness and non-heterosexuality. The Turing experiment articulated what Katherine Hayles calls "the inaugural moment of the computer age" and "set the agenda for the artificial intelligence for the next three decades."[65] If Money believed that he had bravely discovered a new scientific path, Turing offered an algorithm for humanity to discover who people really are. In the imitation game, Alan Turing's famous 1950s imaginary interrogator is given the task of trying to guess the sex of people the cannot see.[66] The question of passing and duplicity is at the heart of what Turing sees as the possibility that machines will think like humans. Turing's question, "Can the machine imitate a man?," is opened up by the question of a scientist guessing a person's gender.[67] To guess one's behavior is not unlike knowing one's gender. The interest in gender is not an accident in the US search for artificial intelligence, but is located at its core. Both Money and Turing need to identify deviants and techniques of passing to justify their methods as scientific and efficient.

Since identity has become the rival theory that surpassed Marxism, psychology and mathematics have to follow new epistemological directions. Money and Turing's methods are based on uncovering the hidden truth of identity. The dominance of identity in scientific inquiry had two major long-term consequences. First, it consolidated the formation of human and sexual identities along a binary. In this framework, opposite categories such as men vs. women, white vs. black, and heterosexuals vs. homosexuals offered the basic pattern to identify normality and deviancy. As Robert Corber observes about the 1950s in the USA, "sexual orientation became as crucial a determinate of social identity as race and gender."[68] Second, the figure of "the enemy within" solidified the assumption that the major threat to US stability was the undercover deviant. The US ideologues located the enemy in the personal identity of various non-normative individuals that could have been corrupted by a rival ideology. In this imagination, the deviant enemy takes over the mind of regular Americans and induces "normal" people to commit criminal and perverse acts.[69] Policing as an operation of surveillance of one's psyche was encouraged as a strategy to identify and neutralize potential dangers. One's gender, race and sexuality were deeply tied to the new category of identity, and were flattened by evacuating their historical transformations. If Marxist dialectics was a scientific rendition of the historical formation of social life, the new epistemology of identity derived its logic from binary thinking and a psychologized view of human action.

The obsession with identity permeates post-World War II cinema in the USA. A key component of identity formation is the capacity to achieve the right gender. This capacity can be realized if one refuses the temptation of deviancy. Alfred Hitchcock's 1951 *Strangers on a Train* is a full exploration of the dangers that threaten the acquisition of the right white male identity. In the film, Guy Haines is young, white and handsome. A successful tennis player, Haines is one step away from achieving the full American Dream. He wants to marry the attractive daughter of a senator and to be fully included in the Washington upper class. Charles Bruno, described as a spoiled "mama's boy" from Long Island, will serve as a formidable obstacle to this plan. Bruno is dominated by unresolved Oedipal problems, such as his desire to kill his rich father. He blackmails Haines and seems to constitute a grave danger to his friends. Hitchcock narrativizes the encounter between Haines and Bruno as a homosexual menace. The first sign of a homosexual flirtation is when Bruno, in his dark wool tweeds and V-neck sweater, accidently kicks Haines's legs in the train.[70] The normal hetero male is exposed to unknown temptations. Bruno is a threat to the American Dream because he does not believe in the law of the father, wears striped pants, engages in unsolicited confessions and dresses in silk robes in the living room of his father's estate. In the discursive construction of white masculinity, not to achieve the right gender role is to fail to resolve the Oedipus complex successfully. Bruno is not only a deviant, but can also easily become a threat to national security. In a key scene, his menacing figure on the steps of the Jefferson Memorial haunts Haines, who is walking towards the monument. To counter this danger, Haines needs the police, and is accompanied by a police detective who can intervene at the right moment. As Corber puts it, the stark contrast between Bruno's "dark silhouette" and the gleaming white marble "makes the government appear vulnerable and unprotected."[71] Haines is made to feel vulnerable to blackmail not only because his heterosexuality is in danger; he is also threatened because his gender is called into question. Bruno is a menace because of the gay overtones of his behavior, which lack gender-correctness. The deviant does not have the masculine desires of Haines, who wants to achieve success by entering into a white upper-class marriage.

In a Cold War rhetoric, deviancy and race deficiency derive from the seductive nature of communism. If one achieves the right gender, one is fighting communism. If one does not, then the danger of becoming a communist is lurking in the shadows. As we saw in *Strangers on a Train*, even an all-American tennis champion can easily be turned into a homo-criminal who hates authority. This anxiety builds on a psychology that posits the resolution of the Oedipus complex as central to the production of white masculinity. The implication of the film is that *all* heterosexual American men are in danger of being corrupted by foreign ideologies. Haines can become Bruno if the Government is not careful enough. Since homosexuality is a defective gender behavior, the threat is that the boundary between active and passive homosexuality can dissolve. While the report by the Senate Appropriations Committee during the Cold War panic distinguished between "latent" and "overt" homosexuals, for Hitchcock, even the most hetero and normative male individuals are exposed to the threat of deviations.[72] In the US Cold War, the right gender could only emerge from having the right genital orientation and family structure, while all possible sexual alternatives needed to be eliminated.[73]

In this section I have continued to analyze the role of identity and gender within the prevailing anti-communism of the early Cold War. In the next I show the relationship between this ideological background and the epistemology of gender. In Money's texts, gender's epistemology was racialized and derived from various threats to white anti-communist ideology.

Gender as racialization in Money's vocabulary

How does Money's epistemology of gender play in this economy of Cold War? Gender emerged in Money's work as a term not only with anti-queer and anti-communist overtones, but also with a racialized baggage. Early anti-communism in the USA functioned not only to conceive an egalitarian society as a utopian nightmare, but also to racialize non-white bodies to establish the superiority of capitalism. In the long history of anti-communist cinema, one of the first anti-Bolshevik films, *Bolshevism on Trial*, attacked socialist experiments as the powerplays of sexist old men. The 1919 *The Right to Happiness* blended the denunciation of utopian socialism with the racialization of Jewish characters, who were shown to raise a communist revolutionary girl.[74] After World War II, US anti-communism insisted on the protection of a nuclear suburban Christian family, which became the core of resistance against anything anti-American. However, as I showed previously, the ideology of the capitalist nuclear family generated its own internal contestation. The challenge to white suburbia was permissible as long as it was framed according to the goals of American Cold War dominance. As Medevoi argues, the Cold War discourse had to maintain the superiority of whiteness and heterosexuality by recasting those who contested such norms as adolescent rebels in search of their identity.[75] Rebels who discover their true hidden identity become figures of political contestation, yet they never become threats to the entire political system.

In this section I trace the racialization of gender by investigating three themes: gender as a superior stage of evolution, blackness as defective gender, and gender as a spatialized norm. Money's epistemology reveals the conditions of producing gender as a scientific term. His strategy was to put a name to various behaviors and bodies that escaped a definition. This methodological maneuver is a point of contestation for queer methodology. Siobhan Somerville argued that the operation of naming is methodologically in conflict with exploring the intersection of queer and racial presences in texts.[76] In following Somerville's suggestion, I trace Money's use of language to a broader racialized anti-communist and anti-queer rhetoric. First, Money deployed gender to indicate that a particular identity can achieve a superior civilizational stage. His model is evolutionary and suggests a shift from sexed bodies to gender roles, which are seen as superior in their complexity.[77] While he believed that gender and sexuality are connected, he was also keen to see them as distinct aspects in one's life. In his argument, "genderology" can become a science that studies how gender is achieved separately from sexual behavior. Differently put, sex can become gender, given the right cultural conditions. This evolution is achieved by eliminating racial and ethnic deviations that are considered a barrier to whiteness.[78] As Somerville argues, scientific racism was underpinned by the assumption that bodies become more differentiated and complex as they evolve.[79] In this scientific thinking, it was assumed that "hermaphrodites" represented a primitive body that needed to be replaced by a superior type.[80] Gender achievement is not unlike this process of evolution, because it is the process of acquiring a male "he," as D. A. Rubin noticed.[81] Gender borrows from the ideology of white masculinity that was enforced during the Cold War. As Money repeatedly tells us, before the 1950s there was no acknowledgment of "the Adam principle."[82] The Adam principle is a stand-in for acquiring male normative behaviors, which presupposes not only a clear differentiation in sexual organs but also in the brain.[83] It presupposes an alignment between one's sex (that is, genitals, or bodily organs that signify sexuality) and one's gender. For instance, boys who do not act like normal boys "may have been subjected to the relative insufficiency of the Adam principle, prenatally."[84] Money discusses the Adam principle to show that gender represents the normative orientation of becoming a white man and the transition to a higher form of humanity, which presupposes the elimination of primitive features.

Second, in Money's work, gender functions as a mechanism to produce the inferiority of black bodies. This inferiority is constructed by placing white bodies at the end of an evolutionary timeline. Even when black culture is considered an alternative to whiteness, it is conceptualized as "more or less" valuable in relation to white hegemonic norms. Blackness becomes a term of praise only if it is attached to a modern project of underscoring its alternative character to white culture.

Money's conceptualization of gender has suffered changes according to various political and historical moments. Whereas in the 1950s it is inspired by a linear evolutionary trajectory, his understanding of the term has changed according to new political contexts in the 1970s. After the civil rights movement of the 1960s, his use of gender reflects historical shifts in the perception of race relations in the USA. In 1972, Money argues that correctives for black populations are needed, while at the same time believing that African Americans' "sexual dimorphism in sexual partnerships" is superior to whites' sexuality.[85] The debates about the role of blackness in North American sociology shaped Money's ambivalent position. He believes that the gender of black people is defective because it does not follow the chronology and temporality of white people's. Sexual dimorphism – what Money means by "gender failures" – are produced by "cultural lags" that are a result of slavery.[86] In Money's explanation, because black women "were obliged, even forced" to breed, then you have a strong differentiation in terms of the "physique."[87] Pregnancy is "a cultural tradition" and black working-class women look different from other women.[88] Culture becomes an explanation for defects in terms of gender appearance; there is a lag between white and black women, and this lag derives from the legacy of slavery. The problem of black people is that "the very condition of slavery thus favored temporary partnerships, or a series of them."[89] As a result, a corrective is needed, and this can be achieved by the necessary enforcement of equal and long-time partnerships. Money tells his readers that "the relationships of human beings who have personally and emotionally experienced no alternative examples of sexual partnerships to fall back on do not change by legal fiat."[90] In Money's racist history of gender evolution, the system of slavery has lingered on because "the master who provided subsistence has been replaced by the Department of Welfare."[91] In rearticulating an anti-federal rhetoric about welfare queens, he conceptualizes histories of slavery as a legacy that needs to be replaced with white norms about gendered long-term partnerships.

Money's intention is not to assert the inferiority of African Americans. He believes that his conception of gender challenges white North American norms about sexuality. He argues that black culture's difference from whiteness gives a historical strength to black relationships, which escape the suburban white model. When he talks about short-term relationships and the raising of children by grandparents in black families, he calls it "a viable system, equal in status to that of the white middle class, if not in some way superior and better adapted to modern urban conditions."[92] However, this assertion of a different system that may seem more viable because of its rejection of the nuclear white norm depends on predictions about the future. In Money's future, the model of white majority has to prevail. His verdict is that black lifestyles cannot compete on equal terms with white culture to become the majority system.[93] In this conservative rhetoric, blacks are dependent on the welfare state and therefore weakened by the master's interest in keeping them subservient. According to his predictions, the future cannot change because history is dependent on a white majority and its interest in cultural dominance.

Third, Money's notion of gender is fundamentally shaped not only by a white Anglo-Saxon ideal, which is seen as the norm of the majority, but also by spatial norms about who counts as superior on a developmental human scale. The main binary within which he operates in his praise of Anglo-American gender is the *public* character of English language, as opposed to the *privacy* of other languages and behaviors. Gender has to be acquired by gender-non-conforming people in the same manner immigrants have to acquire English to speak in public spaces. Like intersex people, bilingualism (which refers in this context to people who speak languages other than English) is confusing to Money because the bilingual person "is likely to be slower than unilingual children in mastering their language."[94] The specific racialization of non-whites appears when Money speaks about the importance of speaking Chinese in private and English in public. In doing so, the acquisition of an English public identity is in contrast to the use of a private Chinese self.[95] This is why speaking English in public is similar to owning a gender role, because similar principles underpin one's use of language and one's gender acquisition.[96] Language defects, such as dyslexia, function in a similar way to racialized differences, such as indigeneity. Defective behavior is associated with indigeneity in Money's early studies on disability and trans questions. For instance, he opens his chapter on dyslexia in 1962 with this statement: "Technically, it is correct to say that an unschooled aboriginal of some primitive tribe is alexic or, if educated sufficiently to be able to decipher only disconnected fragments of written language, dyslexic."[97] His intention in his article is to distinguish between dyslexia and an incapacity to read. What he wants to show is that one can be illiterate without being dyslexic. To do so, Money wants to identify what is specific to dyslexia as a linguistic abnormality. In this regard, he is interested in identifying structural problems at the level of language: "The dyslexic individual is not unique in making reversals and translocations, but he is unique in making so many of them and for so long a time."[98] Unlike the illiterate, the dyslexic is like a person who did not achieve the right gender. The dyslexic has different linguistic structures and makes associations that impede normal development. To understand linguistic structural problems, Money uses the example of indigeneity, and like dyslexia, indigeneity has to be removed from good language acquisition.

Money is interested in a practical way of correcting disabilities. Here is how he proposes a game that shows how to eliminate a non-white part of oneself: "Make a test on yourself. Close your eyes and 'tattoo' a word on a piece of paper held to your forehead. Write you. Take the card down and see that almost certainly you have written ouy.[99] In this game, if you "tattoo" a word on your forehead, you will notice that you can act like a dyslexic. The problem with dyslexia is about one's spatial norms, which are disturbed once one gets to read one's subjectivity as a "ouy." One becomes a "ouy" when one tattoos oneself. One also loses an important part of whiteness if one loses a conventional understanding of space. This sense of losing oneself is articulated at the level of a deep existential confusion, when you "are" something other than you thought you were. This anxiety is deployed through the figure of the tattooed and the indigenous, which has historically represented the racial category that refused the logic of white settlers.

If one discovers a tattooed person within oneself, this experiment troubles your sense of white spatiality. If you discover a different person within your history, such a discovery would translate into failures at the level of writing and identifying linguistic patterns. Money's explanation is that "the visual image on the written surface is obverted" simultaneously with the "obversion of the kinesthetic imagery from the writer's fingers, hand and arm."[100] But the fear of becoming indigenous is deeper than a mere *inversion* of a linguistic pattern. Like the indigenous, the dyslexic is structurally in a conflicted relationship to white norms of writing. As Money warns us, the problem of not having a "normal" sense of perception is not *just* a visual or body-image inversion. It's not *just* a left–right confusion. The confusion is deeper and works at the level of space or, as he puts it, "It is truly a three-dimensional space-movement perception problem."[101] The threat of indigeneity is traced back to spatial discontinuity, as opposed to blackness, which functions on the assumptions of a woman's bodily deformity and promiscuity.[102] In Money's research on gender the question of a normative gender behavior is deeply tied to racialized differences, which are articulated at the level of "defects" such as the legacy of slavery for black culture, the role of speaking Chinese in private spheres, bilingualism, and dyslexia as connected to indigeneity and non-whiteness.

Conclusion

In this chapter, I added a second piece to the story about how Soviet Marxism has been erased as a potential rival epistemology to liberal capitalism. My main argument is that the concept of gender was deployed not only as part of a colonial and neoliberal project, but also because it contained in its epistemological design anticommunist and racialized assumptions. I traced the emergence of gender to a theory of identity, which became a dominant model that offered a competing ideological structure to that of eastern European Marxism. In insisting that gender identity is a territory of freedom and independence for non-normative people, Money coined the term "gender" as an ideal to be achieved under US racial capitalism. To acquire a gender meant to become not only a freer person, but also a successful white person within a capitalist establishment. My reading of Money's texts shows that while he argued that his theory *described* the social world of North Americans, in fact he *naturalized* hierarchical understandings of whiteness and heteronormativity.

The chapter also briefly explored the connections between the theory of social constructivism and the Cold War with an eye to their interaction. The theory of social constructivism sought to explain social life in the United States of the 1960s. It claimed that people's identities become key theoretical analytics to make sense of the social world. In the arguments of social constructivists, identity is a deep reflection of one's psychology, as opposed to a Marxist dialectics that distorts human perception. The theory allowed the positing of a free self as the site of resistance against cultural norms of conformism. To have a gender means that one is capable of changing one's world. This double movement meant that, on the one hand, Money was able to insist that intersex people conform to the values of white male and female gender, while, on the other, it also created the conditions for countercultural movements in the 1960s – including white feminism – to insist on the discovery of a true identity as a counterpoint to American consumerism. The Soviet danger of collectivism was contested when one accepted not only that identities shape themselves in relation to social norms, but also that a free self can resist repressive cultural norms.

For the purposes of this book, the historical account of the emergence of gender is important because it clarifies the conceptual ground for the next chapter, where I investigate the role of gender in queer theory at the end of the Cold War. Unlike Cold War gender, an important thread in post-1990 queer studies rejected the idea that cultural norms construct a biological sex. In making this move, queer theory sought to depart from a Cold War imagination focused individual freedom and the liberation of the self. Yet, queer theory has inherited a liberal and individualist epistemology that blocked many attempts to find a new theoretical path. More than that, post-Cold War gender did not undertake a deep genealogical investigation of its formation. Such neglect made it possible for a Marxist framework to be gradually erased from queer conceptualization of bodies and sexuality.

Notes

1 Jennifer Delton, *Rethinking the 1950s: How Anticommunism and the Cold War Made America Liberal* (Cambridge: Cambridge University Press, 2013), p. 16, argues that US liberals rejected communism on the basis of their faith in individual freedom and democratic self-rule.

The birth of gender epistemology 91

2 Jemima Repo, *The Biopolitics of Gender* (Oxford: Oxford University Press, 2015); and Susan Stryker, "We Who Are Sexy: Christine Jorgensen's Transsexual Whiteness in the Postcolonial Philippines," *Social Semiotics*, 19:1 (March 2009), 79–91.
3 See Repo, *The Biopolitics of Gender*, p. 134: "The accompanying attempt to induce female subjects to 'make choices' that allow them to 'free' themselves from the antiquated baggage of gender roles to both reproduce the species and create capital only makes sense in the context of neoliberal governmentality."
4 *Ibid.*, p. 4.
5 *Ibid.*, p. 2.
6 *Ibid.*, p. 7.
7 *Ibid.*, p. 159.
8 *Ibid.*
9 Stryker, "We Who Are Sexy," pp. 550–552.
10 *Ibid.*, p. 552.
11 *Ibid.*, p. 550.
12 *Ibid.*
13 Hortense Spillers, "Mama's Baby, Papa's Maybe: An American Grammar Book," *Diacritics*, 17:2 (Summer 1987), 64–81; and Mark Rifkin, *When Did Indians Become Straight? Kinship, the History of Sexuality, and Native Sovereignty* (Oxford: Oxford University Press, 2011).
14 Spillers, "Mama's Baby," p. 67.
15 *Ibid.*
16 Rifkin, *When Did Indians Become Straight?*, p. 26.
17 *Ibid.*, p. 6. Refusing the homo–hetero binary that has been the concern for historians of sexuality, Rifkin argues that "civilization" has been part of a project of a heteronormative imaginary that "positioned monogamous heterocouplehood and the privatized single-family household as the official national ideal by the late nineteenth century" (p. 6).
18 Cedric J. Robinson, *Black Marxism: The Formation of the Black Radical Tradition* (Chapel Hill: North Carolina University Press, 2000), p. 42.
19 Repo, *The Biopolitics of Gender*, p. 1.
20 *Ibid.*, pp. 158–159.
21 See Joanne Meyerowitz, *How Sex Changed: A History of Transsexuality in the United States* (Cambridge, MA: Harvard University Press, 2002), p. 3, for a broader explanation of the crisis regarding the concept of sex: "By midcentury this concept [sex] had begun to break down. Various experts used different terms to distinguish one meaning

of sex from another. Anthropologist Margaret Mead chose sex roles to describe the culturally constructed behaviors expected of women and men. Sex researcher Alfred C. Kinsey adopted the term sexual behavior to outline a range of erotic practices."

22 Ibid.
23 For the emergence of identity as a concept in the New Left rhetoric, see Leerom Medevoi, *Rebels: Youth and the Cold War Origins of Identity* (Durham, NC: Duke University Press, 2005), p. 3: "The liberation movements of the late sixties (black, Chicano, women's, or gay) articulated as their political subject an emergent identity, a young self establishing its sovereignty against the forces of a racist, patriarchal, or homophobic 'parent culture.'" As such, "[i]dentity discourse rapidly permeated postwar US culture in no small part through its now largely forgotten relation to two key terms: 'youth' and the 'Cold War'" (p. 6).
24 Ibid.
25 Ibid.
26 See "National Security Council Report, NSC 68, 'United States Objectives and Programs for National Security,'" Wilson Center Digital Archive, https://digitalarchive.wilsoncenter.org/document/116191.pdf?v=2699956db534c1821edefa61b8c13ffe (accessed May 8, 2020).
27 For the prevalence of Cold War liberalism between 1950 and 1980 in the USA, see Delton, *Rethinking the 1950s*, pp. 1–13.
28 Robert J. Corber, *In the Name of National Security: Hitchcock, Homophobia, and the Political Construction of Gender in Postwar America* (Durham, NC: Duke University Press, 1993), p. 2. Cold War liberalism made it possible for Gail Kligman and Susan Gal (*The Politics of Gender after Socialism: A Comparative-Historical Essay* (Princeton: Princeton University Press, 2000), p. 3) simultaneously to criticize Cold War dualisms and to work under the assumption that the western intervention in eastern Europe after 1989 was a democratic project helping to "establish democratic practices." While they part ways with the language of transitologists, ingrained assumptions of Cold War liberalism, such as that democratic practices did not exist under socialism, are part of their analysis. For a similar observation, see Alexei Yurchak, *Everything Was Forever, until It Was No More: The Last Soviet Generation* (Princeton: Princeton University Press, 2005), pp. 7–8, where he argues that Kligman and Gal's emphasis on duplicity and informing on others reproduces an underlying assumption that socialism "was based on a complex web of immoralities."
29 Corber, *In the Name of National Security*, p. 3.

30 Not only is gender studies vulnerable to this critique, but also a larger production of minority discourses that embrace the idea of an identity with a potent forgotten past. As Roderick Ferguson argued (*The Reordering of Things: The University and Its Pedagogy of Minority Differences* (Minneapolis, University of Minnesota Press, 2012), p. 111), black studies was a key site to an academic transformation that provided new modes of liberal discipline.
31 *Ibid.*
32 *Ibid.*, 19.
33 The US suburbs became, in the words of William Whyte, "a Russia, only with money" (see White quoted by Medevoi, *Rebels*, p. 21).
34 *Ibid.*, pp. 46–48.
35 *Ibid.*, p. 24.
36 *Ibid.*, p. 320. The discourse of identity from the 1950s trickled into the rhetoric of radical social movements at the end of the 1960s and led to an imagination of the young rebel pitted against the quasi-totalitarian and conformist image of white America.
37 Meyerowitz, *How Sex Changed*, p. 6: "This new understanding of gender was forged and refined in the discourse on transsexuality."
38 *Ibid.*, p. 67.
39 See Medevoi, *Rebels*, pp. 12–13, for identity as a concept forged as a response to decolonial politics.
40 *Ibid.*
41 *Ibid.*
42 See Money cited by David A. Rubin, "'An unnamed blank that craved a name': A Genealogy of Intersex as Gender," *Signs: Journal of Women in Culture and Society*, 37:4 (2012), p. 895. Rubin also captures Money's scientific dilemma: "studying individuals with anatomical configurations he regarded as anomalous, Money initially and inadvertently proliferated diagnostic categories; his research generated, he says, 'too many words'" (p. 894).
43 See Repo, *The Biopolitics of Gender*, p. 45.
44 See, for the term "imprimatur," John Money and Anke A. Ehrhardt, *Man & Woman, Boy & Girl: Gender Identity from Conception to Maturity* (Baltimore: Johns Hopkins University Press, 1972), p. 2.
45 Intersex people are defined by Money as people who fail to achieve a gender role: "hermaphroditism or intersexuality in human beings is a condition of prenatal origin in which embryonic and or fetal differentiation of the reproductive system fails to reach completion as either entirely female or entirely male" (Rubin, "An unnamed blank," p. 895).
46 Money as cited in *ibid*. See also his commentary on the same page about Money's coinage of "gender": "This 'unnamed blank'

threatened the very semblance of sex. To contain that threat, Money filled the blank with gender."
47 *Ibid.*
48 Money and Ehrhardt, *Man & Woman*, p. 152.
49 *Ibid.*
50 See Rubin, "An unnamed blank," p. 894.
51 *Ibid.*, p. 118: "Even if his neighbors do not know who he is, and even if he himself may forget in the throes of nightmare, he can reassure himself that his 'true self' is an ultimately real entity in an ultimately real universe. The gods know – or psychiatric science – or the party."
52 Repo, *The Biopolitics of Gender*, p. 39, argues that Money's concept of gender "was accompanied by a behaviorist theory of how this active process of psychosexual differentiation occurs."
53 An imprimatur was the statement offered by the Roman Catholic Church that nothing offensive has been discovered in the work of an author.
54 Peter Berger and Thomas Luckmann, *The Social Construction of Reality: A Treatise in the Sociology of Knowledge* (London: Penguin, 1966), p. 14–15: "What he can and must do, however, is to ask how it is that the notion of 'freedom' has come to be taken for granted in one society and not in another, how its 'reality' is maintained in the one society and how, even more interestingly, this 'reality' may once again be lost to an individual or to an entire collectivity."
55 *Ibid.*, p. 18.
56 *Ibid.*, pp. 12–13.
57 *Ibid.*
58 *Ibid.*, p. 198.
59 *Ibid.*, p. 200.
60 *Ibid.*, p. 74.
61 *Ibid.*, pp. 74–75.
62 *Ibid.*, pp. 80–81.
63 *Ibid.*, p. 80.
64 Corber, *In the Name of National Security*, p. 8.
65 Katherine Hayles, *How We Became Posthuman: Virtual Bodies in Cybernetics, Literature and Informatics* (Chicago: University of Chicago Press, 1999), p. xi.
66 See Alan M. Turing, "Computing Machinery and Intelligence," *Mind*, 49 (1950), 433–460.
67 *Ibid.*, p. 433: "The new form of the problem can be described in terms of a game which we call the 'imitation game.' It is played with three people, a man (A), a woman (B), and an interrogator (C) who may be of either sex. The interrogator stays in a room apart front the other

two. The object of the game for the interrogator is to determine which of the other two is the man and which is the woman."
68 Corber, *In the Name of National Security*, p. 9. During its investigations at the end of the 1940s and early 1950s, the House of Un-American Activities Committee did not limit its investigation to communists but extended it to include non-heterosexual people who passed as heterosexuals.
69 *Ibid.*
70 *Ibid.*, p. 71.
71 *Ibid.*, p. 72.
72 *Ibid.*, p. 74.
73 The logic of argumentation suggests that John Money's experiments may also have been driven by the logic of procreation. For Money, *Love and Love Sickness: The Science of Sex, Gender Difference, and Pair-Bonding* (Baltimore: Johns Hopkins University Press, 1980), p. xi, "procreation is the ultimate and irreducible criterion of sex difference." He also argues that because "too many children live in a one-parent household," no society can afford to pay the bill of "so much pathology" (p. xiv).
74 For a discussion of Hollywood's early anti-communism, see Tony Shaw, *Hollywood's Cold War* (Edinburgh: Edinburgh University Press, 2007), pp. 13–14.
75 Medevoi, *Rebels*, p. 47: "Precisely because whiteness and heterosexuality were foundational features of this suburban imaginary, their norms were often exactly what the rebel narrative of identity formation symbolically challenged or resisted, even when the rebel remained manifestly white or straight, as was the case with such figures as Elvis or Norman Mailer's 'White Negro' hipster."
76 Siobhan Somerville, *Queering the Color Line: Race and the Invention of Homosexuality in American Culture* (Durham, NC: Duke University Press, 2000), p. 6: "My readings, therefore, listen for 'the inexplicable presence of the thing not named' and are attuned to the queer and racial presences and implications in texts that do not otherwise name them."
77 See Money quoted in Rubin, "An unnamed blank," p. 898.
78 See Money quoted in Repo, *The Biopolitics of Gender*, p. 34: "Presumably, it is the very ambiguity of the external genitals that makes hermaphrodites so adaptable to assignment in their sex."
79 See Somerville, *Queering the Color Line*, p. 29: "One of the basic assumptions within the Darwinian model was the belief that, as organisms evolved through a process of natural selection, they also showed greater signs of sexual differentiation."

80 *Ibid.*
81 Rubin, "An unnamed blank," p. 898.
82 Money, *Love and Love Sickness*, p. 22.
83 *Ibid.*
84 *Ibid.*, p. 25.
85 Money, *Man & Woman*, p. 130.
86 *Ibid.*, p. 128.
87 *Ibid.*
88 *Ibid.*
89 *Ibid.*, p. 129.
90 *Ibid.*
91 *Ibid.*
92 *Ibid.*, p. 130.
93 *Ibid.*
94 *Ibid.*, p. 18.
95 *Ibid.*, pp. 18–19.
96 *Ibid.*, p. 19: "The same principle applies to the models of gender role from whom a child establishes his or her own gender-identity differentiation."
97 See John Money, "Dyslexia: A Postconference Review," in John Money (ed.), *Reading Disability: Progress and Research Needs in Dyslexia* (Baltimore: Johns Hopkins University Press, 1962), p. 9.
98 *Ibid.*, p. 17.
99 *Ibid.*, pp. 19–20.
100 *Ibid.*, p. 20.
101 *Ibid.*
102 See Rifkin, *When Did Indians Become Straight?*, p. 97, for the confusion of space introduced by indigeneity: "To try to introduce native populations into the space of white nationality produces an 'unnatural' crossing."

4

Marxism and queer theory at the end of the Cold War

Chapter 4 investigates the shift from a Cold War gender, as Money formulated it, to a new post-Cold War gender, which drew its inspiration from a Foucauldian-inspired research on power and sexuality. I continue not only to analyze the erasure of Marxist theory from theories of sexuality, but also to insist on historicizing this process both in North America and in eastern Europe. The first part of the chapter introduces the rise of a gender epistemology in the work of eastern European artists at the end of the 1970s and beginning of the 1980s. While Jimmy Carter and Ronald Reagan's renewed Cold War politics transformed bodies into a contested ideological terrain, an anti-communist orientation was deeply felt, not only in the Unites States but also in the socialist bloc. In drawing on films and artwork, I investigate how gender and non-normative sexuality were mobilized to reject socialism in the East. In the second part of the chapter, I focus on the theoretical split of queer theory from Marxism. Queer theory, the product of post-identitarian theory, initiated an analysis of power relations without relying on a theory of personal identity. As such, it inaugurated a distinct epistemological orientation that tried to part ways with a theory of social constructivism, which became a dominant model in US social sciences. Its refusal of identity became a major theoretical motivation to produce a new field of inquiry that rejected Cold War politics. The driving force of a queer critique is that it returns to an analysis of material bodies and identities to suggest a different subjectless politics, which seeks a different terrain of political possibilities.

The desire of queer scholars to move away from social constructivism has been, however, concomitant with the elimination of Marxist theory and its epistemology.[1] Queer studies have lost an important historical and materialist dimension by keeping studies of sexuality separate from an analysis of Cold War politics. Research in Marxist queer theory has illuminated some of the dynamics of this process, but my analysis focuses on the elimination of Marxist epistemology from influential theories of power and sexuality.[2] In the 1990s, Judith Butler was successful in reconceptualizing gender as trouble (or a subversive coalition of identities), and like Soviet Marxist theorists in the 1920s, queer theorists were interested in the capacity of a new vocabulary for political critique.[3] However, gender has been gradually attached to an epistemology that saw individuals as the product of self-defining acts who confront punitive and exclusionary social conventions. The conceptualization of gender as an identity deeply affected queer theory, although it has explicitly taken an anti-identitarian direction.[4] The current understanding of queerness as "a subjectless critique" derives from the path opened by early queer thinking, but needs a profound analysis of its genealogy to break the impasse of the Cold War.[5] The new conceptualizations of debility, indigeneity and trans seek a better post-identity politics, yet they have to fall back on individual agents who want recognition in the political sphere.[6] The paradox of a theory that advances a critique of queer bodies to propose a post-identitarian conception is at the heart of queer thinking. Queer stutides has shifted away from historical materialism, not only through its reliance on material bodies who seek to become recognized liberal subjects, but also in its reluctance to investigate its anti-communist genealogy.

During the Cold War, not all queer thinkers who utilized a gender analytic rejected Marxist politics. In queer feminist studies, some key scholars argued for the potential of fusing liberated sexuality and Marxism. In Gayle Rubin's work, from the 1974 *Traffic in Women* to the 1982 "Thinking Sex," Marxism was considered a vital tradition for a theory of gender. Rubin argued that Marxism, like feminism, can be a source for rethinking the category of sex.[7] While her ideas became an inspiration for queer thinkers such as Judith Butler, Marxism has gradually lost salience in cultural studies of sexuality. Part of this process, as Hennessey insightfully observed, is the substitution in Butler and Rubin's work of a theory of materiality by an anthropological account of kinship relation (or cultural relations).[8] Also, given the loss of global power of Marxism-Leninism, queer thinkers who theorized the potential of an alliance between queer sexuality and Marxist ideas were more or less ignored. Marco Mieli's gay communism forged an exciting mix of a critique of psychoanalysis, gay liberation and communist ideals, yet his work was practically unknown until his late rediscovery in the 2010s. Similarly, the work of the New York City-based Gay Socialist Action Project (which includes thinkers such as John Katz and John D'Emilio) has been fairly marginal in queer studies, which has been mostly inspired by theorists such as Judith Butler, Eve Kosofsky Sedgwick, Laurent Berlant and Jack Halberstam. When Marxist politics has been incorporated into queer accounts, however, it has shared many anti-communist assumptions about life in eastern Europe. It has also adhered to a philosophy of history that centered on the events and transformations in the USA.[9]

In the last ten years, contemporary queer scholarship has started to investigate more thoroughly the relationship of the development of capitalism and imperialism in the USA with gender theory.[10] This body of work continued, like Gayle Rubin's early Marxist work, to question not only gendered ideas, but a broader racialized gender/sex system and its economical foundations. This study, however, suggests that a different path is needed to rethink queer theory's epistemology. I provide a deeper genealogical critique to advance a dialectical method, with the aim of showing the prevalence of anti-communism in queer epistemology. Also, I introduce a new theoretical ground that transforms the aims of queer theory, particularly in eastern Europe.

Gay communism at the end of the 1970s

In the introductory part of this chapter, I draw a contrast between the use of gender in anti-communist eastern European artwork and proponents of sexual liberation and communism in western Europe. My objective is to show that bodies became a terrain for Cold War politics because they were conceptualized along conflicting ideological lines. In a western liberal program, gender and non-normative sexuality functioned as part of an ideology that celebrated freedom and individuality. In a socialist realist program, bodies were imagined as devices to achieve communism by following contrasting aesthetic guidelines.

After the opening to the West and the 1970s contestations of Soviet dominance by China, ideological lines were redrawn in eastern Europe. In this new political climate, socialist leaders tolerated various modernist art forms that were not directly confrontational to Marxist ideology. As I will show, the category of gender became a vehicle to criticize the politics of Marxism in eastern Europe. This artistic production has been rarely seen and widely distributed in socialist countries. While in the East gender was deployed as an anti-communist weapon, in western Europe a communist revival was brought about by the Chinese Cultural Revolution and May 1968. As a result, this communist renaissance led to an unexpected alliance between non-normative sexuality and Marxist theory. As a powerful example of this revival, Mario Mieli's theory of transsexualism combined New Left sexual politics with communism under the assumption that socialist states are political systems that promote heteronormativity and sexual oppression.

How was gender deployed in art as a criticism of Marxism? In the second part of the 1970s, and at the start of the Ronald Reagan presidency in the early 1980s, the epistemology of productivist bodies has been increasingly depicted as a tired Stalinist convention. The idea that bodies can be produced collectively, along with an understanding of the dialectical transformation of characters, has been almost erased from productions that have abandoned the aesthetic conventions of Soviet Marxism. As I showed in Chapter 3, the Cold War ideological conflict was also a contest over the superiority of epistemological ideas. In the work of rebellious eastern European artists, gender and non-normative sexuality were sites that placed values such as freedom and individualism in opposition to the politics of authoritarian collectivism. In their art, Marxism was denounced as an empty rhetoric and replaced with statements about individual freedom and creativity.

The common ideological ground of new artistic works was that the free subversive individual opposed the conformism of Marxist theory. In Hungarian cinema, heroic characters became leading voices that contested the gender traditionalism and sexual authoritarianism of eastern European communism. Non-normative sex became a device to criticize the conformism of the State ideology in Hungarian films such as Károly Makk's *Another Way* and Pál Gábor's *Angi Vera*. In Romania, the work of eccentric artists such as Ion Grigorescu and Ion Panaitescu presented communism as an exhausted and invasive ideology. For Grigorescu, Marxism threatened the intimate space of bodies and domestic privacy, which were regarded as key sites for political resistance. Grigorescu's "neodocumentary realism" is an aesthetic that is opposed to the Party's socialist realism, which forged a productivist economy of bodies and signs.[11] Like the theory of identity proposed by social constructivists, which I discussed in Chapter 3, Grigorescu's art claimed to document historical times and reflect a need for the concrete, as opposed to Marxist ideological images.[12] Bodies were conceptualized according to the idea that they were the territory of affirmation of a free self that defies a controlling State authority. Masculinity and femininity were devices to reveal the gendered dimensions of repression in State socialism.

In a 1971 artwork titled *Cultural Revolution*, Grigorescu portrayed State attempts to revitalize socialist realism in Romania as "an invasion of parasites" in people's private space.[13] In this work, Grigorescu sought to indict State artistic messages on socialist television that were part of a Romanian Chinese-inspired Cultural Revolution. The construction of an intimate body that is resistant to socialism was imagined as a form of resistance against the invasion of public communist entities. If John Money's gender was a device to racialize the Chinese language as the language of the private space, Grigorescu deployed a different form of racialization, asserting that Chinese communist bodies invade the autonomy of one's mind. The Romanian territory was construed as a territory that was exposed to the infection of communist Asiatic parasites. In contrast with an earlier "thaw" in relation to western European countries, the author criticizes a turn to a Mao-inspired communism in the cultural politics of Romanian socialists.[14] A Cold War frame of reference has been powerfully inserted into the art of artists such as Ion Grigorescu.

Ion Grigorescu's work shows that gender (as indicated by categories such as masculine and feminine) becomes the location for expressing anti-communist politics and rejecting socialist realism as a repressive aesthetic. In 1976, Grigorescu produced a piece titled *Masculine/Feminine*, which was considered a prominent attempt to criticize the official communist ideology.[15] In *Masculine/Feminine*, he continues to theorize his body as a space of freedom against the

Figure 1 *Cultural Revolution*, by Ion Grigorescu.

restrictions that were imposed by socialist regimes. In reflecting on what a body can do, Grigorescu deploys categories such as masculine and feminine to show that socialist bodies live in narrow boxes. The loss of the integrity and wholesomeness of one's body is linked to the repressive nature of State ideology. The piece *Masculine/Feminine* is important because it shows that in Grigorescu's anti-communism bodies become a key site to look for an intimate and materialist day-to-day politics. Masculine and feminine were not yet the location of same-sex politics, as they are deployed in the Hungarian film *Another Way*, but they were fundamental sites to understand socialist repressive effects on bodies.

Ion Grigorescu's art was not unlike the work of another Romanian artist, Ion Panaitescu, who explicitly mixed pornographic images with Marxist slogans. In his work from 1982, Panaitescu deployed ideas such as sexual liberation and freedom of speech to undermine the claims of Marxism, which were treated like empty ideological slogans. His artwork was provocative because it

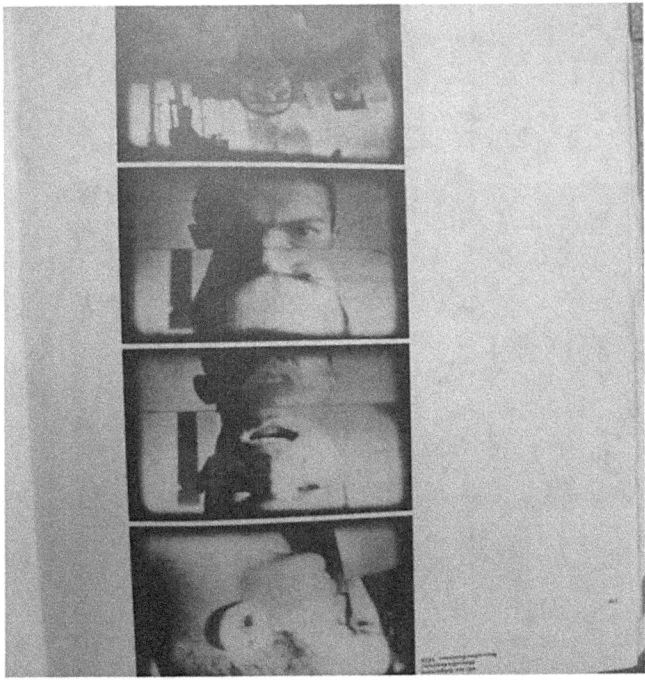

Figure 2 *Masculine/Feminine*, by Ion Grigorescu.

imitated the structure of the avant-garde visual collage. The Tantric art of sexual arousal offered an uncanny and striking contrast to Marxist slogans. Sentences that were widely accessible, such as Marxist slogans that were widely accessible in public spaces, were juxtaposed to images that were almost invisible in the public space, but that circulated as erotic material on private networks. The seductive quality of this artwork is that it is has an ambivalent relationship to the ideology of socialism. On the one hand, the collage could be perceived as undermining the serious claims of Marxism. On the other hand, his artwork could be seen as bringing something new to the Party's rhetoric, given that the normative demands of communism were not in conflict with a call to a healthier sexual life. In a mysterious manner, his sexual imagery added a titillating effect to a communist rhetoric that, because of its ubiquity, became

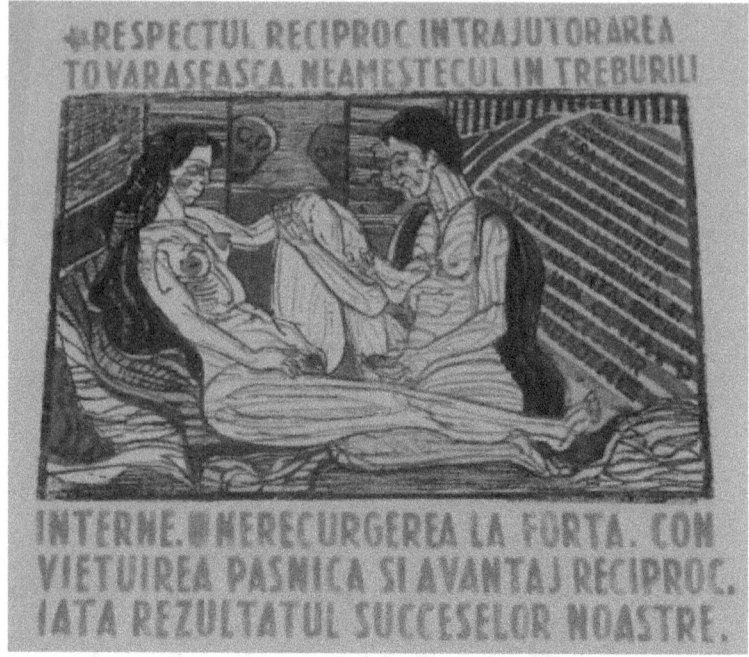

Figure 3 *The 13th Congress: Politics with Sweets*, by Ion Panaitescu.

almost invisible. In *The 13th Congress: Politics with Sweets*, two bodies that were preparing for sexual intercourse were framed by the following text: "Mutual respect[,] comradely help. The politics of non-interference in domestic affairs. Non-violence. Peaceful living and mutual advantage. Here is the result of our successes."

Like Romanian artwork, Hungarian films at the end of the 1970s and beginning of the 1980s deployed a conflict between sexual liberation and communism. For instance, the 1982 film *Another Way* locates a critique of State socialism in heroic accounts of sexual and political resistance to Stalinism. The plot revolves around the relationship between two female-bodied characters, Éva Szalánczky and Lívia Horváth, who fall in love while working for the same newspaper in Budapest. Éva is the most outspoken and courageous of the two, since she pursues a sexual relationship with Lívia. She is courageous not only in private life, but also in her politics. She criticizes the bureaucracy and hierarchy of the Party and writes an article where she denounces the lack of democratic life on a collective farm. Party officials are enraged by Éva's attitude, and she resigns before she is forced to leave the newspaper. While trying to flee across the border, Éva is shot by a soldier. The film is centered on a heroic individual character who is subversive to a bureaucratic socialist ideology. A fearless Éva not only refuses the traits of femininity attibuted to women in socialist Hungary, but also refuses to become a conformist communist subject. She has short hair, is interested in writing and speaking plainly about political matters, spends time by herself in bars, and seduces women. Éva's gender and sexuality offer a standpoint whereby State socialism is seen as repressive and unable to change. Her death is a martyr-like statement that denounces the hypocrisy of the political system.

Unlike *Another Way*, the 1978 Hungarian film *Angi Vera* does not use heroic characters to criticize socialism. Instead, the film leaves to the reader to understand the effects of socialism on people who dare to follow their sexual desires. Angi Vera is an innocent, eighteen-year-old femme-looking orphan, who is sent to a Party school at the end of the 1940s in Stalinist Hungary. She soon discovers that to move up in the Party hierarchy she has to denounce her love for a Marxist lecturer. Angi's public denunciation of her lover transforms her into a Party apparatchik. An important contrast in the film is offered by other characters who ask for reform of sexual attitudes within communism. Mária Muskát, a worker who talks openly about her sexual desires, will have her sexuality repressed in socialism. Anna Traján, a Party member who acts as a puritanical Stalinist, and who plays the role of Angi's tutor and Mária's enemy, is the embodiment of repressive sexuality. If *Another Way* focused on heroic attempts to undermine Hungarian socialism, *Angi Vera* proposes a critique of repressed socialist sexuality that has become the norm in the Hungarian version of 1950s Stalinism.

Hungarian cinema after the 1960s changed the tone of its political critique. The non-conformist radicals of Hungarian cinema began to look increasingly like the rebels in US cinema. The association between gender-, sexual and race liberation in the US politics of identity led to a particular type of self-assertion, which Medevoi described as taking the shape of "a proud declaration of emergence into power."[16] Like the US critics of conformism, the new young heroes of eastern European cinematography criticized the hypocritical world of an older generation. Their rebellion was attached to a philosophy that centers on the value of sexual and individual freedom. In *Angi Vera*, the film shows the desires of a woman for a married man becoming the target of ideological repression. In *Another Way*, the main character comes into her own power by denouncing the perils of Soviet dogmatism and its hold on people's imagination.[17] When Éva comes out as a lesbian, her gender identity is not dissimilar to the Gay Liberation Front's rhetoric of "coming out," which is a process when one discovers a hidden self-determination and power.[18] Also, when Angi's friend, Mária, is explicit about her sexuality and publicly confronts a Marxist lecturer at the Party school, she is not unlike the sexually attractive hero of *Rebel without a Cause* played by James Dean.

Hungarian cinema is not an exception in eastern Europe. Romanian and Czechoslovakian cinema have embraced the new outlaws who seek to live a better sexual life than their parents. In the 1968 Romanian black-and-white film *The Reenactment*, the defiant and open sexual behavior of two teenagers offers a stark point of contrast to the hypocrisy of a communist prosecutor. In the 1963 Czechoslovakian film *The Sun in the Net*, a young girl experiencing her sexual awakening has to address the duplicities of her socialist family life. The aesthetic of Soviet Marxism has not completely surrendered to the new norms of sexual and political liberation. Other genres of Marxist cinematography have tried to subsume the rebellion of a young generation into the codes of the productivist body. In the 1983 Romanian film *Impossible Love* (Constatin Vaeni), an engineer and a worker struggle to maintain a dialectical relationship to recapture the early possibilities of communism. Discussions about sexuality and freedom are part of a strong communist friendship shared by the two main characters. Communist, honest discussion of sexual desire is imagined as a response to the corruption of late socialism. While, in the 1980s, the communist project is still a necessity, it is increasingly seen as part of a difficult attachment to its utopian nature.[19]

If eastern European art tended to draw closer to a western political critique, radical queer activists discovered the potential of communism. Marco Mieli's 1977 book *Gay Communism* is a powerful manifesto not only about gender and sexual disorder, but also about a desire for communism. Mieli was a brilliant gay theorist and Italian radical activist, and a prominent member of the Gay Liberation Front in London. For him, communism is not primarily an authoritarian ideology, but an ideological program that will lead to the destruction of capitalism. If the term "gender" hardly makes an appearance in socialist films, Mieli deploys it when he talks about the transition from a female role of a transsexual male role.[20] Rather than having the same meaning as Gayle Rubin's 1974 use of the term "gender," which she describes as an analytical term, Mieli's "gender role" resembles John Money's use of the category.[21] For Mieli, like Money, gender identifies the capacity of a body to move from one sexed category to another. In Mieli's theory, transsexuality generates a politics of sexual liberation and freedom against a repressive society. Like Romanian anti-Marxist artists, Mieli conceptualizes bodies by insisting on their capacity to become free from conventional restraints. Like heroic characters in Hungarian films, becoming a transsexual is a declaration of one's capacity to emerge into an empowered position.

Yet, unlike Money and eastern European artists, Mieli was a firm advocate of anti-capitalist politics on the basis that capitalism is a system that represses people's capacity to live a sexually free life. His reconceptualization of Marxism breaks with an anti-communist ideological front and anticipates later conceptual moves made by queer theorists such as Gayle Rubin and Judith Butler. Mieli calls for liberation not only from heteronormativity, but also from a capitalism based on the market economy. In making this move, the Italian radical theorist is not an exception in western Europe, particularly in that after May 1968 communism became identified with a project of sexual liberation. In France, Gilles Deleuze and Felix Guattari's *Anti-Oedipus* forged new theoretical routes by mixing Marxism with a critique of psychoanalysis. The theoretical combination of Marxism and psychoanalysis goes back to the avant-garde politics of the 1920s and 1930s, when various thinkers such as Tristan Tzara, who defined the politics of Dadaism, positioned themselves on the side of Marxist revolutionary politics.[22] What Mieli proposes as a novelty is to connect the category of transsexuality to a revolutionary Marxist project, since for Freud "normality" is a result of inhibition and censorship.[23]

What are the reasons for Mieli's interest in theorizing gay practices and communism as part of the same politics? In Mieli's book, transsexuality contains a special potential for revolutionary actions.[24] By transsexuality, Mieli understands "the infantile polymorphous and 'undifferentiated' erotic disposition" that is present in every person.[25] An astute commentator on Freud, Mieli argued that "in adult life, every human being" carries this anarchic sexuality within him "as a latent state."[26] If one does not feel this transsexuality, one is "confined in the depth of the unconscious under the yoke of repression."[27] Mieli's gay communism combines perverse sexuality with equality in a political, radical program.[28] In his theory, transformations in gender and sexual desire have to start from rethinking the pre-Oedipal stage. As a result, transsexualism is for Mieli the capacity of subjects to embody and live the potential of a non-hierarchical and disruptive subjective position.[29] Like the British psychoanalyst and theorist Juliet Mitchell, Mieli wants to liberate an ability to realize radical sexual politics, which he calls "trans-sexual Eros," that derives from "infantile 'perverse' polymorphism."[30] Transsexual politics disrupts a capitalistic organization of sexuality based on hierarchical and exploitative relationships.

What are the differences between Soviet bodies and Mieli's transsexual? Like many New Left theorists, Mieli believes that communism is a possibility that is exhausted in the East, but that can be reimagined in the West. Gay communism is the yearning for novel gender and sexual arrangements on the basis of a universal capacity for erotic desire. This desire is based on a discovery of the potential for freedom, which is a term that signals a new alliance between homosexuality and communism: "a liberated homosexuality is an important condition for the creation of communism, i.e. the (re)conquest of human community."[31] In Mieli's theory, a theory of communism changes from representing an enemy of sexual freedom (as in Cold War politics) to its strongest ally: "Communism is the rediscovery of bodies and their fundamental communicative function, their polymorphous potential for love."[32] In Mieli's gay communism, Soviet Marxism was already a lost cause, because for him "the capital monster" ruled in both the capitalist West and the Soviet East.[33] Within this theoretical framework, assumptions related to the freedom and individuality of transsexual bodes are in direct contrast to the aesthetic of Soviet bodies. For the Italian theorist, to become a transsexual one needs to liberate one's desire, and the revolution will follow. For him, bodies are the territory of a psychic liberatory potential and anti-market ideology where revolutionary changes come from within.

A different epistemology separates eastern European socialism from Mieli's theory of queer bodies. While Mieli's communism is possible because of the liberation of a psychic homoerotic potential, productive bodies abolish the distance between the individual and the social. For Soviet Marxists, communism produces a new understanding of the social, rather than putting an individual in the position to liberate themselves. While Mieli's liberated bodies are possible because of the work of erotic drives, Soviet Marxism contains an imaginary of bodies that enact a communist mode of production. In other words, a communist body is not the body of an individual who sexually liberates himself, but one that is part of a political economy that produces a different ideological life. Moreover, Mieli's transsexual bodies have lost any attachment to a dialectical understanding of their existence. Unlike a Soviet Marxist model, for Mieli communism arrives when labor has lost its sublimating function (in his formulation, when the perversion of sexual deviance will not be directed to the factory line). Individuals can attain full sexual liberation through their deviant practices. When people take on the power of their sexual non-normativity, such a process "will coincide with the fall of capitalism and the rejection of alienated and alienating labour."[34] Unlike Mieli's transsexual, Soviet Marxist bodies are first and foremost imagined as a modality of creating an anti-capitalist system in a dialectical manner.

Mieli's Marxist ideas are severely limited by their individualism and loss of dialectical materialism. The path to communism is primarily a change in an individual gender and sexual identity while it also gestures to the possibility of a new society. For Soviet Marxists, a new socialist mode of production functions when bodies labor with others to transform themselves and generate a new economic and moral system. While Mieli's politics is a function of becoming by activating one's perverse instincts, for a Soviet productivist such as Boris Arvatov a collective and dialectical process of social change leads to individual transformation. Not unlike a communist program, Mieli's transsexuality seeks to "overturn the entire imposed morality." This new stage can be achieved only if one abandons heteronormativity and becomes a different sexual being, a "lesbian, bum-bum, gay."[35] This transformation is not only intimate and relational, but also sidesteps a historical materialist analysis of collective change. The rise of the transsexual as a model for liberating pleasure and discovering the true dimensions of one's humanity signals another chapter in the gradual erasure of the epistemology of eastern European Marxism.

Marxism and gender in Gayle Rubin's work

Given that during the Cold War eastern European Marxists were defined as repressive, authoritarian and coercive, their societies were increasingly positioned as the opposite of sexual freedom. In the next sections of the chapter, I will discuss North American queer theory's relationship with Marxism from the 1980s to the 1990s, with a focus on the term "gender." I discuss primarily the work of Gayle Rubin because her arguments were considered to provide the conceptual foundation of queer theory. She advanced the thesis that sexuality and gender should be not only separated as conceptual terms, but also kept in conversation because of their potential for progressive politics.[36] In this new language, gender became naturalized as a sign of one's sexual identity, and sexuality held an important potential for revolutionary disruption.

The connected but analytically separate relationship between sexuality and gender became an important source of conceptual tension between feminist and queer theory. Rubin's intention was to imagine a theoretical field that would be highly critical of conservative feminism. As she argues, the problem with conservative politics was its embrace of heteronormative feminism.[37] Rubin's position posits what Judith Butler would later call "gender trouble," which is the juxtaposition of the troubling nature of non-normative sexuality and gender presentations. In relation to mainstream feminism, Rubin seems to believe that gender in itself is no longer a concept that generates productive analytic ideas. On the contrary, it has become an identity that functions to limit the possibilities of a feminist revolution. Unlike gender, sexuality has become the new historical and theoretical location for revolutionary feminism.

Was this theoretical move enough to undermine Cold War epistemology? In response to biological descriptions that naturalized conservative assumptions about men and women, a social and political feminist critique asked for a new vocabulary of power in the 1970s. The feminist move to build a new theory drew on the rising epistemology of social constructivism in the social sciences. The Cold War social construction thesis was a dominant model for explaining the rationality of actors according to cultural differences. This idea became a key feminist strategy of challenging arguments that saw naturalized sex as a biological category. In its strongest formulation in 1972, the British sociologist Ann Oakley argued that "sex differences may be 'natural,' but 'gender' differences have their source in culture, not nature."[38] Yet Gayle Rubin rejected this idea. The trouble with this argument was, as Rubin argued, that "even as she challenged the claim that gender roles reflect innate differences between the sexes," "it simultaneously consolidated a binary understanding of gender as the basis of a feminist politics of women's liberation."[39]

In its early formulations, Rubin's queer feminism presented a theoretical perspective that challenged the liberal feminist view that gender was the primary axis of discrimination. For her, rejecting a politics based on the difference between men and women (or what was identified as "gender") was consistent with the embrace of the critique of women's oppression. Rubin was considered a precursor of queer theory because she focused her analysis on sexuality as an independent site of investigation. Like Rubin, Judith Butler accepted the idea that women's oppression is an important analytic for politics, but sought to interrogate the idea that "a natural sex" is the foundation for alternative progressive politics. The problem for queer theorists was how to criticize the essentialism of women's discrimination without abandoning a theory that insisted on the constructed roles of womanhood. To solve this problem, Rubin's strategy was to expand the term "gender" from sex roles, defined as man and woman, to sexual roles, which involved sexually non-normative practices.[40] In doing so, she called for a move away from gender oppression as the primary site of a Left feminist analysis. This move, however, as I will demonstrate, was based on an erasure of Marxism as a theoretical source for feminist theory.

Rubin's theory opposed the Cold War epistemology of social construction at the price of gradually abandoning Marxist assumptions. I briefly compare her 1974 work, *Traffic in Women: Notes on the "Political Economy" of Sex*, with her 1982 piece "Thinking Sex," to show this shift. Rubin's 1974 Marxist framework was a critique of a feminism that operated with gender as a single axis of oppression. By the mid-1970s, "patriarchy" had become a key term in the vocabulary of feminists, meaning the male domination of society. Instead of using the language of male domination, Rubin wanted to illuminate a broader system of inequality that was undergirded not only by men's oppression of women, but also by other oppressions. In her usage of the term, gender is synonymous with the idea of social construction. Gender is what society does to biological sex, and as a result, culture transforms biology: "sex/gender system" is "the set of arrangements by which a society transforms biological sexuality into products of human activity, and in which these transformed sexual needs are satisfied."[41] While using the idea of social construction, she deployed the term "sex/gender system" to challenge the idea of naturalized patriarchical norms. Unlike the psychoanalyst Robert Stoller, who used the term "gender" to highlight a core sense of personality, Rubin did not agree with an essential core of one's self. In turn, she suggested that gender identity can be transformed if patriarchal kinship is overthrown.[42] Because gender is socially constructed and kinship is at the basis of gender oppression, Rubin suggested that changing the rules of kinship changes the structure of gender. While eastern European Marxists thought that changing the economic and political rules leads to the abolition of gender, Rubin focused instead on the transformation of the structures of family.

Rather than looking primarily at gender as a term of empowerment, Rubin has regarded it with deep skepticism and called for its abolition. This elimination of gender was necessary because patriarchal culture had to be eliminated. If one's gender is a product of historical and social norms, gender therefore functions as a *straitjacket*. A feminist revolution has to encompass alternative forms of sexual expression and liberate humanity from gender impositions: "a thoroughgoing feminist revolution" would liberate "forms of sexual expression" and "human personality from the straitjacket of gender."[43] Rubin's vision of abolishing a sex/gender system was part of her broader interest in the revolutionary possibilities of theory. The hope of *Traffic in Women* was to identify a new site for revolution, the sex/gender system, that would transform an entire capitalist system: "The dream I find most compelling is one of an androgynous and genderless (though not sexless) society, in which one's sexual anatomy is irrelevant to who one is, what one does, and with whom one makes love."[44] Her investigation argued that there is "hope for a sexually egalitarian society" and that the analysis of oppression can lead to "a society without gender hierarchy."[45]

The transition to a gender analytic that distanced itself from Marxist theory continued in the 1980s. In the paper that Rubin presented at Barnard College in 1982, which was later published as "Thinking Sex" (1984), she claimed that a theory of sexuality has to change feminists' assumptions about gender. Her main concern was that feminism dealt "inadequately" with sexuality.[46] In a famous sentence, Rubin captures what is at stake in her separation between gender and sexuality: "I want to challenge the assumption that feminism is or should be the privileged site of a theory of sexuality."[47] In mirroring her early argument that Marxism and gender cannot be part of the same investigation, Rubin conceptually distinguishes between sexuality and gender. In making this theoretical shift, she articulates a queer approach that derives from her opposition to the claims of Marxism. As such, queer theory has started from not one conceptual break, but two. Erotic desire and sexuality become for queer theorists the location for a new field of investigation. Yet, queer thought sought to leave behind not only feminism, but also Marxism.

In Rubin's account, queer theory emerges as a direct response to the rise of a right-wing rhetoric of sexuality.[48] In her rendition of the context, gender as a category was overpowered by the presence of anti-porn feminists, who embody a type of conservative, antisexuality feminism.[49] In response, sexuality should move away from a theory of gender (or feminism), and sexuality should become "a nexus of the relationships between genders."[50] Transgender, sex work and sadomasochism have become the new targets of conservative feminism. Yet, in Rubin's opposition to conservative feminism a Marxist analysis of modes of production had lost its theoretical relevance. If in *Traffic in Women* gender was a mode of production, she later embraced a Foucauldian analysis that introduced power rather than class as the main analytic for gender.[51] She rejected traditional versions of Marxism that did not engage with women's oppression because they did not take seriously the specific nature of that oppression.[52] In her argument, Marxism "works best for those issues of gender most closely related to issues of class and the organization of labor."[53] Unlike such investigations, "the issues more specific to the social structure of gender were not amenable to Marxist analysis."[54] Rubin had a clear target, namely the Marxist theory that sees gender as a merely reproductive apparatus of class inequalities. In the version of Marxism that she criticized, women's reproductive role did not have an independent status, but was only an element of a total approach to political change. In criticizing theories of class domination, she introduced a clear separation between Marxism and gender, which have to be viewed as distinct theories of knowledge.

The term "gender" has traveled a long distance between 1974 and 1982 in Rubin's thinking. While "gender" appeared to be an important revolutionary term in the 1974 piece, in "Thinking Sex," as William Turner argued, we have moved to a different temporal interval where the sex wars have shaped the deployment of terms.[55] Anticipating Judith Butler's move to theorizing gender as the formation that produces sex, gender becomes for Rubin a different conceptual site from sex.[56] If gender and sexuality have become a new terrain of revolutionary politics, Marxism is also a lost cause in this process.

Queer theory at the end of the Cold War

Given that Marxist theory seems to have lost its epistemological appeal between the mid-1980s and the 1990s, liberal feminist theory is on the rise. The gradual elimination of socialist ideology in the Soviet Union and eastern Europe has changed the terms of the debate on the American Left. An important consequence of this evolution is the separation of analytics such as gender and queer from Marxist theory, a theory of human emancipation and class struggle. If productive bodies within Marxist ideology are discarded as a relevant epistemology, women's oppression and non-normative sexualities have become a key site of resistance for North American feminism. A growing skepticism about the potential of anti-capitalist theory, not to mention the disregard for any socialist histories, has shaped the articulations of canonical queer and gender theorizing. In Butler's 1990 *Gender Trouble*, Marx has a fleeting appearance at the beginning of the book, where he is briefly invoked as a theorist who urges us to consider "the historical present."[57] From a mere reference in Butler's book, Marx is summoned by Eve Kosofsky Sedgwick, in *Epistemology of the Closet*, in a sentence where she argues that modern Marxists, liberal capitalists and Nazis agree that same-sex desire and "decadence" frame gay people as being in need of a cure.[58] In Teresa De Lauretis's 1991 "Introduction" to a special issue of *Differences*, where she coined the term "queer theory," Marxism and socialism are ignored as a theoretical frame. Instead of Marxism, De Lauretis focuses on how race, gender and sex function as critical intersectional categories.[59]

Within this global political context, I analyze the reconceptualization of gender in the work of Judith Butler, Joan Scott and Hortense Spillers, with an emphasis on the period between 1985 and 1990. While all three theorists want to separate gender from women's sexual identity, their analytical routes are different. Butler and Scott have struggled with Rubin's dilemma about gender as a cultural construction, although they wanted to move forward theoretically. They argued against the essentialism of gender categories but preserved the feminist idea of discrimination against women. While in her early work Butler deploys gender to challenge the idea of gender as a sexed body, Scott seeks to transform it into a category of analysis to explain power. Both theorists reworked a Foucauldian analysis into the analytic of gender to integrate the idea of discrimination against women. Yet neither has conceptualized gender as a category related to histories of colonial violence and slavery. In turn, Spillers's conceptualization of gender traces the production of the category to global capitalism and slavery, and as such, brings back a theoretical link to historical materialism. An analysis of the work of these three theorists shows that the anti-capitalist orientation of sexuality studies had been seriously weakened at the end of the 1980s.

To challenge social constructivism, Butler distinguished between what she calls gender subversion and the sexed body in *Gender*

Trouble. In a direct response to liberal feminism, she argues that feminists lost their capacity to be subversive if women's sexed bodies were viewed as as primary sites of agency. Like Rubin in *Traffic in Women*, Butler suggests that a definition of gender as the social construction of the body is insufficient for radical feminist politics. An interview with Butler from 1994 clarifies why she wants to keep gender separate from a sexed body. Butler seems to agree with Rubin that gender has become the domain of feminism. In Rubin's view, it should be viewed synonymous with a woman's body.[60] Yet, gender as the politics of women's oppression is not enough because women's bodies have become a taken-for-granted site for constructing a Leftist politics.[61] To open up a different view of bodies, gender in Judith Butler's 1990s *Gender Trouble* is defined not only as a subversive mode of living for those who do not conform to regulatory norms and identities, but also as an open coalition of subjectivities:

> Gender is a complexity whose totality is permanently deferred, never fully what it is at any given juncture in time. An open coalition, then, will affirm identities that are alternately instituted and relinquished according to the purposes at hand; it will be an open assemblage that permits of multiple convergences and divergences without obedience to a normative telos of definitional closure. [62]

While Butler conceptualized gender as an open coalition of identities, this intervention fits with calls for solidarity that were part of 1990s politics, which rejected single issue politics. As part of a New Left coalition in the USA, not only women's oppression, but sexuality and race are essential to a broader transformative analytic. In addition, the new conceptualization of gender focuses on political struggles without a teleological goal, as was the case of communism in Marxism. The novel politics had to become different from Marxism, and sought a different type of politics within the framework of liberal capitalism. In Butler's account, New Left politics is one without Marxism, in its intention to make the aim of Leftist politics "an open assemblage."[63] The reference to Deleuze and Guattari's concept of assemblage positions gender trouble in a new field of radical politics, which, as Foucault intimated in the preface to *Anti-Oedipus*, draws on "a movement toward political struggles that no longer conformed to the model that Marxist tradition had prescribed."[64]

In this new model of Left politics, the alliance among various identities was directly linked to the subversion of liberal capitalism, which aimed to replace the old Marxist model of class conflict. Foucault's *The History of Sexuality* was explicit in its rejection of class analysis and Marxist ideological terms. The term "power" was defined negatively with regard to a Marxist analysis. Power is not something that is "acquired," is not exterior to "economic processes" and is not class conflict.[65] If resistance is inherent in power, then subversion of norms becomes the strategy of opposition. In Butler's work, "queer" became a term that articulated a program of what Foucault defined as "a plurality of resistances."[66] Like Foucault's power, Butler conceptualized "gender" and "queer" as terms designed to embrace contingency and complexity, but with the aim of transforming the capitalist system.[67] Instead of constituting an abstract call to solidarity, gender had to perform a specific and contextual task. In *Gender Trouble*, gender was a device of interrupting politics associated with traditional heteronormativity.[68] For Butler, a gender identity that was considered a "failure" was a theoretical ground for new politics, which was later associated with the term "queer." Not only women's alleged failure to become full men, but also queer people's sexuality, racialized bodies and disabled bodies, are part of the potential meaning of gender. In a new coalitional politics, Butler's hope was that differences in relation to heteronormative conventions can generate a transformative political program.

Butler's theory builds on Rubin's earlier gesture of separating gender from Marxism. Not unlike Rubin, for Butler, Marxism is a site for limited theoretical possibilities. The revolutionary aims of the Left theory have changed. Instead of changing the political economy of a society, the term "gender" points to a politics of allyship. If identity by itself is not enough, then Leftist politics needs coalitions. With her reconceptualization of gender, Butler fundamentally challenged a US Cold War tradition that saw bodies as identities constructed by culture. Instead, she imagined a post-identitarian politics that does not derive from the single identity of an oppressed subject. In articulating a linguistic space for various subjects to find themselves, she designed a politics of future alliances that could serve as a replacement for Marxism. The new queer politics has eliminated any connection to either Soviet or

Chinese Marxism while keeping the sociological category of class as a reminder of the possibilities of intersectionality.[69]

The rise of a new deconstructivist Left had an impact not only on sexuality and literature studies, but also on history. The elimination of Marxism was part of a broader move to challenge social constructivism arguments with new theories of gender. Like *Gender Trouble*, Joan Scott's 1986 article titled "Gender: A Useful Category of Historical Analysis" opposed the understanding of gender as a sexed body. Four years before the publication of *Gender Trouble*, Joan Scott called historians to move away from deploying gender as an equivalent of sex.[70] Scott offered two alternative meanings of gender, which, she argued, would help historians perform a different conceptual work that would sharpen their research. Her first step was to anchor gender in a pervading mode of conceptualizing it at the end of the 1980s. According to this, gender is an indicator of social experiences that are constituted by sex differences.[71] Her second step was to invite historians to work with the idea of gender as power.[72] In other words, rather than saying historians need gender to understand the relation between men and women, Scott told them that they need gender to understand power. Like Butler's, Scott's gender was redefined and restructured according to a vision of political and social equality, which would include "not only sex, but class and race."[73] She made an additional move with the term "gender," however. In arguing that the term can serve as an analytic for a historian, she saw gender as a tool to understand historical difference. In her view, it can help investigate the changing nature of the language of sexual difference to create an analytic distance between "the seemingly fixed language of the past" and "our own terminology."[74] In short, gender could no longer be for Scott a constructed sexed body. Instead, gender becomes an analytic that captures the historical shift in the meaning of categories such as man and woman.

In Scott's argument, the Foucauldian concept of power became the primary methodological tool for historical investigation. If understanding power was the primary task of the researcher, then the normative goals of Marxist ideology were eliminated from this Leftist method in historical analyses. What Scott brings to queer theoretical accounts that is new is the historicized nature of gender as an analytic, because neither Rubin nor Butler made a sustained attempt to conceptualize it as such. Yet, what is missing from Scott's analysis is an account that takes seriously broader analytics of historical formation, such as colonialism and slavery, that were available to her. Such analytics preserved Marxist theories of emancipation and anti-colonialism, which remain fundamental sites to interrogate gender and sexuality. Unlike the work of Rubin, Butler and Scott, Hortense Spillers's 1987 article "Mama's Baby, Papa's Maybe" sought to keep gender in conversation with thinking in anti-colonial and anti-capitalist scholarship. Her piece is central to a tradition of reconceptualizing gender in US academia. Rather than a main explanatory concept, gender became a variable in a broader analytic that emphasized racial and imperial formations.

Spillers's article became a critical site for questioning the conceptual language deployed by white North American theorists and their racial underpinnings. She locates gender and sexuality in the colonial history of the Anglo-American world. In Spillers's view, "sexuality" is a term that has not only named white sexuality, but has also emerged as a category from the history of slavery. Given its racialized origins, Spillers asked a key question: Can sexuality constitute a site for political resistance? In her analysis, her answer is rather negative because sexuality is fundamentally shaped by relations of colonial domination:

> We could go so far as to entertain the very real possibility that "sexuality," as a term of implied relationships and desire, is dubiously appropriate, manageable, or accurate to any of the familial arrangements under a system of enslavement, from the master's family to the captive enclave.[75]

Under conditions such as slavery, gender, like other concepts ("reproduction," "motherhood," "pleasure" and "desire") is thrown "into unrelieved crisis."[76] The situation that Spillers describes in relation to the enslaved calls into question not only the language but also the symbolic order that the white masters have built in North America. From the standpoint of the enslaved African Americans, the language of white power is one of domination. Yet Spillers also gestures to the practices and life of the enslaved that can provide a different theoretical angle to rethinking concepts such as gender and sexuality. As with Butler's term "queer," Spillers finds a novel potential in creative practices that build new relationships and kinship arrangements. For her, black life creates new alternative forms of interaction and survival, which are specific to the situation of people being captured and put to work in the interest of white capitalists.

What Spillers brings to the historiography of gender is the realization that the analytic has a weak power to make sense of the life of the enslaved. For instance, the concept is poorly situated to offer an account of black women's capacity to become mothers: "gender, or sex-role assignment, or the clear differentiation of sexual stuff, sustained elsewhere in the culture, does not emerge for the African-American female in this historic instance, except indirectly, except as a way to reinforce through the process of birthing, the reproduction of the relations of production."[77] Spillers's interest is to focus on resources that are part of the historical positionality of black women in the USA. The need to rethink gender emerges from the fact that a "problematization of gender places" situates the African American woman "out of the traditional symbolic of female gender."[78] In Spillers's argument, this refusal of the family arrangements known as "gender" derived from two key developments: (1) black motherhood is both denied and considered as a founding term of human and social enactment, and (2) the black father's name is banished and has a mocking presence. The outcome of this predicament is that the black woman becomes an insurgent ground as a female social subject. As such, an insurgent monstrosity offers the possibility of rewriting white terminology and imagining new terms for liberation.

Spillers deeply interrogated the language that Anglo-American theorists used for political resistance.[79] She calls our attention to the need to overthrow a general syntax of racialized violence. First, a project of liberation is founded on rupturing "violently the laws of American behavior that make such syntax possible." Second, this project calls for a rewriting of "the laws of American behavior" and the creation of a new language that will speak to the conditions of existing power hierarchies.[80] In the end, Spillers's goal is, like Rubin's, to abolish an entire structure of power and privilege. Unlike Rubin's argument, the abolition of the sex/gender system is not conceptualized as a Marxist anti-capitalist call. Instead, the abolition of capitalism is based on its history of racial violence, and a radical overturn of our vocabulary can be accomplished by the invention of a new semantic field.

My interest in this section has been to trace not only the deployment of gender in opposition to Cold War ideas, but also the elimination of Marxist theory in queer theory. While queer theory was created as a post-Cold War theory, it kept its anti-communist history unanalyzed. The authors I have discussed (Butler, Scott and Spillers) tried to reconceptualize gender to part company with a social constructivist gender. These contributions indicate that gender has been differently conceptualized from the tradition of the social construction of the sexed body. Butler and Scott sought to deploy gender as part of a post-identitarian coalition of the New Left in North America. Unlike theirs, Spillers's contribution was to add an anti-colonial and anti-imperial historicized analysis. Her theoretical premises were attached to a black feminist conceptualization of resistance in African American culture. While it moved an epistemology of gender out of the language of personal identity, queer theory has not proposed a definite break with Cold War assumptions. In the next section I briefly articulate two key consequences of this shift to a post-Cold War gender in queer studies and its unanalyzed rejection of eastern European Marxism.

Anti-communism in queer theory?

In this chapter, I have analyzed the transformation of the term "gender" in queer feminism at the end of the 1980s, with a focus on North American theorists of sexuality. To trace the gradual loss of a Marxist epistemology, I analyzed the rise of the term "gender" and its subjectless post-identity epistemology. According to this model, only a broad coalition of racial, ethnic and sexual positions can lead to a new political vocabulary of power. As I demonstrated in Chapter 3, Cold War gender was coined as an alternative to the epistemology of Soviet Marxism. Queer thinking wanted to move away from a conception of personal identity, yet its conceptual apparatus was attached to the vocabulary of rebellious and nonnormative individuals. For gay theorists such as Marco Mieli communism was, unlike Soviet Marxism, an authentic form of political action that wanted a true political revolution. The term "gay communism" was a critique of all State apparatuses and their conception of sexuality, so that Soviet Marxism and liberal democracy were seen as similar repressive structures. Mieli's theory relied on transsexual individuals, who can attain sexual liberation by following an anti-normative behavior.

Gender and liberated sexuality were key terms not only for a countercultural thinkers such as Mieli, but were also becoming dominant: in eastern Europe as a critique of Marxism, and in the USA to inaugurate new conceptual tools. Gender sought to become a subjectless concept, yet it appealed to material queer bodies. While Gayle Rubin's *Traffic in Women* suggested that gender can be abolished, her theory relied on the revolutionary potential of queer subjects. Marxism as a theory of the political analysis of power, but also as a guiding theoretical practice, has gradually disappeared from the concerns of queer thinkers. In continuing this direction, theorists such as Judith Butler, Joan Scott and Hortense Spillers have abandoned any attempt to deploy Marxist categories of analysis. Terms such as "relations of production," "human emancipation" and "historical materialism" were removed from the rising fields of queer theory and cultural studies.

A first consequence of the elimination of Marxism is the abandonment of the idea of changing an entire system of political and ideological production. Butler's post-identitarian theory sought to dismantle the terms of social constructionism that were dominant in North American feminist and cultural studies. Rather than utilizing the thesis that bodies were socially constructed, Butler showed that gender produces what are perceived as biological differences. And here is the twist. In doing so, she not only changed the terms of the controversy between constructionism and natural differences, but also operated within the same conceptual apparatus that was put in place in the 1950s. In undermining the term "gender" but also highlighting its importance, she made "gender" a key term in what is currently attacked as "gender ideology," the name that a conservative body of thinking has used to describe its adversaries. Butler is not, however, the only scholar who echoes the work of a sexologist such as John Money. Theorists such as Jack Halberstam justify the use of the term "trans*" by queering Money's formulation of gender. Trans* was conceptualized to resist the narrow use of the term "transgender."[81] In his own account, Halberstam deploys the asterisk in trans* to mark a blank that could be productive of various gender possibilities. If for Money the term "gender" emerges from a blank that was confusing to him, in Halberstam's theory "trans*" is a term that speaks to a queer resignification of the term "transgender." Like "queer," "trans" becomes a mode of resignifying a term that was coined to function according to ideas of freedom and sexual possibilities. Queer theory is oriented in these formulations towards changing the system from within, rather than putting forward an ideology that wants to abolish capitalism, as Soviet Marxists did after the October Revolution.

Newer accounts of a Left-to-queer theory are exciting in their invitation to produce historical and materialist accounts in queer thinking. They suggest a deeper concern not only with sexuality as a single analytic, but with the totality of social relations. While suggesting a corrective to previous theoretical analyses, their proposals keep some ideas of Cold War anti-communism in place. Eng and Puar's program in *Social Text* suggests a materialist orientation to reveal "how subjects emerge and cohere through geopolitical exceptionalisms that render the material conditions of their production opaque."[82] But the danger is, as Keti Chukhrov argues, that articulating a theory of dismantling alienation is not enough to offer a political alternative to a critique.[83] In Eng and Puar's call, a revived Marxism is based on Althusser's work, which, as Chukhrov reminds us, argued that communism is primarily not a structure, such as eastern European socialism, but a "process of critique and communization."[84] Similarly, queer Marxism in Petrus Liu's conceptualization seeks to synthesize Butler's work and Marxist theory, but this attempt is based on the idea that Marxism offers primarily a theory of social structuration.[85] In contrast to Marxist theories, Butler seems, for Liu, to have a more expansive notion of livability "beyond the production of food and shelter."[86] The entire historical world of eastern European Marxism is erased with this argument, given that an eastern European Marxist world had produced much more than food and shelter. The problem starts with conceptualizing Marxist theory as a specter that haunts queer theory. Instead, eastern European socialism not only offers an alternative epistemology, but also makes claims to a world revolution. In emphasizing the debt to Althusser and its theory of subjectivation, Liu's queer Marxism moves away from a historical materialist view of social life, in spite of his call to forge a materialist methodology. In its neglect of analyzing the Cold War separation between eastern European and western Marxism, a Left-to-queer theory relies to a great extent on a theoretical corpus that rejected the contributions of eastern European Marxism.

A second consequence of the split between queer and Marxist theory was the loss of an anti-capitalist economic program. Soviet Marxism was able to create a political economy of objects and bodies that was designed as a materialist alternative to capitalism. In turn, queer theory has not developed a clear program of analyzing non-normative sexuality that would move beyond cultural transformation. To resist and subvert the economy of bodies in capitalism, which was a major concern for theorists such as Butler, is a different tactic from a program that seeks a collective Marxist transformation of bodies. Queer theorists theorized linguistic interventions as a political platform to change people's attitudes and conceptions, and yet the change of the economic infrastructure of people's lives has hardly become a focus of queer theory. For thinkers such as Hortense Spillers, who use broader analytics such as racialization and colonialism, the solution to inequality was the invention of a new semantics. This move from modes of production to a theory of language signals the transformation of Marxism in cultural politics. Yet as significant economic transformations in eastern Europe and the Soviet Union have indicated, a theory of revolutionary change cannot operate without the social transformations of labor relations and industrial production.

Queer theory that distances itself from queer liberalism criticizes the idea, as Liu argued, that "the primary obstacle facing queer people is discrimination, misrecognition, or other forms of mental judgment that impede parity in participation."[87] The work that I've done in Part II builds on this critique, but what it shows is that any materialist program cannot move forward without historicizing the formation of queer theory. My analysis of eastern European Marxism's epistemology advances a program that derives from a project of human emancipation. This is why in Part III I will change my method. If in Part II I historicized various meanings of gender and as its circulation during the Cold War, Part III dialectically introduces the epistemology of Soviet Marxism into queer theory. The method in this next part of the book is to show that historical materialism can bring new resources to a queer of color critique. Its goal is to create a hybrid analytic, which borrows not only from the

Marxist model of productive bodies, but also focuses on racialized and imperial dynamics after the Cold War.

Notes

1. The criticism made by Leerom Medevoi, *Rebels: Youth and the Cold War Origins of Identity* (Durham, NC: Duke University Press, 2005), that queer theory lacks an alternative vocabulary, is on point, but it does not acknowledge queer theory's *desire* to produce such vocabulary.
2. See Rosemary Hennessy, *Profit and Pleasure: Sexual Identities in Late Capitalism* (New York: Routledge, 2000), pp. 175–203; and Kevin Floyd, *The Reification of Desire: Toward a Queer Marxism* (Minneapolis: University of Minnesota Press, 2009), pp. 1–38.
3. See Judith Butler, *Gender Trouble: Feminism and the Subversion of Identity* (London: Routledge, 1999), p. vii.
4. Medevoi, *Rebels*, pp. 318–319, argues that given queer theory's intention to contest identity, it failed to propose an alternative vocabulary to replace it.
5. David L. Eng and Jasbir K. Puar, "Introduction: Left of Queer," *Social Text*, 38:4 (December 2020), p. 1.
6. See *ibid.*, p. 2, for new reconceptualizations in queer theory.
7. Gayle Rubin, *Deviations: A Gayle Rubin Reader* (Durham, NC: Duke University Press, 2011), p. 193.
8. Hennessy, *Profit and Pleasure*, p. 59.
9. Petrus Liu, "Queer Theory and the Specter of Materialism," *Social Text*, 38:4 (2020), p. 36, noted that D'Emilio subscribes to a US-centric narrative "that locates Stonewall as the putative origin of modern gay identity and liberation."
10. Jemima Repo, *The Biopolitics of Gender* (Oxford: Oxford University Press, 2015); and Susan Stryker, "*We Who Are Sexy*: Christine Jorgensen's Transsexual Whiteness in the Postcolonial Philippines," *Social Semiotics*, 19:1 (2009), 79–91. See also the theoretical accounts mentioned by Jordana Rosenberg and Amy Villarejo, "Queerness, Norms, Utopia," *GLQ*, 18:1 (2011), p. 3, such as the queer of color critique or Jody Melamed's reading of Cedric Robinson.
11. Alina Asavei, "Rewriting the Canon of Communist Visual Art," M.A. dissertation (Central European University, Budapest, 2007), pp. 40–42, www.etd.ceu.edu/2007/asavei_maria.pdf (accessed June 10, 2019).
12. *Ibid.*

13 *Ibid.*, p. 40.
14 For the turn in Romanian socialism in 1971 and Nicolae Ceaușescu's "July theses," which called for an increase in political education and Party control, see Cezar Stanciu, "The End of Liberalizaton in Communist Romania," *Historical Journal*, 56:4 (December 2013), 1063–1085.
15 See Asavei, "Rewriting the Canon," p. 104.
16 Medevoi, *Rebels*, p. 5.
17 *Ibid.*
18 *Ibid.*
19 In contrast to late Hungarian films, the critique of Marxism in the Yugoslav film *Man Is Not a Bird* (Makavjev, 1965) is articulated by deconstructing the categories of socialist realism. Two central figures of socialist realism, the engineer (Jan Rudinski) and the worker (Barbulovic), are revealed as humans who are fraught with strong and unruly sexual desires. Rather than completely excluding socialist realist types, the film works with these two cinematic types to infuse a dimension of reality into Marxist cinematography. In Makavjev's film, freedom and sexual liberation were not directly opposed to Marxism but, on the contrary, were considered to be compatible with the communist project. Yet, unlike an early Soviet aesthetic, the two characters were no longer part of a dialectical process of producing communism.
20 Marco Mieli, *Homosexuality and Liberation: Elements of a Gay Critique*, trans. David Fernbach (London: Gay Men's Press, 1980), p. 27.
21 Rubin, *Deviations*, p. 48.
22 John Middleton, "'Bolshevism in Art': Dada and Politics," *Texas Studies in Literature and Language*, 4:3 (1962), 408–430.
23 Mieli, *Homosexuality and Liberation*, p. 24.
24 Mieli discusses the gay potential of early sexual life, since for the infant, the selection of a sexual object is circumstantial, and "little girls are also lesbian, and little boys are also gay" (*ibid.*).
25 *Ibid.*, p. 26.
26 *Ibid.*
27 *Ibid.*
28 *Ibid.*, p. 135: "Communism is the rediscovery of bodies and their fundamental communicative function, their polymorphous potential for love."
29 Transsexual politics is for Mieli a politics of rejecting Oedipal normative roles regarding man and woman.
30 For perverse polymorphism, see *ibid.*, p. 23. For "trans-sexual Eros," see *ibid.*, p. 27. See also Juliet Mitchell, *Siblings* (Cambridge: Polity

Press, 2003). Both Mitchell and Mieli are fundamentally shaped by London's feminist, queer and socialist movements: Mitchell worked for the *New Left Review* in the 1960s, where she took strong socialist and feminist positions, while Mieli took an active role in London's Gay Liberation Front between 1970 and 1972. Mitchell uses the term "sibling" as a lateral/egalitarian position where a subject is not defined by Oedipal sexuality (and thus by what they miss, for example, a penis or a vagina), but by a capacity to exceed their gender identification.

31 Mieli, *Homosexuality and Liberation*, p. 135.
32 *Ibid*.
33 *Ibid*., p. 16.
34 *Ibid*., p. 38.
35 *Ibid*., p. 118.
36 For Rubin's intervention in feminist debates at the Barnard conference in 1982, see William Turner, *A Genealogy of Queer Theory* (Philadelphia: Temple University Press, 2000), pp. 87–88.
37 Rubin, *Deviations*, p. 294.
38 Ann Oakley cited by David A. Rubin, "'An unnamed blank that craved a name': A Genealogy of Intersex as Gender," *Signs: Journal of Women in Culture and Society*, 37:4 (2012), p. 889.
39 *Ibid*. Rubin is not an exception for academics who use the term "gender" as social construction; Robert Stoller, "Gender-Role Change in Intersex Patients," *JAMA*, 188:7 (1964), 684–685, deployed the formulation "gender identity" in a critique of Money's term "gender."
40 For the feminist debates during the 1980s on sexuality and gender, see Turner, *A Genealogy of Queer Theory*, pp. 83–87. For the difference between sexuality and gender in queer theory, see *ibid*., p. 89.
41 Rubin, *Deviations*, p. 48.
42 *Ibid*., p. 293. For Robert Stoller's understanding of a core in gender identity, see Richard Green, "Robert Stoller's Sex and Gender: 40 Years On," *Archives of Sexual Behaviour*, 39 (2010), p. 1458: "The sense of core gender identity ... is derived from three sources: the anatomy and physiology of the genitalia; the attitudes of parents, siblings and peers toward the child's gender role; and a biological force that may more or less modify the attitudinal (environmental) forces."
43 See Rubin, *Deviations*, p. 72.
44 *Ibid*., p. 75.
45 *Ibid*., p. 33.
46 *Ibid*., p. 294.
47 *Ibid*., p. 191.
48 *Ibid*., p. 280.

49 *Ibid.*, p. 186.
50 *Ibid.*, pp. 185–186.
51 This concept of a sex/gender system, along with ideas such as "the traffic in women," was aimed at constructing better critical descriptions of sexual inequality.
52 *Ibid.*, p. 179: "Marxism, no matter how modified, seemed unable to fully grasp the issues of gender difference and the oppression of women."
53 *Ibid.*
54 *Ibid.*
55 Turner, *A Genealogy of Queer Theory*, pp. 85–90.
56 See Rubin, *Deviations*, p. 284: "I see no reason why feminism has to be limited to kinship and psychoanalysis, and I never said it should not work on sexuality. I only said it should not be seen as the privileged site for work on sexuality."
57 Butler, *Gender Trouble*, p. 8.
58 Eve Kosofsky Sedgwick, *Epistemology of the Closet* (Berkeley: University of California Press, 1990), 128.
59 Teresa De Lauretis, "Queer Theory. Lesbian and Gay Sexualities: An Introduction," *Differences: A Journal of Feminist Cultural Studies*, special issue, 3:2 (1991), iii–xviii.
60 See "Sexual Traffic," interview with Gayle Rubin by Judith Butler, in Rubin, *Deviations*, pp. 276–310. Also, see how Rubin defines a woman's body: "the cultural residue and the symbolic manifestations and all of the other aspects of that system, and the inscription and installation of those structures and categories within people" (p. 279).
61 *Ibid.*
62 Butler, *Gender Trouble*, p. 22.
63 *Ibid.*
64 See Michel Foucault, "Preface," in Gilles Deleuze and Felix Guattari, *Anti-Oedipus: Capitalism and Schizophrenia* (Minneapolis: University of Minnesota Press, 1983), p. xii.
65 Michel Foucault, *The History of Sexuality*, Vol. I, *An Introduction*, trans. Robert Hurley (New York: Pantheon, 1978), pp. 94–95.
66 *Ibid.*, 96.
67 See Judith Butler, "Critically Queer," *GLQ*, 1:1 (1993), p. 19, for the permanent transformation of the term "queer": "it will have to remain that which is, in the present, never fully owned, but always and only redeployed, twisted, queered from a prior usage and in the direction of urgent and expanding political purposes, and perhaps also yielded in favor of terms that do that political work more effectively."
68 Butler, *Gender Trouble*, p. 24.

69 See Butler's debate about class with Nancy Fraser in Judith Butler, "Merely Cultural," *New Left Review*, 1:227 (January–February 1998), 33–45.
70 Joan W. Scott, "Gender: A Useful Category of Historical Analysis," *American Historical Review*, 91:5 (1986), 1053–1075.
71 *Ibid.*, p. 1067, where Scott saw gender to be "a constitutive element of social relationships based on perceived differences between sexes."
72 *Ibid.*, where gender is a "primary way of signifying relationships of power."
73 *Ibid.*, p. 1075.
74 *Ibid.*
75 Hortense Spillers, "Mama's Baby, Papa's Maybe: An American Grammar Book," *Diacritics*, 17:2 (Summer 1987), p. 76.
76 *Ibid.*, p. 76.
77 *Ibid.*, p. 79.
78 *Ibid.*, p. 87.
79 *Ibid.*, p. 75.
80 *Ibid.*, p. 79: "the project of liberation for African-Americans has found urgency in two passionate motivations that are twinned – 1) to break apart, to rupture violently the laws of American behavior that make such syntax possible; 2) to introduce a new semantic field/fold more appropriate to his/her own historic movement. I regard this twin compulsion as distinct, though related, moments of the very same narrative process that might appear as a concentration or a dispersal."
81 Jack Halberstam, *Trans*: A Quick and Quirky Account of Gender Variability* (Berkeley: University of California Press, 2017), p. 4: "The asterisk holds off the certainty of diagnosis; it keeps at bay any sense of knowing in advance what the meaning of this or that gender variant form may be."
82 Eng and Puar, "Introduction," p. 2.
83 Keti Chukhrov, *Practicing the Good: Desire and Boredom in Soviet Socialism* (Minneapolis: University of Minnesota Press, 2020), pp. 185–186.
84 Keti Chukhrov, Alexei Penzin and Valeri Podoroga, "Marx against Marxism, Marxism against Marx," *Stasis*, 5:2 (2017), pp. 279–280.
85 Liu, "Queer Theory," pp. 38–39
86 *Ibid.*, p. 38.
87 *Ibid.*, pp. 41–42.

Part III

De-contextualizing Marxism

The aim of Part III is to bring an eastern European Marxist epistemology into queer anti-racist theory. The method I use in this section takes socialism out of its historical context to create a new analytic. Specifically, I juxtapose the epistemology of Soviet Marxism, which was the product of an eastern European world, with a queer of color analysis, which draws on tactics that racialized queers deploy under US racial capitalism. This part of the book seeks to depart from projects that try either to offer an accurate representation of the communist past or to be subversive within liberal capitalism. My argument is neither a claim to historical truth nor a subversive tactic in liberal capitalism. Instead, I propose to reorient queer theory to a Marxist theory of human emancipation and create a materialist conception of queer studies. In this theory, the story of the communist past and a queer of color theory function not unlike the found footages that Guy Debord deployed in his video art. By mixing video inserts with reflections on the actual state of cultural capitalism, Debord intended to produce a montage that created new images by selecting excerpts from advertising and Hollywood cinema. Like him, I take eastern European Marxist films out of their historical context and seek to insert them into a new setting to produce an innovative relationship to a forgotten aesthetic such as socialist realism. Unlike Debord, I do not seek to combat the alienation under current capitalism, but to produce a new method that moves away from anti-communism into queer studies. The goal of this juxtaposition is to change the conventional boundaries of both socialism and queer theory by generating a third analytic.

What is the goal of applying a socialist montage to queer theory? First, this method asks that a project of abolishing gender norms should be conceptualized along the lines of an eastern European Marxist theory that has a long history of abolishing capitalism. The 2020 responses to the death of George Floyd in the United States made visible the question of the abolition of the police in scholarly conversations about racism and justice. The rise of trans theory and, with it, of the category of non-binary, raises the question of eradicating the category of gender. While abolition is an important current political project focused on future elaborations, eastern European Marxism offers a long history of eradicating private property and capitalist sex roles. In connecting different abolitionist theories, a materialist queer conception suggests that eastern European Marxism provides important lessons for a project of criticizing racial and heteronormative capitalism. It responds to what José Esteban Muñoz calls the increased danger of "the expansion of the normal," which extends the logic of capitalism to all spheres of life.[1] The expansion of the normal is not only the dominance of capitalist straight time, and with that, of the idea that the queer should always fail in a heteronormative world, as Muñoz argues.[2] The expansion of the normal also elides abolitionist projects from the past that offered an important alternative to liberal capitalist politics.

Second, to work with a dialectical method means to introduce a needs-oriented materiality in queer studies. The main theoretical frame for queer studies is current capitalism, as if eastern European socialism had never existed. In its present-oriented methodology, for Jordana Rosenberg and Amy Villarejo queer studies has to foreground capitalism "as the ground and condition of such analysis."[3] Similarly, trans studies often fails to engage with studies of materiality that center on worlds that were imagined as anti-capitalistic. The question of materiality has been approached by trans theorists primarily by focusing on bodies' corporeality to discourage "any particular alignment of sex-as-anatomy and gender-as-role, any predetermined relationship between orientation and act, and reduction of pleasure to genitalia as the primary site of erogenous activity and reproduction."[4] Yet queer and trans theory have not yet confronted what an eastern European Marxist world and epistemology can offer to their theoretical premises. To gesture to a new understanding of materiality, I focus Part III on a historical account that takes the universality of needs as a material ground for social change. As part of the path to human emancipation, this method highlights common enemies, such as an anti-communist discourse, but also various artwork resources such as films about anti-slavery Roma struggles and trans coalitions for labor rights.

In the current anti-communist rhetoric of most of the eastern European states, the accusation of Marxism has the role of shaming a postsocialist generation on the grounds of its alleged criminal past. But, as Eve Kosofsky Sedgwick told us, shame is a queer affect because of its capacity for transformation: shame is a "free radical, that attaches to and permanently intensifies and alters the meaning of – of almost anything."[5] From the alterations of conventional Marxism-Leninism, a method of decontextualizing Marxism can bring forth an alternative to US-centric queer theory. As an example, shame can undo what is taken for granted as "Stalinism" in liberal capitalism and open our imagination to a new theoretical account. To be able to feel shame one needs to take seriously the revolutionary potential that was encompassed by the communist project in its darker moments such as Stalinist times.

To theorize new resources for queer theory, I appeal to film material considered politically irrelevant and dead. As Boris Groys argued, the genre of socialist realism can liberate its revolutionary potential by offering anti-capitalist historical material to future artists.[6] Instead of being stored in a special location – let's say a cinematheque or a museum – Marxist films function in a virtual space (such as YouTube, Vimeo and other media platforms) that is up for grabs. This condition of being up for grabs is important because films are not yet organized in a systematized archive with its traditional curators and gatekeepers. If Marxist films have no value under digital capitalism, then this is a key and strategic position that queer theory can use to develop its anti-capitalist project. A different sense of history is contained in eastern European Marxist films, particularly in Stalinist ones, which are seen as the most backward and unfashionable artistic productions. Marxist theory and artwork have a strategic importance for queer theory because they display a revolutionary imagination that is considered obsolete and totalitarian. This film archive offers what I call "auratic illuminations" from a socialist epistemology and shows how revolutionary moments emerged along with a history of consolidating its achievements.

To indicate some potential routes, I plan to proceed in four steps. In the first I argue that dialectical ideas in eastern European Marxist cinema put forward a compelling model of the abolition of sexuality anchored in private property. In Chapter 5 I explain that the Romanian Marxist film *The Valley Resounds* shows not only communist characters who build a new world, but also a process of abolishing capitalist perceptions and behaviors. Unlike conventional queer sexuality, Marxist films point to a dialectical interaction among communists that leads to a new sexuality. In the second step, I show in Chapter 6 that a theory of counterfetishes (e.g., socialist objects that fulfill people's needs) can infuse queer thinking with a Marxist epistemology. Socialist objects are inspired by a sensuous materiality that was designed to emerge at the moment, as Marx said, that senses have become theoreticians.[7] Unlike the queer emphasis on subverting commodities, the refusal of commodities and the design of counterfetishes was a key strategy of eastern European Marxist planners. In the third step, I show in Chapter 7 that Marxist cinema offers important material to provide not only an anti-racist character to the concept of the unconscious, but also a socialist orientation. My reading of dominant psychoanalytic theory by appealing to Marxist psychology is inspired by anti-slavery rebellions by Roma people, as they are depicted in the socialist film *The Fiddlers*. In the fourth step, I uncover in Chapter 8 the deep ideological currents that connect a widespread anti-communist project in the United States with anti-trans politics. This last chapter makes visible the Cold War dynamics that led to the separation between labor politics and trans politics.

Notes

1 José Esteban Muñoz, *Cruising Utopia: The Then and There of Queer Futurity* (New York: New York University Press, 2009), p. 173.
2 *Ibid.*, p. 155.
3 Jordana Rosenberg and Amy Villarejo, "Queerness, Norms, Utopia," *GLQ*, 18:1 (2011), p. 3.
4 David L. Eng and Jasbir K. Puar, "Introduction: Left of Queer," *Social Text*, 38:4 (December 2020), p. 14.

5 Eve Kosofsky Sedgwick, *Touching Feeling: Affect, Performativity and Pedagogy* (Durham, NC: Duke University Press, 2003), p. 62.
6 Boris Groys, *In the Flow* (London: Verso, 2016), p. 77.
7 "The *senses* have therefore become directly in their practice *theoreticians*"; Karl Marx, *Economic and Philosophic Manuscripts of 1844*, www.marxists.org/archive/marx/works/1844/manuscripts/comm.htm (accessed February 21, 2021) (italics in original).

5

Abolition

In contrast to an orientation either to erase the history of communism or frame it as totalitarian, scholars of Left theory have insisted on history's return as an answer to current concerns about inequality and social justice.[1] Instead of either returning to past revolutionary events or disconnecting queer theory from Marxism, I theorize a tactic of decontextualizing history to insert Marxist epistemology into queer theory's assumptions about sexuality. I propose a different vision of communist gender/sexuality that moves away not only from nostalgic reconstructions of the socialist past, but also from queer anti-communist politics. My method draws on a hybrid analytic that I create from Boris Groys's understanding of Stalinist art and José Esteban Muñoz's queer of color analysis. From Groys's work, I borrow the term "decontextualization" as an invitation to locate Marxist film in a new aesthetic context.[2] Decontextualization derives from the Marxist emphasis on a dialectical process that posits the opposition between two positions as a way out of an impasse. From Muñoz's queer theory, I draw on what he calls queerness, a "jolt" to a capitalist representation of bodies and sexuality.[3] In working with queer theory, my interest is to show that communists' gender and sexuality are not unlike an emergent queer practice seeking to abolish a bourgeois-oriented imaginary. A communist sensorial orientation can help Muñoz's method and infuse it with a strong eastern European Marxist epistemology.[4]

Stalinist art has a strategic importance for queer theory because it displays a vital abolitionist imagination. Currently, socialist realism and its objects function as an aesthetic avant-garde because they are outside a circuit of cultural incorporation, or so Groys argues.[5] If films and artworks have little value under digital capitalism, this is a key position that queer theory can use to develop its anti-capitalist project. For this project, an archive of socialist realist films has two main advantages. Socialist films reverse the flow of time: they grant the spectators "much easier access to documentation" than any other archive.[6] Marxist films are easy to access on a wide range of media platforms, and a new political meaning can be articulated when artists use materials such as found footage for their own purposes. If the value of the socialist aura in art is given by an object's "presence of the present," under new digital conditions the history of Marxism can be reinscribed differently in the flow of circulation of art objects.[7] Rather than historicizing art objects, the goal of decontextualization is to give them a different life in a digital world that is unlike the historical time that they seem to speak about.[8] It would be a waste not to use this material, which has an overwhelming internet presence and rarely functions according to Anglo-American copyright laws.

My analysis in Chapter 5 focuses on the capacity of *The Valley Resounds* sensorially to abolish capitalist perceptions and roles about sexuality. The story of *The Valley Resounds* is about building State socialism in Romania, a country that became a new ally of the Soviet Union after World War II. The Marxist production wanted to capture the construction of an impressive State-funded railroad project, Bumbești-Livezeni, which united two historical regions, Oltenia and Wallachia. While the film highlights the collective effort of Party activists and workers on a State-funded project, it also discusses the sexual relations among different revolutionary and non-revolutionary figures. The main characters, Sanda and Radu, are two working-class people who fall in love by fighting together against their capitalist masters. In contrast to this relationship, the film presents a grey zone of people who are not fully revolutionary. Whereas Ileana is an enthusiastic female-bodied peasant who seeks to become an emancipated proletarian, Niki is an intellectual dandy who rebels against his family and does not know how to join the revolution. Characters such as Ileana and Niki serve as artistic devices to talk about problems that Romanian socialists were confronted with, for example: Is it possible to bring non-revolutionary agents (such as peasants and social democratic intellectuals) onto the side of a communist project? More importantly, how do you destroy an old world in its wider ramifications within not only class relations, but also in terms of power and inequality? How do socialist films produce a revolutionary imagination with the shocking intent to destroy the hold of private property on sexuality? I take the concerns of Romanian socialists and locate them in a new conceptual space derived from both queer theory and Marxism. Muñoz and Groys share important theoretical similarities on the basis of three themes: the meaning of revolutionary time, the role of a counterfetish in capitalism, and the sensorial transformation of the world. However, they diverge with regard to the subjects of their theoretical analysis. Whereas socialist realism was intended to speak to the communists in the Marxist world, disidentificatory practices address queer racialized subjects in North America. In the first section of the chapter, I investigate how both queer disidentification and socialist realism work with the idea of "the future in the present," which means that the future is embodied by collectives that refuse a capitalist present. Rather than locating utopia in the future, both queer practices and socialist realism produce a different understanding of temporality by showing that utopia emerges from concrete actions of revolutionary agents. In the second section, I argue that Muñoz and Groys share an interest in reappropriating aesthetic objects and bodies from the market forces of capitalism. They do so by thinking about the potential of the counterfetish, which is a body or an artwork that reveals the conditions of its own production. In the third section, I argue that Muñoz and Groys discuss the capacity of an artistic practice sensorially to transform objects and people in an anti-capitalist manner. The actions of revolutionary agents produce a sensorial relationship to the materiality of objects that gestures towards a utopian, unrealized potential. In comparing two theoretical models, my intention is to show that Marxist films can be understood as part of a new artistic practice that redeploys video footage and audio sequences in new settings.[9]

Socialist realism needs queer theory, and *vice versa*

I start by comparing José Esteban Muñoz's method of disidentification with Boris Groys's approach to the aesthetic of socialist realism. My choice of these theorists is strategic: while Muñoz's work has become a major analytic in current queer studies, Groys's philosophy of Stalinist art led to a strong revitalization and interest in the link between Soviet Marxism and the traditional avant-garde movements.[10] These two theorists speak to different audiences. Whereas a socialist realist aesthetic wanted to *produce* revolutionary eastern European subjects, queer methods are aimed at working for racialized and gendered subjects who *survive* under conditions of global capitalism. This key difference calls for a reimagining of the role of cinematic objects that are left from State socialism, such as an entire production of socialist realist filmography.

My argument is that the revolutionary possibilities of Marxism can infuse queer theory to offer a new approach to queer tactics in capitalism. Given that the abolition of private property was a key program in Soviet Marxism, it can bring an important new thread into queer theory.[11] Scholars of art theory such as Boris Buden and Boris Groys called for a move away from an understanding of State socialism as primarily traumatic and heading inexorably towards its own demise.[12] While Buden and Groys explore the imagined traumatic nature of socialism and its relation to utopia, they are less concerned with sexuality and gender hierarchies. This is what queer theory can bring to the conversation, given that queer theory and the Soviet Marxist aesthetic are part of a playing field that was constituted by two rival and opposite Cold War universalisms, western democracy and communism. Important scholarship has contested the strict separation between queer theory and socialist histories, yet further research is needed to show not only connections, but also their different conceptualization of sex and gender.[13]

What does eastern European Marxism bring to queer theory? Socialist art rechannels an auratic revolutionary dimension from the Marxism of the Soviet Union and eastern European countries to the capitalist present. By auratic dimension I understand what Groys calls the presence of the past in the present, which can be "experienced only at one moment – namely, at the revolutionary moment."[14] To think about the Soviet past as having "auratic dimension" is possible because of Groys's argument that socialist realism emerged as a product of both avant-garde art and the Soviets' control of power.[15] As Groys argued, socialist realism "was not created by the masses but was formulated in their name by well-educated and experienced elites who had assimilated the experience of the avant-garde and been brought to socialist realism by the internal logic of the avant-garde method itself, which had nothing to do with the actual tastes and demands of the masses."[16] Socialist realism became a dominant, recognized method for all socialist artists until the fall of the Soviet Union and eastern European socialism.[17] Groys's conceptualization of aura points to a potential use of the Marxist past by contemporary artists, provided that the artwork can offer what Muñoz calls "a historical materialist critique."[18]

Queer theory needs an archive of Soviet and eastern European films not only because queer theorists deploy histories that are primarily Anglo-American, but also because its anti-capitalist possibilities are severely reduced by its imagination, which is tied to private property. Given its materialist epistemology, eastern European Marxism has a key role of providing a wealth of militant socialist films that de-center queer theory from its US-based epicenter. The decontextualization of a Marxist archive can be achieved by reconsidering its role, along the lines of a revolutionary practice that, in Groys's argument, will not escape the flow of time by resisting it. Rather, the communist move is to throw itself into an artistic and temporal flow of time, which leads to the eventual disappearance of a socialist film archive as it stands. Groys's theory reveals an important route that queer theory can take in relation to the proejct of communist history. Rather than simply recuperating the aura of utopia, installations of socialist realist art can offer films new meanings, or what Groys calls "liberat[ing] life" in a different setting.[19]

Time: queer theory and "the future is here'

Groys and Muñoz have at the center of their theories the idea of a future temporality that challenges the vision of the capitalist present. They explore the anti-capitalist possibilities that are part of reconceptualizing the relationship between the past and the future. In Groys's understanding, socialist realism draws its program from an avant-garde project that challenged the idea that politics should be a representation of reality.[20] For Groys, socialist realism was an attempt to build on a new aesthetic anchored in a different understanding of the future.[21] Given that in eastern European Marxism the future is here, socialism produces a new model of a human being that dreams in a different way: "socialist realism was the attempt to create dreamers who would dream socialist dreams."[22] In this sense, socialist realist films asked their audiences to disidentify from a capitalist reality and live as if communism was a reality of the present.[23] Like Groys, theorists of socialism such as Evgeny Dobrenko have identified the nature of the future and the present in socialist realism as "a new temporality," in which the future is already achieved.[24] For Dobrenko:

> Stalin introduced a new temporality: the concluded future (a kind of future pluperfect). In order to free the ground for this new future, the present was shifted into the past, and the future-directed future was transformed into the present, as a result of which the present itself underwent complete de-realisation.[25]

In a similar way, the idea of the future as present is at the heart of Muñoz's project of queer disidentification.[26] In Chapter 3 of *Cruising Utopia*, titled "The Future is the Present: Sexual Avant-Gardes and the Performance of Utopia," Muñoz analyzes objects of inquiry such as avant-garde art, queer sex, and a socialist performance of collective labor, which have been rarely thought about together. In Muñoz's conceptualization, cruising utopia can be achieved through the production of spaces and acts that lead to a different anti-capitalist and non-heteronormative future. In them, he finds practices of disidentification from a capitalist present that are also a "backward glance to enact a future vision."[27] Muñoz makes that move on the basis of two Marxist sources. From Ernest Bloch's theory, Muñoz takes the insight that utopia can be born only from situated and historical struggles. This utopian hope builds on a surplus that promises something that is not quite here, defined as a potentiality. From C. L. R. James's dialectical method, Muñoz takes the idea that a communist future is already contained in the practices of socialist workers. This dialectical method actualizes itself in performance art, transgender practices, and socialist workers, which are part of the same project of disidentification from capitalism.

By drawing on C. L. R. James's theory, Muñoz shows that the future can be interrupted as a fantasy of heterosexual and capitalist reproduction that evolves around the idea of a heteronormative good citizen. A concrete future is embodied in what artistic collectives enact through their performances: that is, they embody not an abstract utopia, but a concrete vision that is located in real circumstances. For queer disidentificatory practices, the real utopia is the present of current circumstances that offers alternatives to the impoverished nature of capitalism. "The future in the present" is also a temporality that is not unlike the Stalinist project of derealizing the present with the goal of disidentifying from capitalism. A disidentificatory practice is a project that locates queerness in the future, because queerness is "not here" and "we can feel queerness as the warm illumination of a horizon imbued with potentiality."[28] In short, Muñoz's queerness is not essentially different from eastern European Marxism in its attempt to create a different type of future, a future in the present, that offers hope for a better world to come.[29]

A materialist conception of queer theory offers an analysis of the trope "the future is here" in the Romanian socialist film *The Valley Resounds*. In its cinematographic articulation, the future is presented as a concrete sexual and gender utopia based in Romanian socialism. In a future that already lives in the present, the dynamics between male- and female-bodied people are defined by an abolitionist fight against capitalist inequalities. The film shows gender- and sexual communist emancipation as intertwined: communist sex and gender interactions are articulated in a deep relationship with the Marxist account of class struggle. To love like a communist is to live in a gendered body that has communist tasks. The function of communist gender and sex is to produce a different humanity that challenges western capitalism and its hierarchies of exploitation. Given that a newly achieved temporality has already transformed the nature of social interactions, the practice of communism invites its audience to join subjects that are engaged in a real struggle. The role of the future in *The Valley Resounds* shows that sexual utopia is not a distant ideal but a concrete presence that calls its audience to join the movement to abolish capitalism.

The film provides a dual understanding of a future in the present. On the one hand, utopia unfolds when new revolutionary agents refuse the empty present of the capitalist world. The rejection of capitalism is first an act of negation. The film concentrates on Sanda, a young professional woman and a voluntary worker on the construction site who is harassed by Crețu, a villainous section leader ("șef de echipă"). We are introduced to this dynamic in a key shot. Sanda pushes a wagon with rocks; Crețu touches her body and stops her from doing work. As the communist screenplay seeks to show, the villain is paid by bankers to undermine the efforts of the socialists. To be a capitalist with power means that the villain harasses female workers not by accident, but as part of his ideological orientation. The first direct representation of sexuality in the film is Crețu's gesture of touching Sanda's body and the woman's denunciation of this act. Sanda's "no" is an act of stopping an economy of sexual exploitation, and the film proposes to look at her actions as the actualization of a communist future. Sanda refuses to play the traditional role of a sexual commodity to a superior. Disidentification from a capitalist world is part of the socialist realist idea that the future is here. In rejecting the touch, Sanda not only institutes a demarcation between two worlds but, more importantly, inaugurates the new communist world through her refusal.

But the future in the present is achieved with strategies of sexual disidentification that are also affirmative. Simply put, proletarians destroy bourgeois morality to inaugurate a new world. Stalinist art is based on the rejection of individual sexual desire that does not stem from a revolutionary orientation. Communist sexuality refuses cinematic conventions such as private love and courtship without class conflict. The erotic plot for Sanda and Radu unfolds in a manner that refuses the romantic genre of courtship and marriage. The private does not exist as a space for sexual desire. Sanda and Radu interact when they meet in large groups, and sexuality is an ideological effect of the workers' project of realizing socialism. Radu has worked in Lupeni, a mining site that has historically been a key location for sabotaging Romanian State capitalism. He comes to the construction site to replace his dead brother, a committed comrade who is the socialist martyr in the story. Radu falls for Sanda – or Sanda falls for Radu; it is not clear from the story if we have a point of origin for their relationship. What we know, however, is that their erotic encounters emerge from working together and fighting the enemy. Sexual attraction is not a product of the desire between two bodies, but rather two committed comrades are generating sexual desire when they build a new world. Communist ideology organizes the meaning of sex and gender in Stalinist art and generates a "total" ideological frame for how to feel and love.[30] Socialist realist films present a process of abolishing bourgeois attitudes and power inequalities that functions as a shock to gender conventions. The idea of gender- and sexual utopia derives not only from making gender inequality visible, as much gender-oriented scholarship discusses the relationship between inequality and social roles. By contrast, a gender revolution comes primarily from imagining the destruction of a capitalist world. It is a movement to eradicate private property, and the role of characters such as Sanda and Radu is to set that movement in motion. While desire has fallen upon Sanda and Radu, it did so when they acted together to liberate themselves from an old world. In this sense, they live in a dream: the Stalinist aesthetic asks its viewer to seize the possibilities that are embedded in the idea that dreaming is possible in the here-and-now. It proposes a disidentificatory practice that emerges from Sanda and Radu's struggles against western capitalism.

Becoming a sensorial counterfetish

Both socialist realism and queer disidentification are concerned with the idea of extracting bodies and objects out of capitalism. They do so by reappropriating the past for a future to come. This strategy was at the heart of a socialist realist project that believed the past "has to be appropriated by the victorious proletariat, and put at the service of the new Socialist state."[31] As Groys argues, Stalinist art and the avant-garde share a common project in their refusal of the idea of representation.[32] Yet, unlike the avant-garde, which merely wanted to destroy the past and its representations, a socialist realist aesthetic was invested in taking from the bourgeois world what was "best" and "useful to the proletariat" and "us[ing] it in the socialist revolution and the construction of the new world."[33] For Emma Widdis, at the center of the Soviet revolutionary project was an ideal of "sensory radiance," which can be achieved only by an encounter with the materiality of the world of things.[34] As in socialist realism, a key part of a strategy of queer disidentification is to take a body and reroute it for the goal of queer utopia. The extraction of a body out of capitalist ideology is a deep concern for Muñoz, who seeks to identify modes of imagination that offer alternatives to "the face of here and now's totalizing rendering of reality."[35] Given that past sites of utopianism, as Muñoz tells us, contain ephemeral traces that may appear merely romantic, they assist to "extend a glance toward that which is forward-dawning, anticipatory illuminations of the not-yet-conscious."[36] At the heart of this disidentificatory strategy is the idea of survival of subjects through their interpretation of the past. Muñoz's future is possible because objects change their meaning: minority subjects engage in "a mode of recycling or re-forming an object that has already been invested with powerful energy."[37] This disidentificatory recycling seeks to capture the aura of an object that can be redirected to the future.

The concept of the counterfetish is key to the possibility of a sensorial transformation. Soviet and queer thinkers theorize different types of counterfetishes. Marxist counterfetishes are revolutionary devices for sensorially transforming the world. As Widdis argues, in revolutionary Soviet cinema "bodies act and feel the world" and, in doing so, live "in enhanced sensory relationship with the material."[38] This appropriation asks for a new relationship with the senses, or what Christina Kiaer suggests, by drawing on a phrase of Arvatov's, to be the transformation of objects into co-workers.[39] Such transformation was a sensorial process: it imagined the production of a new human being and objects that generate revolutionary feelings. In the words of the Soviet theorist of film Grigori Kozintsev, the project of new cinema is to make the "celluloid feel."[40] Whereas Soviet cinema seeks a sensorial counterfetish, queer disidentification's main aim is to de-naturalize capitalist bodies and acts. Like socialist theorists, but with a focus on subjects who live in capitalism, Muñoz theorizes the potential of minoritarian subjects to become counterfetishes. While socialists were interested in filling the past with the new in order to win an ideological battle, the queer recycles objects to transfigure them. The goal of Stalinist art is the sensorial transformation of the world, yet in slight contrast with this emphasis on the haptic (or the tactile), the counterfetish in Muñoz has the goal of revealing the conditions of gendering bodies. For instance, the role of the counterfetish is to illuminate the conditions that lead to men becoming butch. For Muñoz, one of the outcomes of a utopian imagination is that it is able to forge an object that produces anti-capitalist desires with regard to gender and sexuality. The queer counterfetish is a practice of survival under conditions of global exploitation of bodies. On the one hand, in relation to Jean-Michel Basquiat's work, Muñoz is interested not in a practice that will triumph over capitalism, but in one that retools and imagines a different space of survival for minority subjects. Rather than actively winning over capitalism, minority subjects can see themselves as "surviving" the nullifying force of consumers' capitalism models of the self. A strategy of disidentification is able to transfigure a capitalist system invested in creating fetishes. Basquiat's work can function as a counterfetish because it shows that magic cannot replace labor and "marketing" cannot erase "intrinsicality."[41] On the other hand, a queer counterfetish is a performance that shows the labor and the intentionality involved in producing it. A counterfetish is promised by something that "is not quite here," which comes from a surplus of an encounter with the traces of what is not-yet-conscious.[42] As an example of a counterfetish, in talking about a black queer performer, Kevin Aviance, Muñoz theorizes how this performance of gender is anti-capitalist: "he is once again a counterfetish, elucidating the material conditions of our gender and desire."[43] By becoming a counterfetish, Aviance is engaged in a critical materialist practice of revealing the capitalist conditions of producing gender. Unlike Muñoz's interpretation of the counterfetish, a renewed, sentient relationship with objects is a precondition for the new Soviet subject. The emphasis on feeling and de-naturalization is not exclusionary, however. While Soviet theorists have theorized the power of de-naturalizing reality, Muñoz sees the sensorial power of the touch to "coanimate" blackness and queerness.[44]

How does the sensorial counterfetish function in *The Valley Resounds*? A counterfetish is not only a device to instigate revolutionary feelings, but is also for de-naturalizing conventions about gender and sexuality. In reaching out to Sanda's body, Crețu seeks violently to stop a revolutionary moment, which is symptomatic of how villains sabotage the socialist world. The act of touching a communist body is highly significant to the central conflict of the film. From the beginning of the story, we are located at the intersection between two worlds: that of western capitalism is slowly disappearing, and another socialist world emerges through labor and vibrant socialist eroticism. The performance of becoming a communist functions as an interruption of conventional expectations around sex. Sanda's gesture to say "no" to her superior is a momentary strike against expectations about power and seduction. Harassment is not only a violation of a working woman's body, but also signifies the entitlement of the old world to assert its privileges and power. The construction of a socialist utopia emerges from the worker's refusal to be touched. The refusal is a temporary stop-gap in the process of gendering women as exploited bodies with penetrable boundaries. Like the counterfetish in Muñoz, Sanda's "no" functions as a technique of defamiliarizing the audience from a widespread convention about female-gendered bodies. It does so by revealing traces of the past in the present. By traces, I understand what Muñoz calls the leftovers, "the remains," or the things that are left "hanging in the air like a rumor."[45] These flickering illuminations that come from socialism can help rethink an aesthetic that is built on a desire that is utopian and queer and also seeks to reforge a "collective futurity."[46] The touch is key to a moment in the practice of disidentification. Sanda's gesture is a sensorial counterfetish because it is not only a rejection of a bourgeois attitude, but also "a practice of world-making."[47] Not unlike Muñoz's performative call for a queer utopia, it constructs a space for imagining an egalitarian world that is opposed to a hierarchy-based and exploitative capitalism. To refuse to be touched is not only a rejection of a sexual demand, but also a strike that calls for a larger front of opposition to the western capitalist order.[48]

Socialist sexuality as totalitarian sexuality has become an important framework that sees socialist people as sexually patriarchal.[49] Yet the film has an irretrievable quality in its queer dimension. Sanda's gesture not only refuses an unwanted contact, but also shows how transforming the surrounding world is a sensorial experience. A sensorial counterfetish that emerges from Marxist cinema is an invitation to rethink affects such as joy and hope in relation to changing the material world. Ileana, Radu and Sanda participate in the construction of communism by breaking stones and touching the new instruments of production. Their tactile engagement with the world is a mode of producing communist affects such as feelings of joy and optimism, which also abolish the world of capitalism.

The limits of reappropriation

Socialist realism is not only a call for the creation of sensorial counterfetishes, but also proposes a discussion on the limits of such practice. Communist ideology can produce revolutionary subjects, but not all people become communists. The attempt to extract bodies from capitalist ideology and reorient them ideologically is a major concern for Romanian socialists in the 1950s. In *The Valley Resounds*, the object of interrogation is the character of Niki, who has strong sympathies with the socialist project.

My goal in this section is to show that Niki's body cannot function yet as a counterfetish, although he is given a chance to join the socialist revolution. Niki is a device to show the limits of capitalist desires to act in a revolutionary manner, and introduces the question of people and objects who are resistant to revolutionary change. In Muñoz's theory, a counterfetish is an object or a performance that shows the limits of commodification. While it is a practice of de-naturalization of a given order, it functions primarily in capitalism. In Marxist art, the conditions of appropriating bodies for revolution are different. Whereas Niki becomes a critic of capitalism, he fails to become a *tovarăș* (comrade). He engages in socialist struggles but is not yet ready for a total transformation. In the aesthetic of realist socialism, only by joining others in common struggles can one become part of a revolutionary avant-garde.

Niki is a student from a well-to-do family who decides to reject a bourgeois lifestyle. In confronting the desires of his uncle, a selfish banker who denies university funding to his nephew, the young man chooses to join the working class at Bumbești-Livezeni. He disidentifies from a history of exploitation, or so we are led to believe. On the construction site, Niki is given a chance to become a communist when he flirts with Sanda's friend, Ileana. Ileana, a female-bodied worker dressed up as a peasant, is introduced to the audience when Crețu humiliates her as being stupid. Sanda rejects Niki's attempt to talk to her, but rather than bluntly rejecting him, Ileana has a different strategy: she invites people to become communists. While Ileana is willing to coax Niki into communism, the student is still immersed in his world of privilege. He wants to join the volunteers, yet his responses show that he is still caught in his bourgeois world. In his dialogue with Ileana, Niki asks her if she was not present at "the bathhouses," which represents a middle-class tactic to open up a flirtatious conversation. In rejecting the language of middle-class flirtation, Ileana tells him that "they did not share the same creek" – that is, they did not bathe together in the River Jiu. By asserting this opposition – the river vs. the bathhouse – Ileana makes clear that their class positions and values are different.

Why does Niki not become a communist? First, he does not see and act as if the future is here, in front of his eyes. He wants to admire nature, while Ileana tells him that the destruction of nature serves the goals of the communist project. He still believes that beauty lies in an imagination that is tied to bourgeois values, rather than looking at the beauty of a new society that he can be part of. Second, he does not have a sensorial relationship to the objects that are co-opted for revolutionary change. He does not know how to handle a spade and becomes the focus of comic relief for other workers because of his inability to break stones. As he reckons with his bourgeois position, Niki speaks directly to us, an imagined revolutionary audience, and confesses that he is unable to fit into the socialist world because he and his family never learned how to work. The lesson about the limits of appropriating bodies is that only the practice of becoming communist makes one part of revolutionary change.

The communist Sanda shares with this rebellious dandy an initial moment where they both refuse a world that seems to be crumbling. If Sanda is a stand-in for a revolutionary consciousness, Niki seems to represent those who cannot transform according to the new revolutionary imagination. The film presents us with grey sexual areas where bourgeois male-bodied characters can flirt with and be erotically interested in committed comrades. Sanda's behavior shows the necessity of confronting the enemies of the new order, yet not everyone acts like her. The Marxist ideology cannot appropriate a body for a communist revolution if the body is not committed to a deep transformative change. When Sanda rejects the section leader, she, like Niki, also refuses the possibility of a better position in bourgeois society. Unlike Niki, she shows a commitment to striking against the enemy, a belief that the future is here and that she can have a direct sensorial attachment to work. Also, unlike him, Sanda is the avant-garde of history and, along with Radu and Ileana, unfolds it in an emancipatory direction.

Abolition and the future of socialist realist films

This chapter has suggested that a materialist queer conception emerges from the investigation of historical practices of abolition. The question that I started from was: What are the conditions that must take place for a productive conversation between queer theory and Marxist art? To answer the question, I argued that they overlap around the idea of a materialist critique of the present and the importance of aura as a "jolt" to capitalist representations of sexuality. Then I showed that a Marxist theory brings two important insights to queer theory. First, a dialectical conception challenges the uninterrogated link between totalitarian and sexual politics in eastern European Marxism. The film *The Valley Resounds* presents a communist understanding of sex and gender that deploys not only an anti-capitalist history, but also a Marxist model of bodies. Like queers of color, socialist characters such as Sanda and Radu offer a counterhistorical narrative to the capitalist vision of progress. In doing so, they reveal that a critical aesthetic of bodies was part of socialist realism. Second, socialist films have been reanalyzed in their historical dimension, but the risk is that they bring back old controversies about the repressive nature of State socialism that were the product of the Cold War. Rehistoricizing socialism can be a mode of betraying the intention of a communist avant-garde impulse to erase a bourgeois world, which, as an emancipatory gesture, is deeply present in socialist realist films. This is why, rather than historicizing socialist art, a different way to stay true to a revolutionary art is to liberate its auratic Marxism.

The current value of *The Valley Resounds* may not lie in the fact that it speaks to the desire to reanimate the socialist past as it was. On the contrary, the film shows the illusion of any attempt that would try to reconstruct Marxism-Leninism as it was articulated in its historical form. A new role for Marxist films is to show what other aesthetic possibilities can be created with a radical act of refusing to re-embody a socialist past. The totalizing gesture of Stalinist art was to create a new aesthetic at the intersection between formal gestures of negation and real-life possibilities.[50] This action emerged from the desire of the avant-garde aesthetic to invent a new future on the basis of a total negation of the past. As Groys argues, "the radical disappearance of the artist into the point zero of art makes it possible to present the context of art as a total context."[51] In reinterpreting *The Valley Resounds*, the gestures of negating the past could be emulated in new art productions. Such new artistic products can be not unlike Sanda's act of refusing Crețu's sexual touch, which gestures to the possibility of new desires in relation to collective life, sexuality and gender presentation. Marxist films can, like the movements of the queer artist Kevin Aviance, perform "gestures that few others can perform."[52] While Aviance's queerness interrogates the strict codes of masculinity in gay spaces, Stalinist art is a refusal of capitalist codes about gender and sexuality according to a global Anglo-American imagination. If Stalinist films are decontextualized, they can provide a gesture of disidentification from accepted norms of the politics of gender. It may be the work of new artists and curators to offer them a new life. Given that the contemporary artist lives and operates "primarily among art producers rather than among art consumers," artists can forge a new revolutionary imagination that takes seriously the past of Soviet Marxism.[53]

A materialist conception of queer theory is not one of resisting capitalism, but of accelerating its movement towards its potential disappearance. If "the revolution is an artificial acceleration of the world flow," socialist films have to be thrown into the flow to make traditional ideas about the past disappear.[54] Like eastern European Marxism, queerness is also a movement that gestures to a transformation of its embodiment by fading away. In the end, queerness is filled with "the intention to be lost," and to accept loss is to accept the destruction of any pretense to a privileged standpoint – that is, "the loss of heteronormativity, authorization and entitlement."[55] Here, to be lost does not mean only to disappear. It means that "to accept the way in which one is lost is to be also found and

Abolition 153

not found in a particularly queer fashion."⁵⁶ In thinking with both Muñoz and Groys, my goal in this chapter has been to reflect on how eastern European Marxist theory can insert into queer theory an abolitionist epistemology. In the next chapter I continue to analyze what eastern European Marxism can bring to queer theory with a focus on a distinct conception of needs-based materiality.

Notes

1 See for instance the discussion of May 1968 in Alain Badiou, *The Communist Hypothesis* (London: Verso, 2010), pp. 43–68, as an indication of the return of revolutionary history in Leftist theory.

2 For the aesthetic of socialist realism, see Boris Groys, "A Style and a Half: Socialist Realism between Modernism and Post-Modernism," in Thomas Lahusen and Evgeny Dobrenko (eds), *Socialist Realism without Shores* (Durham, NC: Duke University Press, 1995), pp. 77–79.

3 For the term "jolt," see José Esteban Muñoz, *Disidentifications: Queers of Colors and the Performance of Politics* (Minneapolis: University of Minnesota Press, 1999), p. 6.

4 In opposition to the present, which functions as a "prison," queerness offers "alternative temporal and spatial maps provided by a perception of past and future affective worlds"; José Esteban Muñoz, *Cruising Utopia: The Then and There of Queer Futurity* (New York: New York University Press, 2009), p. 27.

5 See Boris Groys, *The Total Art of Stalinism: Avant-Garde, Aesthetic Dictatorship, and Beyond*, trans. Charles Rougle (Princeton: Princeton University Press, 1992), p. 7: "socialist realism finds itself in the position to which the avant-garde originally aspired – outside the museums and art history and set apart from traditional and socially established cultural norms."

6 See Boris Groys, *In the Flow* (London: Verso, 2016), p. 7.

7 *Ibid.*, p. 142.

8 For *The Valley Resounds* as a product of totalitarianism, see Aurelia Vasile, "Le cinéma roumain pendant la période communiste: Représentations de l'histoire nationale, " Ph.D. thesis (Université de Bourgogne and Universitatea București, 2011), pp. 89, 95–96. Vasile argues that *The Valley Resounds*, considered to be "the first real appearance of Romanian cinema," emerged from concerns about early socialism's persecution of peasants (pp. 95–96). In most of its

incarnations, totalitarianism equates the Soviet Union with Nazi Germany, and demarcates between an ideal of an Anglo-American liberal democracy and alleged extreme ideologies such as communism.

9 For an example of a transformation of the soundtrack of the film, see the song "The Valley Resounds" ("Răsună valea") by Microlab, www.youtube.com/watch?v=t5P9Z3OVqR8 (accessed May 22, 2020).

10 For Muñoz's influence in queer studies, see the special issue of *Social Text*, 32:4 (2014), dedicated to him. For reactions to Boris Groys, see Christina Kiaer, *Imagine No Possessions: The Socialist Objects of Russian Constructivism* (Cambridge: MIT Press, 2008), p. 27.

11 For the abolition of capitalist sex roles in Marxist theory, see Lenin's statement: "One of the primary tasks of the Soviet Republic is to abolish all restrictions on women's rights," quoted in Alice Schuster, "Women's Role in the Soviet Union: Ideology and Reality," *Russian Review*, 30:3 (1971), p. 261.

12 See Boris Buden, *Zonă de trecere: Despre sfârşitul postcomunismului*, trans. Maria-Magdalena Anghelescu, preface by Costi Rogozanu (Cluj: Tact, 2012), pp. 76–83; and Boris Groys, *Art Power* (Cambridge, MA: MIT Press, 2008), pp. 4–5.

13 See Petrus Liu, *Queer Marxism in Two Chinas* (Durham, NC: Duke University Press, 2015).

14 Groys, *In the Flow*, p. 142.

15 Groys, *The Total Art of Stalinism*, p. 9. See also p. 52: "socialist realism represents the party-minded, collective surrealism that flourished under Lenin's famous slogan 'it is necessary to dream,' and therein is its similarity to Western artistic currents of the 1930s and 1940s."

16 *Ibid.*, p. 9.

17 Groys, *Art Power*, p. 141: "From the beginning of the 1930s until the fall of the Soviet Union, socialist realism was the only officially recognized creative method for all Soviet artists."

18 Muñoz, *Cruising Utopia*, p. 26. By this formulation, Muñoz understands a Marxist interpretation of social and political events that reveals the conditions of production in current capitalism.

19 Groys, *Art Power*, p. 39. See an example of decontextualizing Soviet Marxism in the video production of the St. Petersburg collective *Chto Delat*, https//chotdelat.org (accessed May 22, 2020).

20 Groys, *The Total Art of Stalinism*, pp. 56, 57: "The mimetic nature of the socialist realist picture is a mere illusion, or rather yet another ideologically motivated message among the other messages making up the painting."

21 Groys, *Art Power*, p. 155.

22 *Ibid.*

23 *Ibid.*, p. 144: "socialist realism was oriented toward what had not yet come into being but what it saw should be created and was destined to become a part of the Communist future."
24 Evgeny Dobrenko, *Stalinist Cinema and the Production of History: Museum of the Revolution* (Edinburgh: Edinburgh University Press, 2008), p. 6.
25 *Ibid.*
26 See Muñoz, *Cruising Utopia*, pp. 55–56, and his discussion of C. L. R. James.
27 *Ibid.*, p. 4.
28 *Ibid.*, p. 1.
29 *Ibid.*, p. 55. Muñoz locates C. L. R. James's theory in his post-Trotskyist workerism, and as such, he traces the ideological roots of the formulation "future in the present" to Soviet Marxism.
30 See Groys, *Art Power*, p. 162, for totality in dialectical materialism: "If Stalinism has already managed to unite all contradictions under the sheltering roof of its own thinking, what could be the point of partisanly advocating just one of these various contrary positions? There can ultimately be no rational explanation for such behavior, since the position in question is already well looked after within the totality of Stalinist ideology."
31 *Ibid.*, p. 142: "Being confiscated from the old ruling classes, appropriated by the victorious proletariat, and put at the service of the new Socialist state, old artistic forms become intrinsically new because they were filled with a new content and used in a completely different context."
32 For Groys, *The Total Art of Stalinism*, p. 36, socialist realism and the avant-garde project share important commonalities, such as the rejection of representation in political art: "the Stalin era satisfied the fundamental avant-garde demand that art cease representing life and begin transforming it by means of a total aesthetico-political project."
33 *Ibid.*, p. 37: "The attitude of the Bolshevik leaders toward the bourgeois heritage and world culture in general can be summarized as follows: take from this heritage that which is 'best' and 'useful to the proletariat' and use it in the socialist revolution and the construction of the new world."
34 Emma Widdis, *Socialist Senses: Film, Feeling and the Soviet Subject, 1917–1939* (Bloomington: Indiana University Press, 2017), p. 252.
35 Muñoz, *Cruising Utopia*, p. 1.
36 *Ibid.*, p. 28.
37 *Ibid.*, p. 39.
38 Widdis, *Socialist Senses*, p. 254.
39 See Kiaer referenced in Widdis, *Socialist Senses*, p. 37.

40 *Ibid.*, p. 76.
41 Muñoz, *Cruising Utopia*, p. 41.
42 *Ibid.*, p. 7.
43 *Ibid.*, p. 79.
44 For defamiliarization in Soviet cinema, see Widdis, *Socialist Senses*, p. 42. For the function of touch in a queer of color analytic, see Muñoz, *Cruising Utopia*, p. 93.
45 Muñoz, *Cruising Utopia*, p. 65.
46 *Ibid.*, p. 26.
47 *Ibid.*, p. 1.
48 While sexual consent is currently an important term in the student activist's vocabulary, the coercive touch gestures towards a formation of sexuality in State socialism that has its own particular dynamics. The film explicitly deploys sexuality as the link between labor strikes and sexual refusals. The idea of consent here is different from the one deployed by current student activism. To understand how consent functions in Leftist-oriented student organizations, see Joseph Fischel, *Sex and Harm in the Age of Consent* (Minneapolis: University of Minnesota Press, 2016).
49 See Gail Kligman, *Politica duplicității: Controlul reproducerii in România lui Ceaușescu* (Bucharest: Humanitas, 2000), p. 14, who argues that the State's totalitarian intervention in Romania created patriarchal relations of power.
50 Groys, *The Total Art of Stalinism*, pp. 52–53.
51 Groys, *In the Flow*, p. 112.
52 Muñoz, *Cruising Utopia*, p. 79.
53 Groys, *In the Flow*, p. 112.
54 *Ibid.*, p. 11.
55 Muñoz, *Disidentifications*, p. 73.
56 *Ibid.*

6

Counterfetish

If the previous chapter focused on abolition, the role of this chapter is to show what a theory of socialist materiality can bring to queer theory. My starting point for socialist materiality is the concept of counterfetishes, by which I understand material objects that seek to abolish alienation in capitalism. Unlike capitalist commodities, these objects are either socialist goods, which means they were produced in eastern European Marxist economies, or queer counterfetishes, which are objects that rerouted from a capitalist economy to an anti-capitalist existence.

Socialist goods are different from queer objects in one particular aspect. While socialist objects in eastern European Marxism were designed to produce a world that would fulfill people's needs, queer counterfetishes interrupt a capitalist circuit by changing the role and meaning of commodities. I build on this difference to insist on the different value of a socialist object, which is defined by a sensorial capacity to fulfill a human need. As Agnes Heller summarizes Marx's theory of needs, capitalist society produces not only alienation, but also the consciousness of alienation, which is enacted by the assertion of radical needs.[1] Radical needs, such as the need for education, health care and free time, make it impossible for capitalism to remain the basis of production.[2] From the consciousness of alienation follows 8/"the need to overturn the alienated social and productive relations in a revolutionary way."[3] Soviet Marxism produced not only an ideology, but also material objects that encapsulate this radical need to overturn capitalism. Socialist objects are part of a plan, as Oushakine argued, that was "a historically specific attempt to envision – and build – a community in which dynamic things could speak for themselves, unencumbered by the 'corrupting' influence of money, market, or exchange."[4] The refusal of commodities was a key strategy of Soviet planners, and as Oushakine argues, "It was the discourse on veshchism (literally, 'thingism' or 'thing-obsession') that created in the 1970s and 1980s a negative narrative space in which any passion for material goods was deemed incompatible with the socialist way of life."[5] Material objects such as socialist goods contain a philosophy and material production that functions as a counterfetish in contemporary capitalism.

In this chapter, I read queer and socialist theorists not only to identify common ideas but also to distinguish between the different roles of queer and socialist commodities. My first goal in this chapter is – unlike theoretical accounts that maintain a Cold War split between eastern European Marxism and queer theory, such as Keti Chukhrov's analysis – to underscore potential points of contact that could lead to a queer Marxism.[6] I explore the distinction between a project of political economy, which insisted on a mode of production based on needs (Soviet Marxism), and a project of cultural studies (queer theory), which sought to analyze and produce disruptions in capitalism. This split reproduces itself when scholars address different academic groups. Whereas studies in Soviet Marxism, such as Serguei Oushakine's theory of things, speak to anthropologists, Soviet specialists, and historians of socialism, a queer of color analytic addresses an American studies and cultural studies audience. Given that different fields frame the nature of the investigation, these approaches offer a singular role for counterfetishes rather than a broad analysis of their anticapitalist role.

My second goal in this chapter is to investigate what Marxism can bring to a project of queer anti-racism. The sensuous materiality of objects in eastern European Marxism is what distinguishes analyses such as Serguei Oushakine's from the theories of Fred Moten and José Esteban Muñoz. The Marxist and queer models draw on a theory of objects that seeks to abolish a capitalist political economy. Like the Marxist model of needs, Muñoz believes that their erotic potential helps commodities to transcend the logic of capitalism. Not unlike Muñoz, Moten concentrates on the disruptions in racial capitalism caused by objects that are not yet commodities. Yet, eastern European Marxist political economy has at its core not only a deep rejection of commodities but also a theory that argues that fulfilling needs will lead to human emancipation. This emphasis on counterfetishes as oriented to needs is an important part of

Marxist theory and cinematography. It defined not only its ideological orientation, but also the conditions that made possible its anti-communist critique in late socialism. By decontextualizing the Romanian film *The Cruise* (*Croaziera*, Mircea Danieliuc [1980]), I analyze how socialist cinema not only contains a critique of commodity accumulation, but also shows that queer theory needs a socialist needs-based materiality.

Two different models of counterfetishes

The concept of the counterfetish embodies the possibility that material objects can lead to the abolition of capitalism. To understand the potential of counterfetishes, this chapter focuses on comparing and contrasting a socialist world of material things with queer counterfetishes. In Soviet Marxist theory, the proletariat is the leading class, which unshackles the chains of capitalist oppression and abolishes a world organized around commodity production. As Marxist theorists point out, socialist societies have achieved a political economy where material objects function as "things," in direct contrast to capitalist commodities.[7] By things, Serguei Oushakine understands material goods produced according to the Soviet ideology of production for needs, and not profit. Boris Arvatov's work was hugely influential in redesigning the Soviet political economy according to a theory of productivism.[8] According to Arvatov's productivism, an anti-commodity is a thing that functions against the bourgeois aim of producing art for the pleasure of capitalists.[9] Instead of producing designs aimed to beautify, Soviet Marxism emphasized that communist designs are made to fulfill people's needs according to the principle "form must follow function, and function must follow need."[10] As such, the ornament represents in the productivist critique of art a betrayal of a perfectly constructed object, but also a mode of art that was part of a bourgeois era, since "for a perfectly constructed thing, embellishment is nothing but corruption."[11] A materialist model oriented to needs shows how the working class can be mobilized to transcend capitalism, not only in industrial production but also in art.

Anti-commodities are not only socialist goods, but are also queer counterfetishes. Unlike Soviet theory, a queer of color critique seeks to offer an anti-capitalist meaning to material objects that are produced for profit. Rather than deploying a revolutionary imagination that seeks to overthrow the capitalist system, queer theorists want to take over the meaning of a capitalist commodity and reroute it to a queer use. José Esteban Muñoz suggests that a queer critique operating within capitalist systems will open up a new anti-capitalist path.[12] The failure of queer subjects fully to embody capitalist heteronormativity is the starting point for this method. Because queer subjects fail to acquire a full capitalist status, they are able to take over mass commodities and recreate them as new aesthetic objects. Instead of being merely a product of the market economy, a queer reuse modifies the goal of a commodity object. For instance, even the Coke bottle, which is one the most known examples of fetishized capitalism, can become a potential vehicle for a queer world. In Muñoz's view, a commodity is a "potentiality" that represents a "certain mode of non-being that is eminent, a thing that is present but not actually existing in the present tense."[13] A new, queer time is what is at the heart of the reuse of commodities. Queer practices of reuse offer abolitionist maps that do not emerge from outside capitalism but, on the contrary, arise from within its structures of inequality. Unlike Muñoz, Fred Moten locates the role of a queer reuse of commodities at the level of time disruptions. For him, unruly sounds that come from a black radical imagination disturb a white timeline that builds on concepts such as private property and musicality. Jazz is not just a commodity, but "a temporal warp" that actualizes not only a critique of private property, but the subjectivity associated with it.[14] Unlike Muñoz's commodity, sounds that escape a conventional acoustic register function on a liminal territory: they are neither fully owned by capitalist bosses, nor entities that have only use-value. They are caught in queer territory where they move between use-value and exchange value, without having a single use. Given that they function primarily outside a fully racialized economy, these objects point to an alternative future that is materialized at an acoustic level. They represent a possibility that calls for a new political alternative to a racialized distribution of power.

How does a queer reuse of commodities imagine an anti-capitalist future? In Muñoz's queer theory, failure is a productive moment that has to be supplemented by an imagination oriented to hope as a revolutionary affect. He urges his readers to rethink the potential of failure, since neither queer liberation nor Cuban communism has successfully fulfilled its promise. In *Cruising Utopia*, Muñoz recounts a key conversation with his father where they fought over the meaning of the 1959 Cuban revolution. As the son recounts this conversation, he spent "much of his life" fighting with his father "about revolutions, in relation to both politics and eros."[15] For Muñoz, the Cuban revolution signaled a utopian moment that is located "squarely in the past," but that nonetheless holds a queer potential.[16] The shared impulse that unites communism and queerness is the idea of revolution that ignites the potential of abolishing capitalism. In his back-and-forth with his father, Muñoz brings communist history into a relation with queerness, but such an association is haunted by the metaphor of Soviet Marxism as a totalitarian ideology. His father, a Cuban emigrant, wanted to abandon Marxism and believed in the promise of freedom and the American Dream. Unlike him, his son, the queer theorist, sought a different future that can be imagined in an alliance between communism and gay liberation. For Muñoz, hope here is an alternative to embracing a philosophy of failure. Revolution has a potential that is already present in the political economy of people's lives. It lies in ordinary surroundings that we do not see as containing the seeds of revolution, like "silver clouds, swirls of camouflage, mirrors, a stack of white sheets of paper, and painted flowers," which are all "passports allowing us entry to a utopian path."[17] This potential can only be actualized if it is rekindled permanently so as not to let it disappear.[18]

Muñoz envisions a radical version of democracy that stems from reimagining the role of *all* surrounding commodities. By drawing on Ernest Bloch, he imagines commodities less in Marxist political economy (and thus as material objects in the circuit of exchange value), but more as devices that have an erotic potential for relationality. Queer sexuality is central to his project to revamp material objects, which have been abandoned by conventional Marxist theory as revolutionary objects. In his argument, a queer form of relationality is an excessive addition that changes the role of commodities. Because of their capacity to fail, queers function outside heteronormativity. They can bring a plus to ordinary objects that is not simply a "surplus" that can be easily appropriated by capitalism. This excessive plus is the springboard for non-capitalist modes of being.[19] For instance, a queer relational excess emerges from an encounter around a Coca-Cola bottle, which disturbs with its ornamental structure the economic logic of exchange. A radical version of democracy can emerge from an ordinary commodity.[20] Not only the ornamental map of queer relationality can make possible new forms of anti-capitalism. Like the ornament, the capacity to daydream "represents a reactivation of the erotic imaginary that is not limited to sexual fantasies." This capacity to daydream is more "about a fuller capacity for love and relationality."[21] The route to queer utopia lies through changing our perceptions because their ornamental potentiality can lead the viewer to a different world. This new world is also produced by a thirst for reveries that can imagine anti-capitalist forms of interaction and eroticism.

The relationship between the commodity and the queer world raises several questions: Is eastern European Marxism in direct opposition to Muñoz's theory? Differently put, aren't ordinary commodities such as the Coke bottle already caught in mechanisms of colonialism and anti-communism so that they are unable to be rerouted to an anti-capitalist project? If the Coke bottle is an ornamental sign that gestures to a different world, isn't it also the symbol of the victory of the free market and entrepreneurship? A tentative answer to these questions starts from rethinking the role of anti-capitalist material objects in Soviet Marxism. In working with the dichotomy between early revolutionary moments and a totalitarian phase, Muñoz seems to elide the abolitionist potential that existed in late socialism. The past of Marxism, and implicitly the past of his father, are no longer an important site to rethink utopia. For him, a revolutionary potential is already plagued by reactionary responses that extinguish its initial utopian impulses related to sexuality.[22] In Muñoz's argument, Cuban socialism becomes synonymous with current forms of gay liberation that hide their initial revolutionary impulses. Yet eastern European Marxist theory has important insights to offer about the revolutionary role of counterfetishes.

If Muñoz queers the role of material objects in a capitalist economy, Moten believes that objects that *are not yet commodities* disrupt a white heteronormative timeline. In Volume I of Karl Marx's *Capital*, a famous passage about commodities in the section "Fetishism of the Commodity and Its Secret" presents the reader with the unlikely possibility that commodities can speak about their desires. Moten translated this passage in a commentary on slavery and capitalism. If the enslaved people were also not considered human and they were classified as either animals or unanimated objects, the question of how commodities speak is also the question of how enslaved commodified bodies speak. Can we understand what objects/the enslaved bodies say and feel before they become valuable on a capitalist market? Marx's answer appears to be that capitalism makes commodities perceive each other *only* as commodities. The value of objects is more than exchange value, however: "What does belong to us objects, however, is our value ... In the eyes of each other we are nothing but exchange values."[23] Marx's passage is key for Moten's thinking, because in his interpretation it is not what the commodity says that is important, but what "the commodity, in its inability to say, must be made to say."[24] In a queer manner, instead of finding a problem with the fact that commodities cannot speak in their non-commodified voice, Moten is interested in the potential of their silence. This is why he focuses in his analysis on the *incapacity* of commodities to use conventional language to express their needs. In Moten's interpretation of Marx, he argues that the enslaved disrupt capitalism because they create visual and auditive new aesthetic interventions. The utopian impulse is placed at the level of a "capacity for a literary, performative, phonographic disruption of the protocols of exchange."[25] Exchange value can be abandoned not only in an economy that serves people's needs, but also with a different aesthetic of political action. With this intuition, Moten is not far from the first Soviet theorists, who wanted a mode of production that offered a political and artistic alternative to capitalism.

How does Moten suggest we listen to non-conventional messages from commodities? In returning to Marx's passage where he discusses the capacity of commodities to speak, Moten, unlike Muñoz, finds little value in commodities as such. Accordingly, he claims that commodities retain a value that can be articulated in practices of interrupting the world of exchange, to which they belong. To make this theoretical discussion concrete, the enslaved musical and philosophical tradition represents for Moten a critical instance that can interrupt capitalism. For him, a queer black utopia can emerge from jazz music and disrupt the world of commodities.

Given its roots in the music of enslaved people in the USA, Moten discovers in jazz the potential of unsettling the lines of temporality constructed by a white capitalist narrative. As such, jazz becomes in its materiality "a temporal warp" that "disrupts and augments not only Marx but a mode of subjectivity that the ultimate object of his critique, capital, both allows and disallows."[26] In going back to Marx, Moten sees that capacity of the senses to become "theoreticians in their immediate practice."[27] This is how jazz, in his view, shows the potential of an auditive intervention that is not only affective and corporal, but also incorporates an important theoretical potential.

Can a commodity become a counterfetish? How do Moten and Muñoz approach this question? In queer theory, it seems that an important split emerges from the role of a counterfetish for a queer anti-capitalist future. In a direct commentary on the Marx excerpt, Muñoz believes that an erotic potential helps commodities to transgress the logic of capitalism. Unlike him, Moten argues that we need to educate our ears and eyes to perceive the disruptions caused by objects that are not yet commodities. In a capitalist circuit, commodities can only know each other by being embedded in a mode of social life that is shaped by exchange.[28] This possibility leaves open a space so that material objects that know their value have the capacity to undermine capitalism. In turn, Muñoz's interpretation of Marx's famous passage on commodities starts from the premise that we refrain from taking the *content* of the commodities' speech at face value. For Muñoz, the linguistic content is "the surplus" that emerges from what we perceive as a "sterile container" and is actualized in a different perception of form that leads to a new political imagination.[29] A queer utopia emerges from a surge that represents a reactivation of hidden potential. As it was theorized in his discussion of Aviance's queer practices, the counterfetish denaturalizes capitalism by revealing the conditions of its production. This disidentificatory practice is a surge that comes from a trace of history embedded in a form that is not registered on the radar of straight perceptions.

Queer subjects and communist activists seem to exist in different worlds, given the different traditions of contestation within the West and the East. Unlike queer theories of counterfetishes, Soviet

Marxism is generally located in an ideological thread that is part of an Enlightenment thinking, which wanted to emancipate rational subjects who acted as universal agents. Marxism in its Soviet versions sought to create a world that would function according to the needs of perfectly rational people. As Oushakine argues, Soviet productivism "was a fundamental desire to determine and meet common – universal and rational – needs that defined the view of Soviet commodity and its context."[30] However, queer theory is shaped by deconstructive French thought and critical race theory that have abandoned the idea of a universal rational need. Muñoz's subjects no longer live in the world of rationalized and perfectly universal necessities. On the contrary, they live as minoritarian subjects who are fundamentally different from the universalist models of the Soviets. Their difference in relation to a racialized and heteronormative regime is what makes them unlike the Soviet model. For instance, they are subjects who emerge from the *failure* to embody heteronormativity and not from the *success* of the events of October 1917 and the communist project to spread a world revolution.

Oushakine reads the same Marx passage that Muñoz and Moten discuss, but different theoretical assumptions create two worlds of counterfetishes. Unlike queer theorists, he starts from the standpoint that the counterfetish is a Marxist object. In this analysis, not only does Soviet political economy embody a Marxist ideology, but socialist material goods also are the product of an anti-capitalist ideology. For him, "the importance of this utopian project is not in its failure" but rather in its successful creation of an alternatively political economy.[31] Soviet Marxism is the embodiment of a project that aimed to fulfill radical needs, as Agnes Heller theorized them in a Marxist project.

The idea of radical need is strongly developed by Marx:

> The idea that radical needs are in some sense constituted from labour runs like a thread through Marx's work: either because surplus labour (performed for its own sake) becomes need; or because of the increase in free time, which gives rise to radical needs (and to the need for still more free time); or because of the need for universality which, having arisen in the form of mass production, cannot be satisfied within capitalism."[32]

This situation creates one key difference with regard to queer theory. In the tradition of eastern European Marxism the success of the socialist project was given by its capacity to fulfill the needs of all. Also, the realization of communism was embedded in the capacity of its material production to function as a sensorial counterfetish. As Oushakine notes, the sensorial capacities of the object are fundamental to the socialist mission of realizing new material objects: "The Soviet commodity made itself known first and foremost as a material thing – through its 'sensuous characteristics' and, consequently, through its ability to meet or (more commonly) to fail the requirements of quality and functionality."[33] In opposition to Muñoz, he believes that Soviet Marxism has offered a utopian vision where things were unencumbered by exchange value and were able to exist in a different manner. Because a socialist counterfetish derives from a sensorial relation to the world, its language can hardly be translated into a capitalist world of commodities.

My argument in this chapter is that a theory of socialist materiality can infuse queer thinking about objects. To show why this move is necessary, I argue that a queer reading of socialist artistic objects needs a communist orientation, given that queer theory has not adequately dealt with anti-communism. A communist direction in queer studies shows the importance not only of historicity in reading artistic products, but also of a necessary emphasis on a needs-based materiality.

The Cruise; or, what happens when Marxism is no longer materially seductive

In this section I analyze a Romanian socialist film that focuses on a historical moment when socialist objects are perceived as exhausted in their revolutionary potential. I explore the context and conditions of the film's political message and what alternatives are proposed to replace socialism. A film that is ambivalent towards Marxism, Mircea Danieliuc's *The Cruise* (1981) presents some of the imperatives and constraints that dominated late Romanian socialism. It captures an important moment of contestation in Marxist countries, when the rhetoric of State socialism was considered not only empty, but also repressive. The director's dissatisfaction with actual Marxism articulates his frustration that socialist objects, which were supposed to be committed friends on the path to communism, are no longer seductive. Moreover, Danieliuc inserts into this film a new cinematic convention about life as more important than communist demands. As a counterpart to socialism, sexuality asserts its force despite the political control of the Communist Party.

Romanian socialist films have been heavily influenced by Soviet Marxism, and their ideological requirements were defined by Marxist productivism. Among other films that criticized the politics of socialism, *The Cruise* is important because it locates sexuality as a key critique of the ideology of work and production.[34] The director's critique is based on the fictional Stalinist leader in the film (tovarășul Proca, played by Nicolae Albani), who is dominated by powerful and irrepressible sexual desires. Proca is the Party member in charge of a boat-trip on the Danube that was organized for the winners of various regional competitions. In his activity, tovarășul Proca has to navigate two demands. Like a good Marxist leader, he wants to be perceived as part of the working class – or at least not as a detached and out-of-touch leader. During the 1980s, the Party elite increasingly confronted accusations of acting like a new class – that is, that they were better than the working class, and even worse, that they despised the workers. The socialist ideology called on its leaders to act as if they were part of the proletariat. In one key scene, Proca's response to a rising ideological pressure to be proletarian is to drink water from the Danube. Danieliuc captures well the pressure put on Party leaders to "look" working class but also to show their adherence to a demand to see the ordinary people as a privileged location of value. To reinforce his proletarian credentials, Proca criticizes the doctor, who is his subordinate, for his intellectual and cosmopolitan disdain for the poor.[35]

Yet tovarășul Proca also has to eliminate erotic and ideological threats to his leadership. As in the work of Ion Grigorescu and Károly Makk, which I analyzed in Chapter 4, *The Cruise* suggests that liberated sexuality and Soviet Marxism are incompatible demands. Proca appears to be the Party official who wants to control everything around him but shows openness to the new desires of the young generation. To underline the conflict between sexuality and ideology, Proca's sexual desires are in conflict with what he requires other people to do. In leading people to a better socialism, he has to behave like an upstanding moral guide. Yet his intentions are undermined by different erotic interests that take over the socialist expedition; he becomes attracted to a young member of it. In addition, characters such as Lili (Tora Vasilescu) and Marin (Mircea Danieliuc) have an erotic agenda that is in conflict with Proca's directions. While Proca wants the group to have a collective life, Lili and Marin seek to see each other in private, intimate spaces.

Proca is not a bad Romanian Marxist. On the contrary, like many Party activists, he wants to create forms of cooperation and work outside the standard circulation of commodities. For instance, the members of the expedition have to design their own identification badges, rather than buy them from stores. In Oushakine's formulation, Proca is against "the cult of things."[36] He actively wants to produce counterfetishes that are part of a larger anti-capitalist front. He thinks that the accumulation of things has blocked people's creative inclinations, and he is a firm supporter of producing things in a collective manner. Because he wants athletic and vigorous participants, the participants in the boat-trip have to row to keep themselves fit. *Tovarăşii* (the comrades) have to act and work together in order to gain a sense of collective agency. Like the socialist vanguard, Proca wants to lead and channel the collective energy into an ideological program. But he seems to have lost the upper hand. Socialist things are no longer seductive for people who want western products. Western perfumes are highly praised by Lili, who recognizes their strong erotic charge. The enthusiasm for rowing in a collective is undermined by various clashes relating to debts and private contentions. Serious conflicts emerge when one participant is afraid of losing his property and is followed around by an angry lover.

While in previous Marxist films the dialectical process between the Party activist and the working class transformed society, it has been worn out in *The Cruise*. Proca no longer has a productivist body, and nor have the others, although they are described as working class. The physical education instructor, who could serve as a dialectical partner for the Party activist, is described as a thoughtless person without any independence. He appears as a person lacking any intellectual and political power. If a character such as Kirik in *The Parisian Cobbler* was praised for not being like the highly articulate Party activist, the new socialist instructor in *The Cruise* is more like an example of how ordinary people have stopped thinking for themselves.

The Romanian film seems to say that socialist things have lost the ideological competition because life itself asserts its power. Life, and not ideology, has become the moving force in this production.

The director shows life outside the socialist world by focusing on the contrast between ideology and other forms of language.[37] The artistic techniques are organized to highlight this split. The director films Proca and two young people so that the camera moves back and forth between the Party leader and the dissenters who break the line. While the Party leader articulates his socialists demands, Lili and Marin flirt with each other by ignoring the ideological guide. Not surprisingly, Proca uses Marxist ideology to organize the group's distribution of time and work. In contrast, Lili and Marin deploy non-verbal language to communicate with each other and flirt. A libidinal parallel economy emerges as opposed to the official demands. The film's contrast with an earlier project of Soviet Marxism and productivist bodies is clear. In *The Parisian Cobbler*, Kirik's sign language showed that Soviet Marxism can be lived affectively and politically in a powerful manner. Kirik's life was the best argument that people need an ideological belief. In *The Cruise*, non-verbal language and sexual drives have become the strongest reason to show that Marxism is an empty ideology and that life itself opposes ideology. Like the Polish director Krzysztof Kieślowski, who in *Camera Buff* (1979) was interested to tell the story of a disabled worker who was a threat to the socialist bureaucracy, Danieliuc shows the emergence of sexual interactions that destabilize the rule of Party activists.

To reinforce the critique of the Party's ideology, *The Cruise* suggests that the official discourse about representing the working class is part of a repressive apparatus. Like Kieślowski, Danieliuc shares a rejection of a particular type of socialist realism that asks for truthful account of the working class. He is critical of the official TV propaganda that centers the reality of the working class in its representation. This intention is explicitly articulated in the sexual scene that embodies a key conflict in the film's story: "the game with the spoon." In playing this game, Proca's wife and his collaborators touch each other's bodies with a spoon under the pretext of discovering the other players' identities. This game of discovering what is hidden has a strong sexual undertone, since body parts are touched and exposed to the gaze of the others. The climactic moment of the scene is when the group watch the central player, the one who has the spoon, seeking to guess the identity of the speaker on the TV set. There is general amusement, and the TV speakers are laughed at. This moment is interrupted by Proca, who interprets the scene as a reactionary moment. To him, the players are mocking socialist ideology and the working class and, by inference, they are mocking his authority and power. He is not wrong, of course. The players are mocking the Party's claim to represent reality, which, instead, is performed by Danieliuc. Unlike Marxist ideology, Danieliuc centers his realism on the exposure of how socialist TV has lost its appeal to its intended audience. In this scene, he de-centers a representational discourse about the working class as the source of true political power. He does so by showing how power functions in the Party's ideology and makes the irritated Proca the target of our indignation. In Danieliuc's critique, Proca behaves like a communist who fears losing power and acts like an authoritarian leader.

Why have socialist things stopped being materially sensuous and seductive in Danieliuc's interpretation? First, Proca is depicted as a coercive leader. The implication of the film is that if only threats make things happen, then socialist claims have become an empty rhetorical gesture. Collective actions such as rowing and working to help the socialist factories are deployed to consolidate socialist ideology, but they stopped functioning as a communist program. The film speaks to the situation of socialist State regimes that struggled to keep their appeal to the working class in 1980; as such, productions such as *The End of the Night* (*Sfârșitul nopții*, Mircea Veroiu [1982]), *Impossible Love* (*Imposibila iubire*, Constantin Vaeni [1983]) or *Mirror for a Hero* (Зеркало для героя, Vladimir Khotinenko [1988]) made this loss of trust a key issue to socialist idealists who wanted to fight for social justice. In *The Cruise*, parody has replaced the discourse of socialist things. The man who plays "the spoon" mocks the discourse of socialist representation of reality, and with it, the leaders who exercise power according to a Marxist program. Proca is a very accurate reader of the threat that is deployed when the players stop acting as though they believe the rules of the game. To use his own words, "asta depășește orice închipuire" ("this is unbelievable"), and his frustration signals that he reads this incident as an act undermining the socialist rhetoric.

Second, socialist things have stopped speaking because racialized people are doing the hard work of making the system functional. Danieliuc presents a hierarchy within the working class. The workers at the bottom of the hierarchy are darker-skinned and use a less educated language. They complain about being ruthlessly used to row the boats. The winners of the contest have a better position than the lower workers, who are only hired for their labor and not for their putative position at the vanguard of the revolution. Unlike the badly paid workers, the former politically appropriate Romanian Marxist jargon about "the family as a basic cell of society" or wanting "to give our love to those who organized this expedition." They deploy socialist rhetoric simply to climb the hierarchy. Racialized workers behave as if they are commodities that cannot articulate their demands in the language of the leaders of the expedition. By choosing to give us a representation from the standpoint of the working class, Danieliuc challenges the claims of Party leaders that they are speaking on its behalf. When he shows us that socialist counterfetishes have stopped talking, his claim is not just representational, but also creates the possibility that Marxism can be abandoned. The objects in *The Cruise* do not seduce anymore because they are no longer speaking to people's real needs and desires.

The Cruise: why queer anti-racism is not enough

The Cruise gestures to a crisis in the world of socialists when their material production has stopped being seductive to its citizens. I argue in this section that merely a queer anti-racist analytic is poorly located in challenging the anti-communist ideas in Danieliuc's film. In a queer anti-racist interpretation, eastern European films can currently be seen as uncanny and queer objects. As a digital presence on *YouTube*, the film is not a socialist object anymore because of its distance from the world that it left behind. Like the work of Ion Grigorescu and Károly Makk, it functions in a space outside Marxist ideology. Moreover, the socialist film is not a capitalist commodity that functions exclusively according to the rules of exchange value on a global market. Rather, it is an object that exemplifies the transitioning between two worlds: it moves back and forth between the new capitalist Romanian State and the old socialist past. My argument, however, is that the film is not only a document that shows the Cold War existed, but also an object containing a surplus of desire, a desire for a capitalist world that will come after the formal end of socialism. It represented a direct attack on an ideology that sought to justify its revolutionary legitimacy through the capacity to fulfill people's needs.

The curious positionality of a socialist film is not the only strange feature of this material object. Danieliuc's sexual world is unruly and filled with chaotic erotic impulses, which are hard to control by the ruling elite. In contrast to a socialist order, the film's opening shot illuminates the world of fishermen, their songs and their desires. One can hear a song in the background, from among images of boats, that tells the banal story of a deceived lover. A mysterious song evokes a sexual, racialized world, which can offer the material for a queer anti-racist interpretation. Here *the style* of the story is what matters in relation to modernizing ideals of the socialist rhetoric. Because songs like this not only talked explicitly about sexual desire but were also shot through with racialized references, they were considered vulgar, subversive and anti-socialist. This song in particular, "Magdalena, Magdalena," functioned during socialism as a forbidden commodity because of its association with the racialized underworld. In its lyrics we can hear the male lover complaining about the deception and ies that he had heard from a woman lover. The complaint is not only erotic but also racialized, and as such, it challenges the limits of ideological socialism.

An important feature of the song is the ambiguity of the racial positions within its narrative. The listener does not know who is or is not Roma, and that lack of knowledge changes the conventions of listening to Romanian songs that deploy racist tropes. It allows those who identify as ethnically Romanian to see themselves in the position of people who were slaves. Not only because it affirms a space for racially ambivalent positions, but also because it opens up an ambiguous portal that intensifies a desire for bodies and pleasure, the song "Magdalena, Magdalena" has a revolutionary grammar. From its first shot, *The Cruise* tells us a different story about utopia, which is no longer located in the imaginary of tall and brazen socialist engineering projects. In turn, the counterfetish – the song that we listen to although we were not supposed to – introduces the audience to a different imagination of desire and life:

> Magdalena, tell me the truth, who bit your chest?
>
> Magdalena, who was it that bothered you, and why is your chest black?[38]

In the song, the erotic messages locate utopia in the struggles of the racialized and it stands in contrast to the communist message, where racial and ethnic divisions are formally abolished. The disparity between the opening shot and the main character of the film, the Stalinist leader, is critical. Whereas Proca, the mouthpiece of Marxism, articulates a rhetoric that no one seems to want, the song speaks about the desire to be wanted and loved. It is a performative of desire and need. As part of this opposition, the point of view of the racialized and poor subalterns – or those who live outside the official apparatus of power – is directly contrasted with the ideology of the ruling class. The song speaks about a working-class male who is driven by sexual desires, which are articulated in the language of domination and possession of women's bodies. The first shot warns its audience that we'll see a story told not from the perspective of official ideology, but from the standpoint of a poor worker who struggles in State socialism.

What the film presents is a powerful alternative to Marxist films, which were inciting people's desire to become communist. While Marxist films were devised to fight for a new world on behalf of the downtrodden and the proletariat, the song in *The Cruise* speaks about a rebellious subject who is abandoned in a world that has forgot to fulfill its promises. Danieliuc deploys a sensorially focused approach against the socialist rules of property and desire. The loss of a lover is a generative space for actualizing a conflict that was erased from official Marxist narratives. The world of racialized people comes through in the song to disrupt the illusion of a State-realized equality. Also, the visual focus on boats reveals a desire to travel that is forbidden and materially articulated by sounds that were not supposed to be heard.

Yet a queer anti-racist interpretation alone is not enough to make sense of the historical role of the film in socialist history. In queer anti-communism, *The Cruise* can provide moments of escape and disidentification from socialism. By using Moten's framework, one can see the film as a call to the formation of a new public, perhaps "an undercommons," which can lead to the transformation of an excessive affect into public property.[39] One can read the film as enacting a critique of socialism and the desire to steal back from those who have benefited from racial hierarchies. In this interpretation, *The Cruise* can show how racialized commodities such as the song "Magdalena, Magdalena" open the possibility of a queer utopia that is not yet present. Since racial violence is not directly represented in *The Cruise*, a lot of the work of gesturing towards the Roma working class is deployed at the level of sonic and affective moments. These moments function as instances that point to a significant potential that lies in undoing the linear time of racialization and exploitation.

But these critics would mistake the anti-communist goals of the film. A theory of socialist materiality can de-fetishize its queer interpretation. As I observed before, a queer anti-racist analytic can travel to eastern Europe and miss its socialist histories and legacies. *The Cruise* is seductive because it places in conflict an anarchic sexuality along moments of racialized transgressions, but it does so to undermine the project of needs-based socialist materiality. In this respect, in traveling to countries that have been shaped by eastern European Marxism, a queer analytic needs a Marxist-focused theory of human emancipation that was designed to speak to all. A theory of needs concentrates on the radical possibility that education, health care and free time can be the sources of overcoming human alienation. In the Romanian film, a queer anarchic sexuality is placed at odds with a project of human emancipation, but my aim has been to show that a Marxist theory of needs asks us to rethink the bases of a queer of color analysis.

The life of material socialist objects

In conclusion, eastern European Marxist theory offers queer theory a distinct materiality of universal needs, which was designed by socialist theorists to function at the heart of their societies. I have argued that socialist material objects are different from queer counterfetishes because they were conceptualized to actualize radical human needs and function as sensorial vehicles for this transformation. Unlike queer counterfetishes, socialist objects were theorized not only as anti-capitalist, but also as overcoming the alienation in capitalism. They were producing a new economy with a different system of production that sought to articulate a radical alternative to capitalism. Second, the main difference from a queer of color analytic is that in eastern European Marxism an entire material production has been deployed against the theory of exchange value. This ideological discourse has generated an important infrastructure that has survived the fall of socialism. The conceptualization of socialist goods as anti-capitalist objects illuminates a broad spectrum of material things, such as practices and aesthetic objects, which are left after the fall of eastern European Marxism.

In my analysis, I have focused on a socialist film, *The Cruise*, which made an anti-communist claim: that socialist objects have stopped being materially seductive. Danieliuc's film can be redeployed by using the vocabulary of queer anti-racist theory to solidify Cold War binaries between sexuality and communism. According to this anti-communist framework, queer anti-racist theory can ignore the role of a Marxist ideology and its counterfetishes in its historical actualization. In turn, focusing on a socialist understanding of materiality, I have shown that queer theory needs a theory of materiality that derives from a needs-based Marxist framework and a careful historical understanding of its materials. The translation of a theoretical framework to an eastern European context can only broaden the divide between queer studies and eastern European Marxism.

In the next chapter I continue to investigate what eastern European Marxism can offer queer studies, but my emphasis will shift to the relationship between materialist psychology and racism.

Notes

1 Agnes Heller, *The Theory of Need in Marx* (London: Allison and Busby, 1973), p. 94.
2 *Ibid.*

3 *Ibid.*
4 Serguei Alex Oushakine, "'Against the Cult of Things': On Soviet Productivism, Storage Economy, and Commodities with No Destination," *Russian Review*, 73 (April 2014), p. 222. For his reference to Karl Marx, see *Capital*, Vol. I: "Could commodities themselves speak, they would say: Our use value may be a thing that interests men"; www.marxists.org/archive/marx/works/1867-c1/ch01.htm#S4 (accessed July 5, 2020).
5 *Ibid.*
6 Keti Chukhrov, *Practicing the Good: Desire and Boredom in Soviet Socialism* (Minneapolis: University of Minnesota Press, 2020).
7 *Ibid.*, p. 204.
8 *Ibid.*
9 Boris Arvatov, *Art and Production*, ed. John Roberts and Alexei Penzin, trans. Shushan Avagyan (London: Pluto Press, 2017), pp. 99–100.
10 *Ibid.*
11 *Ibid.*
12 José Esteban Muñoz, *Cruising Utopia: The Then and There of Queer Futurity* (New York: New York University Press, 2009), p. 9.
13 *Ibid.*
14 *Ibid.*, p. 11.
15 *Ibid.*, p. 145.
16 *Ibid.*
17 *Ibid.*, p. 146.
18 *Ibid.*, p. 146: "It is important not to be content to let failed revolutions be merely finite moments."
19 *Ibid.*, p. 147: "In Ernest Bloch's work, surplus becomes that thing in the aesthetic that exceeds the functionalism of capitalist flows. This supplementary value, which is at times manifest as aesthetic excess and at other times as a sort of deviance from conventional forms, conveys other modes of being that do not conform to capitalist maps of the world."
20 *Ibid.*, p. 145: "That Warholian notion of a radical idea of democracy via commodity form, taken alongside the image of the flowering Coca-Cola bottle, a natural surplus that surges from the apparently sterile container, illustrates Warhol's particular version of the queer utopian impulse."
21 *Ibid.*, p. 144.
22 *Ibid.*, p. 145: "In much the same way that many people think the Cuban socialist revolution succumbed to totalitarianism, I consider gay liberation to have strayed from its earlier idealism."

Counterfetish 177

23 See Fred Moten, *In the Break: The Aesthetic of the Black Radical Tradition* (Minneapolis, University of Minnesota Press, 2003), pp. 8–9.
24 *Ibid.*, p. 9.
25 *Ibid.*, p. 10.
26 *Ibid.*, p. 11.
27 *Ibid.*, pp. 8–9.
28 *Ibid.*
29 See Muñoz, *Cruising Utopia*, pp. 7–9: "the Coke bottle is the everyday material that is represented in a different frame, laying bare its aesthetic dimension and the potentiality it represents."
30 Oushakine, "Against the Cult of Things," p. 204.
31 *Ibid.*, p. 222.
32 Heller, *The Theory of Need*, pp. 90–91.
33 Oushakine, "Against the Cult of Things," p. 222.
34 Danieliuc is a director who adheres to an aesthetic that challenges bureaucratic socialism and the idea of socialist "truthful" representations of reality. See Constantin Pârvulescu, *Orphans of the East: Postwar Eastern European Cinema and the Revolutionary Subject* (Bloomington: Indiana University Press, 2015), pp. 92–117, where he discusses the conflict between State bureaucrats and a new generation of film directors in Krzysztof Kieślowski's *Camera Buff*.
35 This scene anticipates a powerful rhetoric in Romania in the 2010s about the rise of global and urban elites, condensed in the threat of the billionaire George Soros.
36 Oushakine, "Against the Cult of Things," p. 198.
37 Constantin Pârvulescu has noted that the emergence of auteur cinema in eastern Europe can be traced to the development of eastern European political dissidence. In his example, Krzysztof Kieślowski has become an eastern European arthouse name precisely because of his political opposition to socialist bureaucracy. See Pârvulescu, *Orphans of the East*, pp. 92–93.
38 In the original Romanian: "Magdalena, spune-mi drept, cine te-a mușcat de piept? Magdalena, cine te-o fi necăjit, că ți-e pieptul innegrit?"
39 See Moten, *In the Break*, p. 12: "the universalization or socialization of the surplus, the generative force of a venerable phonic propulsion, the ontological and historical priority of resistance to power and objection to subjection, the old-new thing, the freedom drive that animates the black performance."

7

The unconscious

Chapter 7 draws on eastern European Marxism to introduce historical materialism dialectically into the psychology of queer theory. To propose a new political role for unconscious messages and desires, I conceptualize the unconscious as a psychic device that is shaped by class- and racial dynamics. On the basis of a Soviet Marxist theorist, Nikolay Marr, who argued that linguistic expressions are materially produced, I seek to reveal the potential of dreams and sexual desires for revolutionary actions.[1] The direct consequence of this materialist understanding of consciousness is that every linguistic expression is a product of a historical social formation. In my argument, historical materialism not only attaches a class character to the unconscious, as Jean Laplanche explained Marr's position, but shows how unconscious elements can serve as catalysts for anti-capitalist actions.[2]

How does Marr's historical materialism bring a new understanding of the unconscious to queer theory? Queer theory and Soviet Marxism have been kept apart, particularly in their conceptualization of psychological concepts. Given the Cold War, a Freudian theory of the unconscious was kept at odds with Soviet Marxism. More recently, Gilles Deleuze and Félix Guattari's *Anti-Oedipus* constituted a major theoretical influence for queer theorists, from Jasbir Puar's critical account of intersectionality to Lucas Cassidy Crawford's concept of transgender without organs.[3] Yet, *Anti-Oedipus* presumed that Soviet Marxism is a dead political project, and reinforced the Cold War separation between anti-colonial/anti-racist theory and Soviet Marxism. The book advanced new conceptualizations of terms such as "unconscious" and "sexuality," but these categories deployed a binary interpretation of politics that equated Soviet Marxism to US liberalism.[4] The division between Freudian ideas and Soviet Marxism was not only a western project, but emerged as a result of the tensions that arise in the relationship between Soviet Marxist critics and psychoanalytic theory. Martin Miller investigated some of the potential factors that led to this ideological split within the Soviet Union (Freud's statement that "communism is an untenable illusion," Trotsky's enthusiastic support of psychoanalysis, and Soviet psychologists' criticism of the individualist bases of psychoanalytic theory), which all seem to point to a rejection of Freudianism.[5]

My premise in this chapter is that psychoanalytical concepts such as the unconscious not only were very influential in queer theory but were also shaped by the Cold War. One of the most important consequences of the erasure of Soviet Marxism was the widely shared assumption in western psychoanalytic studies that the unconscious is a feature of the human mind that has neither a class dimension nor a racial structure. As such, the unconscious can generate contents that can be analyzed politically but, as a part of an individual psyche, it lacks a political logic for sexual desires and dreams. This view of the unconscious shaped a whole range of ideas in gender- and cultural studies so that, for instance, Judith Butler's theory of gender trouble sees the unconscious as a source of subversion. The unconscious can undermine rigid masculine and feminine identifications, but that concept is not, in itself, structured by capitalism.[6] *De-centering queer theory* appeals to eastern European Marxism as an alternative epistemology to the conventional understanding of the unconscious. Prominent postcolonial scholarship has investigated how the unconscious is shot through with heteronormative and European understandings of sexuality and gender. In *Unconscious Dominions*, race- and literary scholars have investigated "the extent to which the psychoanalytic subject, that figment of European high modernism, is constitutively a colonial figure."[7] In the argument of Warwick Anderson, Deborah Jenson and Richard Keller, psychoanalysis was "a mobile technology of both the late colonial state and anti-imperialism" that not only produced a universalist framework with models of assimilation and association, but also generated a postcolonial frame with its specific potential for destabilizing colonialism.[8] They show the need to unpack a history of resistance to European epistemological categories, but, more importantly, gesture to the relationship between the unconscious and broader historical formations, such as colonialism and the Cold War. In addition to this call, more research is needed to show how epistemological categories such as the unconscious have been theorized in an anti-communist framework. Important work has been carried out that gestures to the consequences of anti-communism on the unconscious. Histories such as Dagmar Herzog's *Cold War Freud* argue that Freud's exploration of sexuality and psychological categories has been Christianized and de-radicalized in psychoanalytic theory during the Cold War in the United States.[9] In Herzog's interpretation, the Cold War divide was primarily a question of demarcating between psychology and other structural factors:

> Psychoanalysis had succeeded so brilliantly in the first half of the Cold War, especially in the USA but by extension also internationally, precisely by shedding whatever socially subversive potential it had once had. Concomitantly, many leading figures in the psychoanalytic community had lost interest in seriously theorizing the complex interconnections between the self and the wider society.[10]

Yet Herzog's analysis ignores not only eastern European Marxism but also how western critical theory has imported anti-communist ideas into its epistemology. She argues that versions of psychoanalytic theory such as Lacanian-influenced theory and Deleuze and Guattari's *Anti-Oedipus* remained attached to a radical project of psychoanalysis, unlike other psychological projects.[11] What she does not account for is that the important divide *Anti-Oedipus* produced was not only between Soviet Marxism and the New Western Left, but also between Soviet Marxism and anti-colonial critiques of race and gender. If Deleuze and Guattari's book has served as a "switch-point" in the Cold War, it did so because Soviet State socialism was positioned in the role of a colonialist power and enemy-in-the-mirror to western capitalism.[12]

While Soviet Marxism after the 1930s seems to have lost interest in psychoanalysis, Western New Left thinking continued after the 1970s to strengthen a divide between psychoanalysis and eastern European Marxism. Soviet Marxism has been conceived as a repressive State project not only in *Anti-Oedipus*, but also in the work of theorists of sexuality such as Jean Laplanche. A major influence for Judith Butler, Laplanche opposed Freud's

Copernican revolution – or what he calls the de-centering of human agency – not only to phenomenology but also to Soviet Marxism.[13] In Laplanche's view, if Husserl's account focused on the idea of a subject, Soviet Marxism has proposed an extreme position of de-centering language by appealing to the idea of a "proletarian speak."[14] In contrast to positions that privilege either the human subject or class analyses of the unconscious, Freudian psychoanalysis is a revolutionary method because it conceptualized the unconscious as an alien object in itself.[15] Laplanche's position is very close to *Anti-Oedipus*'s denunciation of Soviet ideology. Deleuze and Guattari have abandoned the concept of ideology because it masked relations of power within the Soviet Union.[16] For Deleuze, "[the idea of ideology] suits orthodox Marxism and the Communist Party so well. Marxism has put so much emphasis on the theme of ideology to better conceal what was happening in the USSR: a new organization of repressive power."[17] While arguing that desire is what overcomes any ideology, Deleuze and Guattari have insisted that sexuality and political economy are strongly interconnected.[18] Unlike them, yet arguing strongly against Soviet Marxism, Laplanche claims that the unconscious may not have anything to do with class- and racial positions, since it is primarily a device only to alienate one from oneself.

Given that queer psychoanalytic theorists have been inspired by Laplanche's theory of the unconscious, I introduce Soviet Marxism into this conversation to rethink the premises of queer psychoanalytic theory.[19] I focus on a Soviet movie that emerged during the Cold War to ally critical race studies with a Marxist analytic, which extends the work of abolishing capitalism to queer theory.[20] My argument is that a film made in the Soviet Union about Romanian Roma, *The Fiddlers*, offers important anti-racist and anti-capitalist tactics to conceptualize a materialist unconscious. I claim that unconscious messages, such as dreams and sexual desires, can function as devices that challenge the standpoint of capitalist disciplinary institutions. What interests me in this film is that, by deploying a Soviet Marxist lens, the memories of the main character (Toma) are located in a time of Roma slavery, but emerge in his post-slavery recollections to create moments of diversion and panic within capitalism. Toma's dreams will lead to tactics that respond to racialized violence either by terrifying the oppressors or by taking back resources from them. I conclude by reflecting on what a materialist conception of the unconscious offers to psychoanalytic queer scholars.

The queer unconscious and black anti-capitalist studies

The unconscious is a key term for queer theoretical accounts that conceptualize the term gender. Judith Butler's psychoanalytic theory in *Giving an Account of Oneself* draws on Laplanche's understanding that the unconscious of the subject is born in relation to the "other"'s desire.[21] For Butler, the unconscious becomes the site of a radical dispossession from a given rigid psychic structure, or "what defies the rhetoric of belonging, a way of being dispossessed through the address of the other from the start."[22] In addition to the unconscious as a practice of dispossession, queer theorists have found in unconscious infantile sexuality the terms to challenge the linearity of sexual development. At the heart of Laplanche's notion of the repressed unconscious is what he calls *the sexual*, which represents the polymorphous perversity of children's sexuality and its capacity to undo the so-called adult, genital sexuality. For Laplanche, infantile sexuality "is auto-erotic, connected to fantasy, and not procreative; it comes prior to differences of the sexes, prior even to the differences of gender."[23]

The role of *the sexual* in Laplanche's theory has led to a queer reflection on the value of its conflict with the ego and its relationship to messages from early seducers. Leo Bersani's infamous "self-shattering," which builds on Laplanche's enigmatic signifier, has provoked a long conversation about perversion and sex in queer theory.[24] For Bersani, cruising is a practice that can lead to the shattering of the self, because "the sign and the consequence of resurrecting of the enigmatic signifier in an object of desire is sexual passion."[25] Self-shattering cannot only, as Bersani tells us, lead to either "the prospect of breakdown of the human itself in sexual intensities" or "a kind of selfless communication with 'lower orders of being,'" but also generates therapeutic benefits. such as psychic labor.[26] Avgi Saketopoulou's interpretation of Laplanche's unconscious argues that perverse sexual experience "allows early parental infusions" to become available for reconfiguration in novel and unexpected ways.[27] A key problem for scholars working with Laplanche, however, is the unidirectionality of the seduction in the formation of the unconscious. What Laplanche calls "the fundamental anthropological situation" is a scene where infants *do not* have a sexual unconscious, while they are cared for by adults who do.[28] This unidirectionality – for example, that the parent is *always* the seducer – leads to problematic psychoanalytic articulations such as Bersani's, where presumably high orders need to communicate with lower orders of being.

Unlike most of these queer conversations, which sidestep a racialized unconscious, Lisa Baraitser deploys psychoanalysis to address the racialized structure of social interactions between adults in power (the seducers) and those who are seduced (the seduced). By taking the history of slavery and its aftermath as a formative moment of this structure, Baraitser urges her readers to think about working through the afterlives of slavery. At the heart of Baraitser's intervention is Laplanche's idea of "the unconscious" as constituted by remainders of messengers from seducers, and "temporalization" as a process of instigating psychic time.[29] In Baraitser's account, the endurance of anti-blackness can be challenged by creating the conditions of remembering its structural conditions and legacies. Laplanche shows that time itself is produced by *an analytic effort* to decode messages from the past. Given that memory is a tool of producing time, this practice responds to what Christina Sharpe calls the possibilities of living in "the wake," which represents "the continuous and changing present of slavery's as yet unresolved unfolding."[30] In short, decoding slavery means to live in a different anti-racist time, which suggests alternatives for a less exploitative world. Also, enduring time will mean not only the creation of the conditions for remembering slavery's legacies, but also a collaborative, arduous and temporarily unsettled practice of dismantling its effects. Laplanche's "enigmatic signifiers" bring out the idea of "enduring" as taking care of time, which leads to a practice of creating a new world. The work of creating an anti-racist imaginary will address and reimagine life in new way, but this effort needs a continuous practice of decoding and working through slavery's messages.

I identify an important anti-capitalist and anti-racist potential in Laplanche's concept of the unconscious, but I also ask for a reinterpretation of what he calls "the primary scene of seduction."[31] A racialized and exploited figure of the seduced shifts our understanding of the potential of Laplanche's theory. For Laplanche, the unconscious is a collection of "left-over bindings," which carry an enigmatic sexual code and generate a psychic time devoted to decoding such messages.[32] To reconceptualize Laplanche's enigmatic messages – or what he calls "noises" – in relation to racialized structures of power, I take two additional steps. I ask first what if "the adult" – and not the child – receives messages to be translated in the primary scene? In following Laplanche's intuition that the child is the cause of the adult, this change of locations will put the adult at the receiving end of enigmatic unconscious messages.[33] This reversal of positions calls for a second theoretical move. Rather than conceptualizing the child as white and unmarked, I see the figure of the seduced (or the child) as a racialized and exploited person who has to live with the legacy of racial violence and exploitation.

I show that the notion of noise has the task of conjuring the imagination of a different world, which builds on the reversal of status and power. The unconscious produces enigmatic messages that have the potential to "disturb and compromise" a legacy of slavery and class-based violence.[34] As part of being declared as valueless, noises are illegible to a white progressive imagination. In my reconceptualization, Laplanche's "enigmatic" suggests that the radical potential of the noise resides primarily in a mode of communication that is fundamentally at odds with structures of representation that emerge from racial capitalism.[35] For Laplanche, "noise" is constituted by messages that come from the other ("parental messages") and are given to children as their legacy to decipher.[36] Laplanche's concept of noise functions to undo the rigidity of psychic structures that undermines our capacity to change our defensive mechanisms. For instance, it emerges from a process of seduction to undermine the legacy of "gender assignment," which distributes people into two sexes, male and female.[37] The problem with gender assignment is that it offers a "rigid" code that instantiates "the logic of presence/absence, of zero and one, which has experienced an impressive upsurge in the modern universe of computer science."[38]

I want to follow Laplanche's call to rethink the relationship between the child and the adult, but my suggestion is to follow a Marxist critique and reconceptualize the primary scene of seduction.

The unconscious

Laplanche's unconscious has emphasized the unrepresentable character of sexuality: unlike what is already known, Laplanche's enigmatic articulation of *the sexual* is what forces "the limits of representation."[39] "Noises" have value not only because they create psychic time and illuminate the story of colonization, capitalism and slavery, but also because they show the threat of a reversal of power positions. Unconscious messages can produce a different power dynamic between the racialized and those who benefit from racial capitalism. "Noises" are often articulated in their friction with a linear progressive history, and offer modes of countering the fetishized commodification of blackness.[40] Emerging in a traumatic and haunting interval, the memory of being property is brought back to threaten the very institutions of coercion and violence that generated slavery.

The counterfeit

In black Atlantic abolitionism motion, migration and flight have become key tropes in the production of slave narratives. However, the scholarship illuminating black abolitionism has focused not only on fugitive tactics that disrupt white epistemologies of time, but also offer tactics to disrupt systems of racialized violence that emerge from an unconscious memory of resistance.[41] In this section, I want to address how, by feigning death, Toma, an ex-slave and the main character of *The Fiddlers*, deploys effective tactics against institutions that enforce racialized violence. Roma histories need a better exploration, given that they created important tactics to fight racialized capitalist codes and institutions.[42]

In Wallachia and Moldavia, the Caragea and Callimachi laws racialized the term *țigani* to designate the Roma people as the enslaved.[43] But, as I will show, the enslaved revolted against the police and deployed techniques of struggle such as the counterfeit. Roma fugitives fought the police, because the police sought not only to impose an order of violence but also to maintain a capitalist system of exploitation. In *The Fiddlers*, the irruption of dreams is a terrifying moment that reverses the coercive power of the slave owners. The role of enigmatic messages that come from slavery is to make Toma turn fear back against the institutions of racialized violence. "The noise" in *The Fiddlers* echoes the process of materializing the infamous Jean Zombi, the mulatto who had the reputation of killing a great number of whites during the Haitian revolution. Like the figure of the zombie, Toma has access to his power through a specific reversal of what counts as value in a white, straight time: "slave turned rebel ancestor turned lwa, an incongruous, demonic spirit recognized through dreams, divination or possession."[44]

The plot of the film focuses on the story of a great Roma master of the violin, Toma Alistar, who is searching for his lost childhood love. The main action takes place after the abolition of slavery in the Romanian principalities, which took place gradually by 1855–1856. Now in a post-slavery time, Toma's mind goes back to his childhood as a slave and recalls a traumatic memory that shaped his life. To show this transition between the two times – before and after slavery – we are invited to move between the so-called actual, real time, and the dream. To locate the action in the time of post-slavery, the first shot focuses on a band of Roma musicians who are traveling in Bessarabia, but then we effortlessly move our focus to pre-abolition time. This transition is performed by the movement of the camera, which gets close to Toma's face while he is in the middle of a powerful dream. Although the dream takes us back to the time of slavery and the traumatic, it functions in a counterintuitive way because it "represents" a time of sexual desire and pleasure. Instead of the hypervisibility of slave suffering, what we are offered in pre-abolition is perhaps Toma's happiest memory. The setting is idyllic and highly eroticized. He and his lover, Leanca, are adolescents and fully living their love. With its sexualized frame, the dream speaks to Carolyn Dinshaw's observation that queer hauntology draws on the energy of sexual arousal, because "being haunted" is "a profoundly erotic experience, one that ranges from an acute visual pleasure to mystical jouissance."[45] In Toma's dream, the lovers are two wild creatures whose relationship is threatened by slave owners and the police.

This moment is a paradox because of the conflicting structure of the memory. At the precise moment that Toma's body is considered living-dead, he, however, feels intensely alive, if not the most alive. The shock of seeing a happy moment in the time of slavery opens a space to reflect on the value of Toma's memory. While the period of slavery as "happy time" was a highly used racist trope and has the potential to be deployed as such in the future, here I want to see the potential of the unconscious to trouble the so-called "real time" of slave dehumanization. The memory functions as an unsymbolized enigmatic message that, as we'll later see, will push Toma to navigate his relationship with the police skilfully. It is a noise that has the capacity to show, in Fred Moten's terms, "that there are flights of fantasy in the hold of the ship."[46] Like Laplanche's temporalization, Toma's dream, which reflects the gap between a memory and its actualization, *is* the moment of creating psychic time.[47] Yet this time emerges also in the presence of both the pain of domination and the resources that are mobilized to counteract it. In *The Fiddlers*, Toma's dream not only contains joy and excitement, but also provokes the spectator to understand the dangers that the enslaved face. Toma's memory is the enactment of a scene where the audience witness not only the pleasure of being in love but also a feeling of the danger that this bond will be crushed by the force of the police.

To historicize Toma's dream, this imaginary sequence takes us to a time before the abolition of slavery in the Romanian principalities, where Roma slaves were sold like cattle in public markets.[48] Because the Roma are historically a population that served as chattel slavery in eastern Europe, they owned neither their bodies nor their labor. However, besides the deep domination that was exercised against them, which has been documented, what else do we know about them? What do the enslaved dream? How do they react to the violence exercised against them? The film suggests that some of the enslaved dream about the possibility of becoming fugitives, which takes the shape of Toma and Leanca planning to run away. Still in pre-abolition time, the two Roma adolescents entertain the seductive fantasy of leaving a world where their bodies are dead. As we know from Moten, fugitivity is a practice of reimagining liberation, a movement of escape from the constraints and enclosures of whiteness and capitalism. Yet, imagining becoming a fugitive suggests that the enslaved may have another drive, in addition to the libido and the death-drive: a drive that "pressures the assumption of equivalence of personhood and subjectivity."[49] Toma's senses are leading him not only to a traumatic moment in time but also to a moment filled with possibilities of *destroying slavery as an institution*. This potential for destruction lies in abandoning the chronology that separates slavery in the past and a time post-slavery. Moreover, the message of the dream points to a time where Toma's sensuous activity, his dream noises, are not just *his* property, *his* dream and *his* sensorial production.

Toma's dream opens up the possibility that this time of trauma – of a past that does not let go of his body – holds a potential and a future that are not yet actualized. In the following scene the audience is sent to the post-slavery period, where an accident happens. The musicians' cart gets broken; fiddlers fall on the ground. Having had such a scary accident, we would expect the Roma group to feel angry that their plans are interrupted. Yet, rather than seeing Toma being angry about the loss of property, we see him arguing furiously that he lost a dream. As a spectator we could feel confused because we would expect Toma to feel some relief: he just left a traumatic state of mind where he was enslaved. Yet, to attest to the power of the gap between the act of seduction and the moment of living it, which Laplanche would call "the unconscious," what Toma is really angry about in real time is that he cannot feel he is living-dead anymore.[50] When he tells his fellow travelers that he lost a dream that "one could have once in ten years," we realize that there is something about "the noise" in this dream that is highly seductive for Toma.

The gap between the moment of being a slave and the dream is not only highly seductive but is also productive of new ways of acting against the police. In the film, Toma materializes this noise as "a counterfeit," which is a response to how one's body and property are stolen by racist structures of power. It shows that the enslaved body can take back the power that was stolen from them. After Toma's dream, we move to the actual harassment of the fiddlers. While the Roma musicians are repairing the cart, a group of police officers on horses are heading towards them. Toma sees the danger and realizes that they are in trouble. He asks for a candle, and then calls the musicians to put their money in one basket. He knows he has to protect the group's money and, while their dog barks at the police, the camera focuses on an improvised funeral where one man at the center of the frame mourns the deceased. We realize that the dead person is Toma, the leader of the band, and the group is orchestrating a diversion to escape police harassment.

Although Toma is formally a citizen who pays taxes and has the right to own property, he willingly transforms himself into a corpse. In slavery time, he is harassed by the police because his body is intended to be sold to slave owners. In post-abolition time, the police officer tells the musicians that he is there to tax them because they have not payed their State taxes in the last two years. We understand that the police are harassing the Roma musicians and that they are after their money. There is an implicit contrast here between stealing bodies and stealing money, which subtly suggests the story of emancipation. If one is only harassed for money, it seems that one is less subjugated than one has been in the past. We gradually understand, however, that this distinction may not hold, and that these new times are not as different as we are made to believe. When the musicians tell the police that they do not have money to pay, they are asked to undress, and their instruments and clothes are stolen. The difference between stealing bodies and stealing property does seem to matter anymore. The cruel infliction of violence on Roma bodies shows us that the transition to post-abolition time is not linear and may even be a plot that hides the continuities of violent racism. The police, however, can be made afraid that their power is temporary. The living-dead is there, in front of the police, and they know it, and fear it. The police's anxiety translates into a nightmare that is articulated by the officer's curse: "the one who steals from the dead will see *strigoi* in their dreams and wet their pants."[51]

While the statement is half mocking, it is also an articulation of dread. It is a direct commentary that they could lose their power and that the enslaved person, who is materialized in front of their eyes, coud haunt them. Where does this fear come from? The *strigoi* is looking at the police and the police cannot see it. The specter can see you without you seeing "it," and in doing so, it functions as a disappearing appearance.[52] While Toma's counterfeit mobilizes the fear of being looked at in this moment of danger, his action reverses a strict hierarchy of power. It locates the officers in a time of fear where they are looked at by their actual victims. Here Toma is not a terrifying specter such as "the brave Medusa," a beautiful apparition who laughs in front of danger.[53] Toma's specter is rather a tactical response to racialized violence, and discloses to the film's Soviet audience what the police are after: to extract obedience and resources from the Roma. The unique material force of the counterfeit is that in the time of emancipation the police are afraid and thus become transformed into "boys," overwhelmed by an enigmatic message. This enigmatic message is also a performative of an erased history that functions as a shock to the minds of the police officers.

In this section I have sought to show that "the noises," which are enigmatic messages articulated from a history of slavery, can lead to the abolition of capitalism. The scholarship on fugitivity has previously explored how the enslaved have performed counternarratives to the minstrelsy's master script.[54] In these Afro-alienation acts, "the trauma of captivity and subjugation" has been turned into a mode of defamiliarizing tropes of blackness by way of performance in order to generate alternative gender- and racial epistemologies.[55] In conversation with tactics of defamiliarization, this section has shown that noises have the potential to produce tactics to reverse the power dynamic between the racialized and the police.

The curse

> We are all stamped on our foreheads
>
> Toma, *The Fiddlers*

In this third section I show that not only was the counterfeit a method of struggling against capitalism, but also that curses can be a powerful tool against the capitalist bosses. By "curses" I understand social roles that were generally attributed to Roma ex-slaves, such as "a fiddler" or "beggar," which the racialized have to accept in order to make a living. In addition to the counterfeit, the curse is the practice of transforming a situation of racialization, such as a social role, in a practice of reversing power.

In *The Fiddlers*, the Roma musicians are cursed with their profession, but this curse is not only an "omen" in their life. The curse of being a musician literally marks a Roma person as different from other human beings, a "chattel" rather than human. In the film, *the curse* is a literal inscription on Toma's hands. Rather than looking at a curse in its negative dimension, I want to show that a curse could become a mark that opens up a new life on a different temporal dimension. To reimagine the possibilities of the value of an alternative time, I draw on Moten's idea that jazz music can be seen as noise, or "a problem that is here to stay."[56] For Moten, jazz is multiple things: not only is it a stop-gap in the theory that slavery has been left to the past, but it is also an articulation of the pain of exploitation. According to these new terms, jazz is almost "a curse" that cannot be eliminated. Similarly, I want to think that curses *are* literally the problem that will not disappear, precisely because the time of racialization has not stopped. The curse is a response not only to a past event, but to a history that actualizes itself permanently. To think about the continuity of slavery under new circumstances, Moten argues that slavery should be seen differently from an event. In a white abolitionist framework, scholars tend to give too much credit to a temporal construction that sees "events" as fleeting moments in the progression of time.[57] In turning this tradition on its head, Moten asks us to think about the capacity of the formerly enslaved to leave this time of racialized violence. The term "fugitivity" indicates a line of escape to a different free world, which may be less racist than our actual racial capitalism.

What if slavery, rather than a dead institution, becomes a focus for our thinking about the presence of racial hierarchies in a longer durational field? In *The Fiddlers*, after the police raid, we witness the following scene. One of the youngest members of the band, a character who resembles a young Toma, is whipped by one of the officers in their enraged search for the musicians' money. The young man is badly hurt, and the discussion between Toma and the young musician is a direct commentary on Moten's understanding of black music as "the problem that does not go away." In this conversation, for Toma "to be cursed" is a way not only to be attached to a history of violence, but also of trying to transform it so as to interrupt the white linear time of violence.

Here is the dialogue between the two Roma men. The young musician, whose name is Dingă, is crying in pain, and Toma Alistar, the older musician who used the counterfeit to remain unscathed, seeks to alleviate that pain:

DINGĂ: I cannot do it anymore. I cannot. To hell with our craft.
TOMA: You can do it.
DINGĂ: I'll run, and you'll not get me again.
TOMA: Where are you going to run? This is the play, this is the music. You are a person with a mark on your forehead, you.

> We are all marked like cattle. They did it with an iron, and this is worse than a curse.

The reference to being cursed as literally branded references how the enslaved "criminal" was marked and tattooed, so that slave catchers would have an easier time finding them.[58] But in *The Fiddlers*, the curse of being a musician is not only a sign for the slave catchers; it functions to offer a certain solidarity and unanticipated future to the formerly enslaved.

Like Moten, Toma Alistar believes that being *the fiddler* is a curse, a problem, and it is here to stay. But this curse is not only a trap. In the fiddlers' imagination, the "curse" of being inferior is transformed into a different curse: a special and unique ability to use one's hands. In the film, after the police officers have left, the Roma band are able to retrieve their money, which they had hidden in a hat. A conversation takes place that focuses on the route the young generation has to take.

> TOMA (*to Dingă*): Come on you, Dingă, do not cry any more. You are making a fool of yourself. Live with your pain. The one who got to dance in this game will die, so you know that from me.
>
> ANOTHER MAN: You are wrong, Alistar. I will leave [the fiddlers] as soon as I have made enough money. I will buy land, do you hear me? At least a small patch, hear me, one that I can call mine.
>
> TOMA: Do you believe?
>
> THE OTHER MAN: I believe.
>
> TOMA: The hands. Look at your hands. They are able to work neither the horns of the plow, nor the gun. We are all stamped on our foreheads. I have known this for a long time. Look at your hands.

What Toma tells young Dingă is that *the curse* of playing music is here to stay, and perhaps a tactic of surviving by extracting resources from those who keep them in racialized role. In a different scene, Toma remembers another moment when he was a boy and deployed his musical skills to make money for himself and his musical group. While this moment happened after abolition, Toma is still seen as "the enslaved" and at the mercy of those who had the power to sell him. In facing a racist world, for Toma it is important to think that he can transform his music into a tactic to navigate the financial and ideological world of his ex-masters. The performance of being liberated is a mode of surviving the violence of the State and the police.

In putting on this show, the musicians also imagine how they can get back resources from those who stole from them for generations. How does this performance work? They stage a moment when a wild animal, "a wolf" (Toma's dog) will leave its cage and be tamed by Toma's music. For the white master's gaze, this scene signals a certain performance of becoming civilized through music. It is the old racialized trope, that of the wild beast or the racialized being tamed. To the master's gaze what is threatening is a performance of a wolf, or untamed beast, that is ready to attack the social order. In their act, and in response to this threat, the Roma musicians tame the anarchic wild beast. This perspective shows that the rage and threat of so-called animality can be transformed into healthy emotions that strengthen a hierarchical social order. But this performance is also a spectacle designed to fool the master, and the fiddlers are getting money by exploiting the master's gaze. From the standpoint of the enslaved, the scene serves as a sign for a different code, a Roma code, where a new future of liberation is prefigured in this moment of abolishing slavery. Toma takes the chain off the wolf and a new alliance between animal and enslaved is created. Unlike what the master's gaze wants, which is to see how Romanians liberate the enslaved, here the moment of liberation generates the practice of an unlikely deviant coalition between those who are deemed "non-human."

In the Soviet film *The Fiddlers*, Roma tactics anticipate communist revolutions by showing how people fight for human emancipation. The Roma fiddlers are part of a broader historical process that leads to a more humane society. Toma's alliance with the dog, for instance, suggested that is possible to imagine a broader alliance of exploited figures, both human and animal, that fight against capitalism. At the end of the performance, Toma says to his beloved dog, "We've impressed them. We are stealing from their pockets, darling" ("I-am dat gata. Îi avem la buzunar, băețaș"). If racial exploitation is a continuous mode of living in history, then deviance is not only an aberration as a response to racism, but may be the condition of prefiguring alternative modes for human emancipation.

Conclusion: a materialist unconscious?

I started this chapter by drawing on Nikolay Marr's theory to insert historical materialism into queer psychoanalytical studies. In translating Marr's theory to sexual desires and dreams, I wanted to show that unconscious elements can become resources for communist and anti-racist politics. I first examined the consequences of the divide between Soviet Marxism and the New Left for theorizing the concept of the unconscious. My argument was that Jean Laplanche conceptualized the term "unconscious" against Soviet Marxist psychology, yet in the process his theory eliminated the basis for a materialist understanding of the unconscious. I proposed that the Soviet ideology in *The Fiddlers* not only shows a different theory of human psychology, but also offers the historical material to start reconceptualizing a materialist unconscious. In the film, Roma tactics are modalities to reverse the power dynamics against capitalist institutions of repression and initiate a process of social change.

Like in previous chapters of Part III, my goal was to insert a Soviet Marxist film into a queer anti-racist analytic. The pay-off of this method was to show that unconscious messages can lead to tactics where the enslaved struggle against those who exploit them. Specifically, to show that a psychoanalytical scene of seduction is shaped by the history of slavery, I claimed that tactics such as the counterfeit and the curse work against the idea of racialized exploitation. Laplanche located the potential of the noises in the challenge that they pose to a legacy of strict gender assignment. In his theory the message from the adult is something like this: "I am showing you – or letting you see – something which, by definition, you canot understand, and in which you cannot take part."[59] My redeployment of enigmatic messages showed the potential of a materialist unconscious, defined along the lines of "something you cannot understand, and in which you cannot take part," to work against racial capitalism.

The reconceptualization of human psychology has important consequences for queer psychoanalysis. My interpretation of the unconscious asks for a thorough examination of the premises of queer psychology. What Laplanche calls the "the fundamental anthropological situation" is no longer tenable without understanding anticapitalist racialized dynamics and histories. Lisa Baraitser proposes that an anti-racist politics can emerge by listening to enigmatic messages in a psychoanalytical manner. In this interpretation, the value of the psychoanalyst's interpretation is to create a psychic time that undermines the legacy of slavery. Instead, I proposed a different value attached to enigmatic communication. The noises of the counterfeit and the curse do not have value according to a capitalist temporality, but they become valuable in the process of changing the nature of capitalism. In faking his death, the Roma musician gestures towards a time that is at odds with the linear time of the abolition of slavery. As a strategy of power reversal, Toma's actions defy the logic of private property that led to the transformation of racialized bodies into chattel slaves. Differently put, rather than merely creating psychic time, enigmatic messages can generate a strong communist politics where the enslaved are in a leading position.

The second consequence of my argument is that Marxist films challenge the *longue durée* of endurance as the strategy to confront anti-blackness. In Lisa Baraitser's argument, it seems that the longer the period of temporalization, the better are the resources to fight legacies of slavery. Laplanche's understanding of the unconscious seems to refuse the language of causal directions.[60] But causality seems to come back in Baraitser's account when she praises "endurance," which is "the capacity to live time in and through the possibility of political change in the now."[61] The unconscious of the racialized, however, brings a different understanding of temporality that does not operate with a psychoanalytic time of integration. The materialist time of the unconscious one when the police need to feel afraid. It is also the time when deviant alliances articulate a different politics against people who benefit from racism. In Baraitser's view, a theory of care has a representational quality that makes it translatable to a wide audience.[62] In turn, I suggest that the counterfeit and the curse can materially threaten the capitalist bases of people's lives. As *The Fiddlers* shows, these actions emerge from the position of those who are racialized and whose memory and temporality contain other enigmatic messages.

Notes

1 Marr's theories were influential in the Soviet Union until they were criticized by Stalin. Marr was a strong critic of orientalism in

language theory and his theory claimed that language derives from material productions that were designed as anti-colonial structures. See Michael G. Smith, *Language and Power in the Creation of the USSR, 1917–1953* (Berlin: De Gruyter, 1998), pp. 82–86.
2 Jean Laplanche, *Essays on Otherness* (London: Routledge, 1999), pp. 59–60.
3 See the use of Deleuze in Jasbir K. Puar, "'I would rather be a cyborg than a goddess': Intersectionality, Assemblage, and Affective Politics," *transversal texts* (2011), https://transversal.at/transversal/0811/puar/en (accessed August 28, 2020); and Lucas Cassidy Crawford, "Transgender without Organs? Mobilizing a Geoaffective Theory of Gender Modification," in Susan Stryker and Aren Aizura (eds), *The Transgender Studies Reader 2* (London: Routledge, 2013), pp. 473–482. See also Dagmar Herzog, *Cold War Freud: Psychoanalysis in the Age of Catastrophes* (Cambridge: Cambridge University Press, 2017), p. 155, for the role of *Anti-Oedipus* in queer theory, disability work and anti-racist scholarship.
4 For this argument see Herzog, *Cold War Freud*, p. 156: "*Anti-Oedipus* needs to be understood also as a psychoanalytic text, not just an attack on psychoanalysis."
5 See Martin Miller, "Freudian Theory under Bolshevik Rule: The Theoretical Controversy during the 1920s," *Slavic Review*, 44:4 (1985), pp. 644–646.
6 Judith Butler, *Gender Trouble: Feminism and the Subversion of Identity* (London: Routledge, 1999), p. 85, introduces historicity into the structure of the unconscious, but not a historical materialist view of history. For an analysis of the role of the unconscious in Butler's theory of performativity, see Bogdan Popa, "Shame and Cognitive Strikes: What Would It 'Really' Mean for Queer Psychoanalysis to Enter the Perverse?," *Studies in Gender and Sexuality*, 19:2 (2017), pp. 150–151.
7 Warwick Anderson, Deborah Jenson and Richard Keller (eds), *Unconscious Dominions: Psychoanalysis, Colonial Trauma, and Global Sovereignties* (Durham, NC: Duke University Press, 2011), p. 1.
8 *Ibid.*, pp. 1–3.
9 See Herzog, *Cold War Freud*, p. 22.
10 *Ibid.*, p. 157.
11 *Ibid.*, p. 168.
12 *Ibid.*, p. 157.
13 Laplanche, *Essays on Otherness*, pp. 59–60.
14 *Ibid.*, p. 59.
15 *Ibid.*, p. 63.
16 See Herzog, *Cold War Freud*, p. 163.

17 *Ibid.*
18 *Ibid.*, p. 164.
19 For this scholarship, see Judith Butler, *Giving an Account of Oneself* (New York: Fordham University Press, 2005); Leo Bersani, "*Is the Rectum a Grave?" and Other Essays* (Chicago: Chicago University Press, 2009); Avgi Saketopoulou, "To Suffer Pleasure: The Shattering of the Ego as the Psychic Labor of Perverse Sexuality," *Studies in Gender and Sexuality*, 15:4 (2014), 254–268; Tim Dean, "Uses of Perversity: Commentary on Saketopoulou's 'To Suffer Pleasure,'" *Studies in Gender and Sexuality*, 15:4 (2014), 269–277; and Lisa Baraitser, *Enduring Time* (London: Bloomsbury, 2017).
20 For attempts to bring socialism into conversation with race and psychoanalytic studies, see Neda Atanasoski and Kalindi Vora, "Postsocialist Politics and the Ends of Revolution," *Social Identities*, 24:2 (2017), 139–154; and Neda Atanasoski and Erin McElroy, "Postsocialism and the Afterlives of Revolution: Impossible Spaces of Dissent," in N. Pireddu (ed.), *Reframing Critical, Literary, and Cultural Theories* (London: Palgrave Macmillan, 2018), 273–297.
21 See Butler, *Giving an Account*, pp. 54, 72–75, 97, for the enigmatic sexual message implanted by the "other."
22 *Ibid.*, p. 54. Given that this psychic structure is heteronormative and oriented towards achieving property, Butler suggests here a practice of imagining other worlds of relationality and politics.
23 Hélène Tessier, "The Sexual Unconscious and Sexuality in Psychoanalysis: Laplanche's Theory of Generalized Seduction," *Psychoanalytic Quarterly*, 83:1 (2014), p. 180.
24 For self-shattering, see Bersani, *Is the Rectum a Grave?*, p. 24: "a shattering of the psychic structures themselves that are the precondition for the very establishment of a relation to others." For a discussion about perversion and self-shattering, see Saketopoulou, "To Suffer Pleasure."
25 Bersani, *Is the Rectum a Grave?*, p. 57.
26 *Ibid.*, p. 29.
27 Saketopoulou, "To Suffer Pleasure," p. 256.
28 Tessier, "The Sexual Unconscious," p. 171.
29 See Baraitser, *Enduring Time*, pp. 115–139. For a clear presentation of Laplanche's "unconscious" and "enigmatic signifiers," see *ibid.*, p. 104.
30 Cristina Sharpe, *In the Wake: On Blackness and Being* (Durham, NC: Duke University Press, 2016), p. 14.
31 See Tessier, "The Sexual Unconscious," p. 171, for Laplanche's "primary scene of seduction."
32 Baraitser, *Enduring Time*, p. 104.

33 Laplanche, *Essays on Otherness*, p. 212.
34 *Ibid.*, 215.
35 For racial capitalism, see Cedric J. Robinson, *Black Marxism: The Formation of the Black Radical Tradition* (Chapel Hill: North Carolina University Press, 2000), p. 11.
36 Jean Laplanche, "Gender, Sex, and the Sexual," trans. Susan Fairfield, *Studies in Gender and Sexuality*, 8:2 (2007), p. 215.
37 *Ibid.*, p. 205.
38 *Ibid.*, p. 217.
39 See Gila Ashtor, "The Ideology of Transference: Laplanche and Affect Theory," *Studies in Gender and Sexuality*, 19:2 (2018), p. 103: "what distinguishes the 'enigmatic' from other affective phenomena is not simply that it refers to what we didn't know but can know now; what's enigmatic is what could not be translated into language, what drives the bewildering contortions of affective life."
40 To the extent that these events have a sexual component, they provoke a pleasurable shock. For a commentary on sexuality as "painful shock," see *ibid.*, p. 98.
41 Daphne Brooks, *Bodies in Dissent: Spectacular Performances of Race and Freedom 1850–1910* (Durham, NC: Duke University Press, 2006), p. 67.
42 For the role of Roma slave jesters in Wallachia and Moldavia between the 1830s and 1860s, see Mihai Lukács, "Roma Slave Jesters: The Origins of Theater in Wallachia and Moldavia," *Romarchive* (2018), www.romarchive.eu/en/theatre-and-drama/roma-slave-jesters/ (accessed August 6, 2020).
43 Anca Parvulescu and Manuela Boatcă, "The *Longue Durée* of Enslavement: Extracting labor from Romani Music in Liviu Rebreanu's *Ion*," *Literature Compass*, 17 (2020), pp. 1–2, https://doi.org/10.1111/lic3.12559 (accessed July 11, 2021).
44 Joan Dayan, *Haiti, History and the Gods* (Berkeley: University of California Press, 1998), p. 37.
45 Carolyn Dinshaw, *Queer/Early/Modern* (Durham, NC: Duke Univesity Press, 2006), p. 91.
46 Fred Moten, *In the Break: The Aesthetic of the Black Radical Tradition* (Minneapolis, University of Minnesota Press, 2003), p. 94.
47 Baraitser, *Enduring Time*, p. 104.
48 For a history of anti-Roma politics, see Shannon Woodcock, "Gender, Sexuality and Ethnicity in the Stereotypical Construction of Ț. Slaves in the Romanian Lands, 1385–1848," in Jan Selling, Markus End, Hristo Kyuchokov, Pia Laskar and Bill Templar (eds), *Antiziganism: What's in a Word?* (Cambridge: Cambridge Scholars, 2015), pp. 176–186.

49 Moten, *In the Break*, p. 1.
50 See Baraitser, *Enduring Time*, p. 104, for this particular understanding of Laplanche's unconscious.
51 *Strigoi* are entities in popular culture that function as ghosts.
52 In queer studies, the closet, in gesturing towards what is assumed to be concealed, had a strong connection to the specter as a device of representation. The closet introduces the fear of unnatural desire, which could emerge when one is not prepared. See Dinshaw, *Queer/Early/Modern*, p. 77.
53 *Ibid.*, p. 78.
54 See Brooks, *Bodies in Dissent*, p. 2.
55 *Ibid.*, p. 5.
56 Fred Moten, *Black and Blur* (Durham, NC: Duke University Press, 2017), p. xii.
57 *Ibid.*
58 Cuts, long scars and tattoos were heavily used in the British Empire, for instance, both to help authenticate the property of the slave owners and to aid recognition by those who were enforcing such laws; see David Olusoga, *Black and British: A Forgotten History* (London: Macmillan, 2016), p. 93. In Georgian England, the notice of rewards in the newspapers was accompanied by descriptions of particular signs of disfigurement; see *ibid*.
59 Laplanche, *Essays on Otherness*, p. 174.
60 For instance, Laplanche argues that causality cannot operate backwards in time; see Baraitser, *Enduring Time*, p. 104.
61 *Ibid.*, p. 117.
62 *Ibid.*

8

Trans

In Chapter 8, my argument takes a different turn. I claim that historical materialism offers to trans studies a broader historical and analytical understanding of possibilities of revolutionary action. To do so, I shift my focus to analyzing the role of a revolutionary imagination in US films, with a particular attention to anti-communism as a historical formation that shaped both trans and revolutionary politics. A Marxist dialectical method draws on history to show the potential not only of a traditional working class for abolishing capitalism, but also of transgender agents. Trans politics, as a politics of expanding the strict binary between men and women, and Marxism, as a politics of revolutionizing a capitalist political economy, can be conceived as part of a similar alliance to disrupt racial capitalism in the United States.

To show why trans studies need a Marxist analytic, this chapter first illuminates the connections between a widespread US anti-communist project and anti-trans politics. If one of the outcomes of the Cold War was to set Marxism and trans politics in conflict, a historical method reveals a shared anti-communist opposition to both projects. Susan Stryker's piece "My Words to Victor Frankenstein" illuminated an important genealogy of trans people who have historically been perceived as monsters.[1] While her conceptualization of "trans" as a term that is located in "an antagonistic and queer relationship to a Nature" was deeply influential, trans theory has to be put into relation with anti-communism.[2] To do so, I analyze a science fiction Cold War film, *It Came from Outer Space*, and a recent independent production, *Tangerine*, to reveal the possibilities of connecting trans politics and histories of labor resistance. In my analysis, I seek to uncover potential historical and contextual junctures that can materialize a politics of solidarity.[3]

Second, I argue that the pay-off of historical materialism is to show the contributions of trans and queer subjects to the abolition of a regime founded on private property. If a Cold War narrative kept Soviet Marxism and queer anti-racism in conflict, Neda Atanasoski and Kalindi Vora argue that the term "queer postsocialism" seeks to bypass the divide and offers the possibility of thinking about the circulation of Marxism beyond eastern European socialism.[4] In this account, queer postsocialism displaces the narrative that socialism is relevant only to those parts of the world that have lived behind the so-called Iron Curtain.[5] Yet, when Atanasoski and Vora argue that postsocialism needs to "disrupt teleological narratives of oppositional consciousness tied to a demand for a transformation or a revolution in the future," they gesture to the end of a Soviet Marxist belief in a future revolution.[6] While their suggestion is that this tradition is worn-out, I seek to keep alive the hope for potential radical transformations in the future. Unlike their methodology, my historical materialist analysis builds on the gradual transformation of the social world that can lead to human emancipation.

Chapter 8 challenges the assumption that Marxist politics died as a rival political ideology to liberalism after the 1990s. It identifies the threat of labor resistance in cinematic representations not only in the 1950s, but also in late 2010. I draw on what an an anticommunist rhetoric in the United States finds as a common enemy. This politics refuses not only a history of labor resistance, but also a project of abolishing gender roles. Since work and sexual pleasure have been theorized as being necessarily in conflict, my aim is to theorize an alliance where the two converge to point to future revolutionary alliances.[7] While the concept of queer postsocialism offers a "space to work through ongoing legacies in the present," it also needs a materialist analysis of the potential for future emancipatory politics.[8] Queer postsocialism provides a politics that seizes revolutionary actions in settings designed to work in a market economy, but it also has to imagine a world beyond actual capitalism.[9] To develop this argument, I analyze in the first section of the chapter the imagination of future communism, and discuss Susan Stryker's trans theory in dialogue with Jacques Rancière's idea of communism. In the second section I investigate the production of Cold War films in relation to transgender/queer politics and labor resistance. Unlike Tony Shaw, I read the film *It Came from Outer Space* as a clear statement in the war against communism.[10] In the third section, I offer a reading of the film *Tangerine*, and conclude by reflecting on how this chapter helps to show new theoretical routes in trans theory.

Trans* and communism

In Susan Stryker's conceptualization, trans politics refuses heteronormativity by generating a terrifying politics of rage.[11] In her words, "transsexuality more than any other transgender practice or identity represents the prospect of destabilizing the foundational presupposition of fixed genders."[12] She theorizes a trans attitude at the level of rage, which is the affect that materializes an imaginary endpoint to one's monstrosity. Rage is specifically transgender when "the inability to foreclose the subject occurs through a failure to satisfy norms of gendered embodiment."[13] If Stryker's trans theory undermines rigid gender identifications, it originally lacks a strong anchor in a visible anti-capitalist and anti-colonial project. Such a relationship, however, has been gradually theorized by Stryker and other theorists who sought to move away from a queer theory that failed to engage seriously with colonial and imperial histories. In Susan Stryker's 2004 retrospective take on her 1994 piece "My Words to Victor Frankenstein," trans theory is the evil twin of queer theory because it has a special sensitivity to how non-western identities are subsumed by Euro-American privilege.[14]

However, this decolonial turn historicizes the queer revolution of the 1990s only in relation to US imperial history and "the inescapable context of globalization."[15] Stryker wrote an article in 2012 that positions trans theory in the biopolitical turn. Its goal, unlike the 1994 piece, is to analyze the production of identities such as transsexual according to colonial and imperial power dynamics. In following Stryker's research, I seek to build not only on the queer potential of the word "trans," but also on its anti-capitalist promise. A potential tactic is to reveal the intensification of policing regarding trans people of color if one deploys the analytic of anti-capitalism. Dean Spade, for instance, sees the antagonistic potential of trans not only towards reified understandings of gender essentialism, but also against a capitalist system that produces hierarchies of inequality and power.[16] What I focus on is a materialist strategy that underscores key historical moments in the development of anti-communism. The alleged victory of Anglo-American liberalism in the Cold War defined the liberal consensus about the market and private property as the only legitimate rhetorical and political game. In turn, I seek to bring back the relevance of labor politics and the geography of imperial domination to grasp potential moments of revolt.

A Marxist queer politics was extracted from Jacques Rancière's theory, which opens important theoretical lines to understanding what communism can offer to queer and trans politics.[17] Rancière provides a framework of understanding trans not as a minoritarian position, but as a position of enacting a politics of equality. His vision of revolutionary politics is a revolution that seeks a collective reappropriation of labor, since communism "turned out to be the *only* form of possible community still remaining after the collapse of all other communities."[18] Current capitalism is marked by the conflict between equality and the rise of inequality, and, as a corollary, it generates a process of eliminating places where equality and inequality meet.[19] Like the politics of communism, queer and trans politics have the capacity to contest an order of inequality.[20] If for Stryker the monster emerges in a conflict with gendered normalized assumptions, in Rancière's view a political actor emerges through an act of politics when it disrupts a given hierarchy of proper roles and representations.[21] Both thinkers share a strong interest in how the unintelligible can produce new forms of politics.[22] Moreover, both are interested in how new actors and forms of politics can change a given status quo. If Stryker's monster disidentifies from nature, the act of politics for Rancière involves a disidentification from a given hierarchy of roles. Transgender rage is not unlike what Rancière calls an act of disidentification from hierarchies. One refuses the order of the gender police when one disidentifies from it; the other refuses the hierarchies of inequality when one disidentifies from it.[23] Rancière shows that equality operates not in terms of a politics of what should be, as it is abstractly conceptualized by theorists of equality, but as a process of emergence in the here and now.[24] Similarly, Stryker argues that queer fury can create actual conditions for inventing new forms of life that do not pre-exist in a heteronormative linguistic representation. Rage that is articulated in the emergent here and now can inaugurate new modalities to design a future-oriented political imagination.

While Rancière and Stryker's theories can open up a dialogue between communism and trans politics, they focus on interventions that do not fundamentally change the political economy of a society. I draw on a dialectical method to underscore not only the potential moments of revolts but also broader historical transformations that make these actions possible. For Rancière, a communist orientation is contingent and rare. It aims not at radically inaugurating a new social order, but at extending the possibility of equality in societies that are fundamentally shaped by a logic of exchange value. For Stryker, trans politics is primarily one of gender trouble and ignores the possibility that it is part of a bigger project of human emancipation. Their politics has a utopian potential emerging from contingent possibilities, but it does not interrogate the possibility of larger historical transformations.

Trans monsters and the picket line

To forge a queer communist analytic, I argue that in both Rancière's and Stryker's analyses a politics of collective opposition to capitalism is less articulated. While they seek to show new ways in which the unintelligible emerges as a political category, neither theorizes collective forms of struggle that constituted the basis of traditional Marxist politics, such as the strike or the picket line. Unlike other individual forms of resistance, a picket line is a strategy that creates not only political conflict, but also the possibility of imagining a collective space for rejecting capitalism. Labor strikes, particularly in coal mines, have historically constituted a privileged tactic to interrupt the flow of commodities in capitalism. Timothy Mitchell argues that strikers in the coal mines have been seen from the 1880s to World War II as threatening to carbon energy, the primary source of power in the new industrialized countries.[25] Strikes in coal mines were more frequent and lasted much longer than other industrial conflicts, probably because of the miners' freedom from supervision: the opposite of the modern machine-user.[26] "The coordinated acts of interrupting, slowing down or diverting" the movement of coal energy created "a new form of collective capability built out of coal mines, railways, power stations and their operators."[27]

By the 1950s, the threat of the working class had shifted from the miners' strikes to the foreign invasion of communism, and primarily the Soviet Union. The successful Soviet tests of the atomic bomb generated strong anxiety about invasions and the end of liberal order. The politics of describing the communist danger, however, was never about white workers as inherently monstrous. Instead, white workers needed to be saved from communist aliens who were taking over their souls. Workers were ordinary Americans living a life of leisure and comfort until their bodies were occupied by monstrous figures. The representation of workers as bodies who have been colonized by communist politics becomes particularly acute after World War II.[28] During the Cold War, threats of monster aliens invading the heart of racialized capitalist politics become intensely articulated on the screen.[29] In the Cold War sci-fi films of the 1950s, workers are aliens with non-human features who often enact the orders of the superior members of the alien communists. Their transformations during the unfolding of the plot are marked either as an illness or as a refusal of normal heterosexuality.

Among the better-known films of the alien invasion genre, several, such as *Invasion of the Body Snatchers* (1956), *Revenge of the Creature* (1955) and *The Creature Walks among Us* (1959) have been remade or had sequels. *It Came from Outer Space*, however, has a unique history as part of Cold War science fiction. This was the first sci-fi film for Universal, and when it premiered in 1953 it was "the first 3-D film on a wide screen with stereophonic sound."[30] The film shows how aliens threaten couple John Putnam, a scientist, and Ellen Fields, a schoolteacher. The scientist who acts as the savior of the free world is a cinematic trope that is part of a larger rhetoric of US Cold War sci-fi films. John Putnam is a down-to-earth pragmatist who seeks to find a solution to the problem of the alien invasion. He is cool-headed, has the intelligence to deal with extra-terrestrial threats, and is responsible for managing the invasion. Unlike the scientist, the Government and the police are generally hotheads who want to obliterate the threat. In acting differently from the forces of repression, the scientist seeks to understand the monsters, who are often represented as having a superior technological infrastructure. Because of their technological edge, aliens threaten easily to occupy the heart of America, which is located in the minds and bodies of ordinary workers. The working class acts as if effortlessly modified by an unknown technology, and demonstrates little resistance in face of the insidious alien presence. The scientists see the danger and fight with the monsters to retain the supremacy of the free world. While the aliens do not face a lot of resistance in converting the working class, the real battle ground for ideological supremacy is the white female teacher. As a future key element in the nuclear couple, she is the scientist's closest ally and also the most vulnerable element in the plot. The white teacher is in danger of being corrupted as easily as the white working class, but the scientist saves her to liberate her from ideological and technological brainwashing.

Coal mines are key in understanding 1950s Cold War science fiction. At the beginning of the film, the alien ship and its monsters land in abandoned mines, where the aliens seek to continue their mission and repair their ship. Since coal mines were the battle ground for highly efficient actions undertaken by trade unions, it is not a coincidence that aliens live in the mines. Such a setting is part of the privileged imaginary of early-twentieth-century communist politics. Coal miners were seen as the vanguard of the revolution because of their capacity to organize and successfully strike against the capital. In the rhetoric of Cold War films, however, the alliance between workers and monsters can be defeated only if male scientists and female teachers will join forces against its power. Victory requires a specific strategy that will keep the threat of high technology and labor's resistance to capitalism separated.

In *It Came from Outer Space* the working class is queered when it is threatened by communism. Cold War ideology frames communism as a disturbance of basic human primary needs, which transforms white Americans into creatures who will behave according to unknown norms and desires. Their imagination of time is in danger of being taken over by monstrous creatures, but normal time will be restored to its rightful place when the heteronormative couple are united against the communist threat. Working-class Americans act as though they have stopped believing in white North American values. They have strange looks, do not eat, and stop having sex with their wives and lovers. For instance, a female character describes anxiously the erratic behaviour of her working-class husband: "Something is wrong, I know it. He was so pale, he had the queerest look in his eyes and he never touched his food." To become part of an alien universe is to stop feeding the normal flow of the reproductive family. It means literally to stop eating. Another woman, depicted almost as a sex worker with strong sexual urges, complains about the loss of virility of the male workers. She gives a frightened account of what happened to one of her lovers, who happen to be a miner: "Same for George. His landlady told me he skipped dinner. I thought I liked George with his appetite." The primary needs of life – sex, food and health – are all disturbed by the alien invasion. This fear of the unintelligible has to be met, and the role of the white middle-class nuclear couple is to take measures against this threat. It faces the enemy at a critical moment of their world, because aliens show up when they plan to get married.

What we witness in the film is the formation of space that functions as a buffer between invaders and the free world. This political site is defined by Cold War liberalism, which sought to introduce a wedge between communist invaders and the North American working class. In a key scene at the end of the film the scientist seeks to save his lover, as well as other working-class people who have been abducted by communist aliens. In the visual representation of the Cold War, the US expert in technology has the task of drawing clear lines between enemies. What the scene seeks to achieve is to make visible conflicting ideological positions.

Scientists are not neutral observers of the invasion; they act as if they are in a privileged position to defend white heteronormative ideology and break potential anti-capitalist alliances up. Among immediate threats to the USA, trans-like figures function not only to make visible new dangers about changing meanings of gender but also to control and manage them as biopolitical weapons during the Cold War. As Susan Stryker argued, since the birth of transsexuality was linked to the scientific awe and anxiety generated by the atomic bomb, a transsexual figure such as Christine Jorgensen functioned as an "emblem of a new era," an ontological practice that resignified the relationship between gendered subject and sexed flesh within post-World War II biomedical and technocultural environments.[31] The film needs to demarcate the antagonistic invaders from the friendly bodies of white Americans, who can be saved by the liberal hero. In participating in the dramatic events, the spectator has to take sides in the process of ideology formation. The scientist is put in the position of affectively separating between a group that can be recuperated from communist illusions and the creatures that are lost to the enemy side. In this scene, the white teacher, Ellen, is looking to the audience, wanting to be saved, while the white scientist, John, is passionately waiting for her. As part of this romantic encounter, the white miners who have been brainwashed by aliens follow the enraptured woman teacher.

This film produces an imaginary space of liberal North America not only by showing how ideological lines can be created but also by channeling its audience's emotional responses to repudiate communist-oriented politics. In the next section I show that this representational device is not the only affective response that can be produced by aesthetic objects. In a film such as *Tangerine*, rage against the conditions of work and love under racial capitalism can mobilize a different revolutionary imagination.

Trans black sex workers and postsocialist taxi drivers

The Cold War politics of dividing a potential working-class alliance did not conclude with the end of socialism in the Soviet Union and the eastern bloc. After the 1990s, global capitalism has led to a massive migration from former socialist countries to western Europe and the USA, which generated a process of precarity and the loss of traditional working-class spaces such as factory floors and mines. Yet, rather than demonstrating the death of socialist politics, this process has also brought class solidarity into spaces that are produced by exploitation and white hierarchies.

Unlike a politics of racial capitalism, which distinguishes between labor politics and queer pleasure, *Tangerine* gives us a plot about a desire for their convergence. It is the story of how two black trans women (Sin-dee and Alexandra) and an Armenian cabdriver (Razmick) negotiate a hostile environment in contemporary Los Angeles. From its first frame, Sin-dee and Alexandra talk about a utopian wish to ally their desires with their working conditions. After spending twenty-eight days in jail to preserve the freedom of Chester, their pimp and lover, Sin-dee finds out that he is cheating on her. The pimp has slept with another sex worker, a white cis woman. Cheating here is not simply an act of infidelity because Sin-dee makes some claim of property or ownership over Chester's sex life. Sin-dee's desire for revenge is not even about sex as a loss of trust. What is at stake here is "cheating" as a political act of denying solidarity to someone who fought for you as a trans woman. Chester is unforgivable because he betrayed a deep code of solidarity with Sin-dee, who went to prison for him to protect him. What Sin-dee asked from her pimp/lover is that his desire *and* politics at work should be aligned. From "I helped you not go to jail because I care for you," Sin-dee expects something in return: "I want some form of solidarity and love because I did that for you."

Tangerine is about not only this alignment, but also an invitation to act together, which is a call to others to participate in one's actions. Working-class characters need a friend or a comrade in the pursuit of their goals. Sin-dee needs Alexandra to help her get to Chester; Alexandra seeks to bring friends such as Sin-dee and Razmick, the Armenian taxi driver, to her musical performance; Razmick needs Sin-dee and Alexandra for reasons that have to do with pleasure, solitude and solidarity. And their goals, in the end, are not as divergent as the may seem. In the development of her dramatic pursuit of Chester, Sin-dee brings Razmick and Alexandra to a restaurant where their relationships are interrogated and rearticulated. Alexandra's performance of Doris Day's "Toyland," a sad song about the loss of the magic and innocence of childhood, becomes a reason for celebrating unlikely friendships under very hard conditions. While our characters seem to navigate their world by themselves, they are constantly asking others to join in. Desire needs solidarity, and the call to one to be with others is also a call that makes politics happen. In singing, Alexandra wants Sin-dee and Razmick to experience a part of herself that she could show only to her friends. In wanting to be with Sin-dee and Alexandra on Christmas Day, Razmick chooses to be a part of a group with which he shares the experience of working the streets late at night. The alliances are fragile, contingent and easy to break, but they nonetheless happen. These moments of meeting with friends are where the new and the surprising can appear, such as the revelation of Chester's infidelity, or Alexandra's moment of magic when she sings about the fantasy of unbroken toyland.

Trans black people and the emigrant postsocialist driver navigate a difficult working environment that is marked by precarity and humiliation. While Sin-dee and Alexandra share a strong intimate friendship, Razmick struggles between conflicting allegiances to both his family and his fellow workers. Both trans workers and immigrant drivers deal with privileged whites who either insult you as a monster (in the case of Sin-dee and Alexandra) or vomit in your car and call you Mr. Falafel (in Razmick's case). What is at stake in the unexpected relationships between characters is the potential of an anti-capitalist coalition. Such an alliance derives from the entanglement between sexual desire and a working-class positionality, which creates the conditions for labor resistance. Although the alliance momentarily fails, it calls us to think about Razmick's desire to be with, and for, trans sex workers. Razmick *wants* trans black women. Although his desire is marked as pleasure and an escape from work, it is also a feature of how this particular worker navigates the structural hierarchies of a white Anglo-American world. Rather than extracting surplus value from the vulnerable, Razmick's desire is a utopian call for a world that builds on solidarity, pleasure and non-normative kinship. Such desires underpin our workers' attempts to live better lives, yet extractive and appropriative capitalism seeks to destroy these vulnerable alliances.

The stage for creating alliances does not appear randomly by the sheer contingency of events, however. Sin-dee's feeling that she has been wronged drives the action of the story. When she is hurt, her queer rage creates the conflict of the plot. When she finally finds Chester, the audience realizes that the conflict here is not only a lovers' fight but is also a work conflict. Sin-dee is not happy with her boss, and she came to make a point about this dramatically at *his* workplace. Stryker conceptualizes trans* as "an antagonistic and queer relationship" to nature, but here I want to show that trans politics is an antagonistic relationship to a capitalist system of exploiting bodies.[32] Instead of the owners of a coal mine, Sin-dee confronts a boss with a hoodie, who endlessly talks about his professionalism and business in a fast food outlet. Because she feels that harm has been done to her, she wants to change her relationship with Chester. To do so, she creates "drama," as Alexandra puts it, or, in the words of Samuel Chambers, a political theorist who writes about radical political subjects, Sin-dee brings "the stage into being."[33] In Sin-dee's wish to confront Chester, her mad desire for justice and her disappointment that her lover had let her down make a particular politics exist. To put it another way, in articulating a dramatic stage, Sin-dee creates trans black politics as an assertion of a wrong and a call to strike against her boss.

At the heart of the film we find a call for a utopian imagination regarding work and sexual desire. From the outset, the film presents us to with two parties, the trans* workers and the hooded boss. What Sin-dee does is to make visible a space and world that have been invisible. Despite a work conflict, or perhaps because of it, we witness a deeper conflict about how work and love should be negotiated. Sin-dee is in this line of work not just for the money but also because she likes her employer. Unlike Alexandra, who seeks to draw a clear line between work and love, Sin-dee's feelings are a bit confusing to the audience. Chester is her pimp, but she seeks a more honest and equal relationship to her employer, who sells her on the sex market. This is an impossible claim. Let's put it another way: Sin-dee knows that her boss wants to exploit her, but in spite of that she makes a claim to an equal relationship. At this point, one would ask: Why would you even do that? Why would you call for equality knowing that you are already an exploited worker? Yet, while some of us distinguish sharply between desire and a workplace, Sin-dee tells us that we may be the ones who are confused. Sex and work are inherently tied up, and Sin-dee wants a different relationship with her lover and employer because he failed to reciprocate in that relationship. She is not the only one for whom love and work are inherently intertwined; Razmick is not that different from Sin-dee, because he seems to be in some sense confused among workplace, family and sex. He is supposed to spend Christmas night with his Armenian family, but we realize that he is emotionally much closer to sex workers than to his traditional kin. In the same state of confusing work and love, he seeks the company of sex workers on the night he is supposed to be with his family.

What desire does in the lives of Sin-dee, Alexandra and Razmick is to confuse an organization of places that are to remain undisturbed. Rancière calls this naturalization of hierarchies in capitalism *the police*.[34] Sin-dee strikes against her employer and tells Chester she will stop working if he does not change his behavior. While we know Chester functions as the boss, she wants a different relationship to her lover. In her confrontation with him, Sin-dee asks for the impossible: not an impossible claim, but a way for us to rethink what possible is. And one way to make us rethink the possible is to understand the emergence of picket lines and working-class alliances. While our characters are not the working-class proletariat who would strike by defending the line in an actual factory, trans friendship actualizes novel forms of labor resistance. Alliances emerge from refusals to act according to heteronormative white norms. For instance, Alexandra's "no" to one of her clients who wants free sex functions as an interruption of the expectations around sex work. Her gesture in saying "no" to her client is a momentary strike against expectations about why sex work happens in the first place. While he assumes that she just wants sex, Alexandra is very clear that she does her work because she needs money. Like Alexandra, Razmick strikes against expectations associated to heterosexuality and whiteness. As a clear instantiation of his politics, Razmick refuses to have sex with a black sex worker because she is not trans*. Razmick also understands well that because he is not a white American his work and life put him closer to the trans black sex workers than to an idealized version of family that his relatives urge him to occupy. Along the same lines, what Sin-dee seems to value much more than her fierce desire to revenge herself against her boss and lover is the intimacy she shares with her black trans* co-worker. In spite of her own desire to humiliate her boss, she finds time to go and be with Alexandra when she gives her musical performance. Towards the end of the film Sin-dee's body is exposed to direct violence and exploitation when a group of white men insult her and destroy her wig. In response, Alexandra gives her own wig to Sin-dee. In this gesture, we can see a picket line against white normativity emerging in front of our eyes, and a friendship being called again into an actual presence. In that moment of exchanging the wig, the alliance between workers in their workplace is reconstituted and takes the form of a friendship. Or, differently put, a friendship that has been broken becomes a friendship again.

Gestures of refusal are a danger to heteronormative authorities. Chester is not an obvious member of what we traditionally call *the police*. Rather, he is the embodiment of the young boss of neoliberal economics and a person who sees himself as the opposite of the police. He sells drugs and sex and seeks professionally to appropriate the values of his workers. The pimp/drug-dealer/lover Chester, a white man who shamelessly performs every linguistic and behavioral stereotype about black people, is not the embodiment of the authority of the State. By contrast, Razmick's mother-in-law, who wants to preserve the normative family, seems to function as a stand-in for the police and their moral normativity. The mother-in-law wants to call the police to punish Razmick because he breaks the conventions of a white heteronormative world. Unlike the mother-in-law, Chester is the businessman who is only interested in making money, running a clean business and using his charm to make his workers productive. Yet both Chester and Razmick's mother-in-law seek to destroy the potential alliance among Alexandra, Sin-dee and Razmick. How do the police function to destroy their solidarity? Razmick's mother-in-law sees his desires as a threat to his wife and child. She successfully removes the taxi driver from the fast-food restaurant, the scene of the emerging working alliance. Like the mother-in-law, Chester wants a clear separation between sex and work. Under these conditions, the real enemy for Chester is the friendship that Sin-dee has already developed with Alexandra. He realizes that Sin-dee's strike is threatens his profit, and provokes a fight between the two black trans* women, knowing that Sin-dee will get hurt. To do so, he divulges that he and Alexandra have slept together. A story about sex is utilized here as a counter-strike to a picket line.

In a key scene in the film, Chester has three sex workers in front of him, and the way to break the emerging picket line is to create a conflict between them. He allies himself with the white sex worker. The white cis woman is interpellated in joining the boss, because she does not want to see that she is, like trans black workers, on the side of working-class labor. The white sex worker who rejects the strike is part of a strategy to break the solidarity between workers. Chester manipulates Sin-dee into feeling bad not about her boss but about her comrade. While this is a move that will fail in the end, the emerging picket line has momentarily been broken.

Conclusion: trans communism?

In this chapter, I have compared two unlikely films – *It Came from Outer Space* and *Tangerine* – to analyze potential alliances between trans of color subjects and postsocialist immigrants. My argument is that eastern European Marxism offers the standpoint for a historical analysis of anti-communist and anti-trans projects in the USA. In contrast to Jacques Rancière and Susan Stryker's conceptualization of disidentification under capitalism, I argue that their work needs a broader perspective, locating contingent moments of rebellion in a movement that leads to human emancipation.

The chapter addresses what Marxist dialectics can bring to queer and trans theory. First, it shows that it can generate a narrative that historically connects distinct historical and geographical sites in global capitalism. Rather than looking at postsocialist countries as the only site for Marxist politics, I investigated the alliance between labor and trans politics in the USA. In engaging in a historicized analysis of films, I notice a shift from the central figures of US capitalism between the 1950s and 2010. While, during the Cold War, the liberal scientist was the main cinematic placeholder for the values of capitalism, in the post-2008 financial crisis the white entrepreneur is an important character of capitalist expansion. I identified a shift in terms of the spatiality of labor resistance, which changed from the coal mine to ordinary sites of consumption such as fast-food restaurants and the streets. Under new conditions of production and exploitation, *Tangerine* shows that a picket line emerges to interrupt the flow of capitalist extraction of value. Not only has the spatial arrangement changed, but also the meaning of class struggle. In the 1950s, Cold War cinema described the monsters/communists as *already defined* monsters, who were taking over the minds of the working class. A monster/communist was a technologically superior creature, who becomes a threat neither through work nor through forms of collective action such as strikes. *Tangerine* shows that a trans threat, unlike the monster as a threat already formed, emerges within and from the solidarity of workers who struggle against racial capitalism. Rather than a superior technology, in *Tangerine* communism is a coalition that is made possible by the feeling that you have been cheated by your employer.

What *Tangerine* also shows is that the instantiation of socialist solidarity among co-workers is potentially threatening to capitalism, but young white entrepreneurs and self-righteous Armenian mothers-in-law seek to protect heteronormative families and undermine the lines of emerging worker alliances. Like the imagination of a coalition that abolishes capitalism, the alliances that seek to suppress it work in a similarly unpredictable manner.

The second theoretical contribution of this chapter is to think about a future trans politics that seeks human emancipation for all. A Marxist call for a utopian future has the capacity to arouse a desire that seems impossible: the alignment of queer sexuality and working-class politics. If work and sex have traditionally been seen as two distinct areas of human life, trans black workers in *Tangerine* ask their audience to seek the imagination of their alignment. Such yearning for a different world is not unlike Muñoz's argument about Vaginal Davis's performance of a terroristic drag, which can stir up desires that are barely felt.[35] Like Vaginal Davis, Sin-dee and Alexandra create a sense of unease in desire, which challenges conventional assumptions about what is possible sexually and politically. Like Stryker's queer rage, trans disturbs the naturalization of the convention that sexual desire and work are two separate spheres of life. The imagination of their alignment is what is terrifying in this desire, which seeks to transgress current capitalism.

A historical materialist method can bring back a hopeful theory of human emancipation. The affective terror that Sin-dee unleashes towards Chester in *Tangerine* is an important element that emphasizes hope as the primary affect. Sin-dee's rage is both stuck in the past of a relationship where Chester seems to have loved her but also hopeful that a new relationship can be imagined with a lover. Both Sin-dee's rage and Alexandra's singing performance bring in and articulate a belief in a critical need such as the desire for friendship and affection. Yet trans theory has to conceptualize and theorize such moments in a broader narrative that captures developments and opportunities in their historical emergence. Rather than taking for granted the liberal discourse of rights, trans studies can push forward to bring about the fulfillment of the radical needs of all. This chapter is an indication of how this work has begun, and why it needs to continue in a trans communist direction.

Notes

1. Susan Stryker, "My Words to Victor Frankenstein above the Village of Chamounix: Performing Transgender Rage," *GLQ*, 1:3 (1994), p. 238.
2. *Ibid.*, p. 243.
3. For an insightful genealogy of queer studies, see William Turner, *A Genealogy of Queer Theory* (Philadelphia: Temple University Press, 2000). For transgender studies, see Susan Stryker and Aren Aizura, "Introduction: Transgender Studies 2.0," in Susan Stryker and Aren Aizura (eds), *The Transgender Studies Reader 2* (London: Routledge, 2013), pp. 1–12.
4. Neda Atanasoski and Kalindi Vora, "Postsocialist Politics and the Ends of Revolution," *Social Identities*, 24:2 (2017), 139–154.
5. *Ibid.*, p. 141. For an insightful article discussing socialist anti-capitalist connections, see Nikolay R. Karkov and Zhivka Valiavicharska, "Rethinking East-European Socialism: Notes toward an Anti-Capitalist Decolonial Methodology," *Interventions*, 20 (2018), 785–813.
6. Atanasoski and Vora, "Postsocialist Politics," p. 141.
7. For a classic account of the conflict between sex and work, see Herbert Marcuse, *Eros and Civilization: A Philosophical Inquiry into Freud* (Boston, MA: Beacon Press, 1955). With "trans*," I follow Jack Halberstam, *Trans*: A Quick and Quirky Account of Gender Variability* (Berkeley: University of California Press, 2017), p. xiii, and his understanding that the term "trans*" "puts pressure on all modes of gender embodiment."
8. Atanasoski and Vora, "Postsocialist Politics," p. 141.
9. For important historical work on the connections between eastern European socialism and global capitalism, see Neda Atanasoski and Erin McElroy, "Postsocialism and the Afterlives of Revolution: Impossible Spaces of Dissent," in N. Pireddu (ed.), *Reframing Critical, Literary, and Cultural Theories* (London: Palgrave Macmillan, 2018), 273–297.
10. For Tony Shaw, *Hollywood's Cold War* (Edinburgh: Edinburgh University Press, 2007), p. 139, the film is part of a liberal dissidence against the Cold War.
11. With "trans*," I follow Jack Halberstam, *Trans*: A Quick and Quirky Account of Gender Variability* (Berkeley: University of California Press, 2017), p. xiii, and his understanding that the term "trans*" "puts pressure on all modes of gender embodiment."
12. Stryker, "My Words," p. 238.
13. *Ibid.*, p. 249.
14. Susan Stryker, "Transgender Studies: Queer Theory's Evil Twin," *GLQ*, 10:2 (2004), p. 214.

15 *Ibid.*
16 Dean Spade, *Normal Life: Administrative Violence, Critical Trans Politics, and the Limits of Law* (New York: South End Press, 2011), pp. 160–161.
17 Samuel Chambers, *The Lesson of Rancière* (London: Oxford University Press, 2013).
18 Jacques Rancière, *Disagreement: Politics and Philosophy*, trans. Julie Rose (Minnesota: University of Minnesota Press, 2010), p. 170.
19 Jacques Rancière, *The Method of Equality*, trans. Julie Rose (Cambridge: Polity Press, 2016), p. 113.
20 See Chambers, *The Lesson of Rancière*, p. 165.
21 *Ibid.*, p. 43.
22 *Ibid.*, p. 153.
23 Rancière explicitly theorizes politics as undermining "proper representation." See Rancière, *Disagreement*, p. 29.
24 Rancière cited in Chambers, *The Lesson of Rancière*, p. 29: "I mean equality not in any objective sense of status, income, function, or the supposedly 'equal' dynamics of contracts or reforms, nor as an explicit demand or a program, but rather as something that emerges in the course of the struggle and is verified subjectively, declared and experienced in the here and now as what is, and not what should be."
25 Timothy Mitchell, *Carbon Democracy: Political Power in the Age of Oil* (London: Verso, 2011), pp. 19–20.
26 *Ibid.*, p. 20.
27 *Ibid.*, p. 27.
28 The history of representing workers and socialists as threats is connected to the emergence of US cinema. For a history of representing strikes on US screens in the 1930s, see Russell Campbell, "Radical Cinema in the 1930s: The Film and Photo League," *Jump-Cut*, 14 (1985), 123–133.
29 See Victoria O'Donnell, "Science Fiction Films and Cold War Anxiety" (1990), *History of the American Cinema*, www.encyclopedia.com/arts/culture-magazines/science-fiction-films-and-cold-war-anxiety (accessed March 1, 2021): "In these films, aliens represent what some Americans feared about the Soviets. Invaders, friends or enemies, and often with the help of robots, either come to warn earthlings or to destroy them with superior technology. Sometimes the invaders use the strategy of infiltration, taking over the minds of the people, making slaves of them, or appropriating their bodies, thus making war unnecessary."
30 *Ibid.*

31 Susan Stryker, "*We Who Are Sexy*: Christine Jorgensen's Transsexual Whiteness in the Postcolonial Philippines," *Social Semiotics*, 19:1 (March 2009), 79–91.
32 Stryker, "My Words," p. 243.
33 See Chambers, *The Lesson of Rancière*, p. 9: "A radical democratic subject of politics does not just appear on the stage; it brings the stage into being."
34 *Ibid.*, p. 10.
35 José Esteban Muñoz, *Disidentifications: Queers of Colors and the Performance of Politics* (Minneapolis: University of Minnesota Press, 1999), p. 100.

9

The future of queer communism

This book sought to initiate a conversation between queer North American theory and the theoretical and artistic world of eastern Europe. I responded to David Eng and Jasbir Puar's invitation to move beyond the idea of a "proper" object of study in queer theory and concentrated on an ignored anti-capitalist world.[1] Rather than opposing eastern European Marxist and queer ideas, I drew on a materialist method to show how queer theory emerged in relation to Marxism-Leninism. I argued that a Marxist epistemology can offer queer theory not only a historical standpoint to understand its vocabulary, but also a new methodological orientation that is inspired by the world of eastern European socialism. Previous formulations of queer Marxism wanted to find shared points of contact by bringing western Marxism into queer studies. *De-centering Queer Theories* has a different goal. I want not merely to underscore the shared impulse for a total sexual critique, which, as Kevin Floyd has argued, exists both in Marxism and in queer theory.[2] I have not sought to criticize the reification of sexual identities, which have been included as valuable commodities on a global market. Rather, my book claims that the actualization of historical materialism in eastern Europe constitutes an important moment for understanding the development and the future of queer studies. I argue that queer theorists have incorporated many assumptions that are part of historical anti-communism in the USA. I have also shown how to bring together two conceptual projects that were theorized on conflicting epistemologies.

De-centering Queer Theory offers four directions for rethinking the field of queer theory. First, in a Marxist theory of communism, bodies and their sexualities constituted an important element for the future of human emancipation. For Soviet and eastern European theorists, communism cannot be achieved without abolishing a capitalist theory of bodies and sexual desires. This is a tremendous political intervention that has been ignored by scholars who sought to forge a queer Marxism from western theoretical resources. While the dialectical and historical philosophy of eastern European Marxism has been mostly ignored, it shows that a project of human emancipation is available to all, and is not only reserved for a minoritarian class of queer subjects. It centers on a theory of radical needs, such as education, health care and free time, which collide with a world dominated by private property.

This book suggests that eastern European Marxism offers a window onto what can come after the end of capitalism. In this respect, abolitionist eastern European theory shares, with a queer abolitionist project of dismantling the police and prisons, an interest in how to materialize a post-capitalist society; queer scholars who have contributed to the pathbreaking book *Captive Genders* underscore the close connection between abolishing gender norms and abolishing the prison industrial complex.[3] Yet, in adding to an impulse to recover radical histories and movements, this book provides the modality by which queer theory can be provincialized not only as a US-centric production but also as a particular development on the broader historical route to human emancipation. Marx and Engels advanced a historical method that can suggest that the defeat of socialism in eastern Europe may be a phase in a longer process of abolishing private property. In this respect, queer theory and its historical interventions actualize an emancipatory component that has its own contributions and drawbacks. Future research in queer theory might develop this argument further so that we can understand its potential for abolishing capitalism.

Second, the book calls for a centering of queer theory on a concept of materiality that not only has a subversive relation to capitalism, but is also based on a different conception of the human. The socialist person, as eastern European Marxists have imagined, should become a better human under a mode of production that promises a fuller and richer life. This is why the book appealed to an eastern European theoretical and art archive that described how this process of forging a communist person was achieved. As I argued in Chapter 6, the main difference from a queer of color analytic is that in an eastern European Marxism an entire production of material objects has been deployed against the theory of exchange value. Communist material objects were designed as counterfetishes: namely, they embodied a revolutionary struggle for a communist world. Eastern European Marxism contributed to the production of a world of objects that were designed as comrades on a path to emancipation, which embodies a different route that a queer reflection on materiality might take.

Scholars such as Rosemary Hennessy, Kevin Floyd and Petrus Liu have analyzed cultural objects and literary texts, but have stopped short of understanding the value of Marxist material objects that were aimed at building a communist world. Marxist films provide a historical narrative distinct from the conventional queer plot about sexuality. My analysis of *The District of Gaiety* reveals that a communist aesthetic of productivism was gradually replaced by conservative tropes of abortion in Romanian socialism. I also show that the Stalinist production *The Valley Resounds* underscores important connections between an anti-capitalist materiality and queer theory. I suggest that *The Cruise* captures an important moment in the life of Romanian State socialism, when socialist objects were considered failures in the achievement of communism. In contemporary circumstances, Marxist films circulate without the need to pay for access on YouTube, and are available use for free by artists and theorists. These objects show that it was possible to live in a world where the meaning of free commodity was not that one should not pay for it, but one must produce counterfetishes.

Third, the book seeks to part ways with a dominant understanding of the unconscious in queer theory, which distinguishes between psychology (e.g., unconscious desires) and the structure of capitalism (the material production of capitalism). The assumption that the unconscious by itself can serve as a site for liberation from capitalism has deeply affected queer theory. Kevin Floyd observed that psychoanalysis had an important impact on gay liberation, and in particular, Herbert Marcuse's idea that polymorphous desires are able to work against capitalism has been very influential.[4] This liberationist thesis is premised, however, on the assumption that unconscious desires are untouched by a capitalist mode of production. I am not the first to make this critique in queer studies. Rosemary Hennessy suggested that in the 1980s the gay left distinguished between cultural politics, including the use of psychoanalytic terms, and the structural analysis of capitalism.[5] As a result of this split, queer theory has inherited an understanding of the unconscious as unaffected by changes in capitalist production.[6]

Unlike previous critics, I drew on a Soviet Marxism's psychology to show that unconscious elements such as dreams and desires can lead to revolutionary actions. Eastern European Marxism offers an important ideological challenge to the thesis that unconscious productions such as sexual desires and dreams are, as such, a site of resistance to capitalism. By acknowledging that they are a product of capitalism, I claimed that this mutual interdependence is not only troubling, but that it can also generate a new anti-capitalist politics. I read Jean Laplanche's idea of enigmatic messages through a Marxist lens and argued that the unconscious can be a resource for economic struggles against exploitation. More specifically, I analyzed tactics of unconscious rebellion as they are depicted in a Soviet film that shows how Roma outlaws survive a post-abolitionist mid-nineteenth-century Romania. In short, my argument is that anti-slavery practices can emerge from unconscious dynamics, but that they need to be inserted into a Marxist model of human emancipation.

Finally, none of the previous works in queer studies have paid attention to the relation between eastern Europe and the emergence of categories of sexuality. While my book concentrates on eastern European Marxism, a queer communist analytic needs to address the role of anti-communism in the Anglo-American world. Rather than thinking that eastern European Marxism was relevant only to eastern Europe, I showed that trans politics and Marxist politics share a common critical project in the United States. By using a dialectical method, I connected histories of anti-communism with anti-trans politics to highlight the historical links between the fear of gender monstrosity and communism.

Transgender studies need deeper materialist histories that move beyond their narrow focus on bodies and sexuality. Such a move can counter current developments: namely, that transgender politics is becoming highly visible because it is inflected primarily by a philosophy of individual liberation. Historical materialism can reveal how collective trans politics can put into practice the struggle against economic exploitation and genderism. I suggested that the historical connection between anti-trans politics and anti-communism has to be further investigated. In eastern Europe, as in the USA, one of the main electoral ideological divides appears to have been organized around non-normative sexuality and gender. Currently, rhetoric against trans politics is deployed as part of the "nation first" ideology. "Hungary first" and "Romania first" have become acceptable slogans of the new anti-trans and anti-migration politics. A current important divide between conservative and progressive liberals is whether they embrace LGBT politics, with a particular focus on trans politics. Elections and laws in Poland, Russia, Hungary and Romania show that this divide continues to solidify, provided that more progressive liberals will defend the acceptance of minoritarian sexual groups.[7] In response to anti-trans politics, the book traces a historical connection where trans sex workers and immigrant postsocialist bodies shared a common world of exploitation.

In the Anglo-American context, queer liberalism was successful because it asserted an alleged civilizational superiority that saw non-western countries as located in backward modernity.[8] As Puar argued, the success of queer liberals was based on a right to maim, to debilitate racialized non-western populations with the goal of promoting a biopolitical logic of security.[9] The alleged success of queer liberals in eastern Europe derives from an attempt to erase the infrastructure and theoretical production of eastern European Marxism. Historical socialism seems to have become the main enemy of liberal democracies in eastern Europe. It is not the only threat, however, and other foreign ideas such as gender theory are considered to be menacing the postsocialist order. I am writing this last part of the book in 2020, when in Bucharest the mainstream conservative press has intensified its criticism of political correctness and gender ideology.[10] The press uncovers these two dangers as emerging from the totalitarian nature of communism. A law banning gender theory from the educational system has been passed by Romanian legislative bodies but has been contested by the president on the grounds of unconstitutionality.[11] The leading public arguments against the ban have come from underfunded LGBT associations, which appeal to the value of freedom and free speech to defend the lives of non-conforming trans and queer people. What critics and defenders of gender identities have in common is that they both see communism as the main ideological adversary. The

LGBT organizations see socialism as a dark period that repressed non-normative sexualities, while the conservative critics see communism as the starting point of gender ideology.[12] Advocates of LGBT argue primarily on the grounds that non-normative sexuality should be tolerated as the option of a minority. In its rejection of communism, a new homonormativity emerges that privatizes the sexual according to formulas such as "queer people just want to love each other."

Simply put, global anti-communism has advanced American liberal politics as the territory of discursive opposition to eastern European Marxism. This book's warning is that many threads in queer studies – if not all, given its predominantly Anglo-American focus and audience – may solidify this dynamic rather than undermine it. The future of queer communism, if it has one, is necessarily attached to a dialectical method that builds on the experiences and lives of eastern European people.

Notes

1 See David L. Eng, and Jasbir K. Puar, "Introduction: Left of Queer," *Social Text*, 38:4 (December 2020), p. 16, for queer theory as "objectless critique."
2 Kevin Floyd, *The Reification of Desire: Toward a Queer Marxism* (Minneapolis: University of Minnesota Press, 2009), p. 6.
3 See Eric A. Stanley and Nat Smith (eds), *Captive Genders: Trans Embodiment and the Prison Industrial Complex* (Edinburgh: AK Press, 2011).
4 Marcuse cited in Floyd, *The Reification of Desire*, p. 123.
5 Rosemary Hennessy, *Profit and Pleasure: Sexual Identities in Late Capitalism* (New York: Routledge, 2000), pp. 49–52.
6 Hennessy, *Profit and Pleasure*, p. 52.
7 Mark Gevisser, "Duda's Victory in Poland Helps Draw a 'Pink Line' through Europe," *Guardian*, July 17, 2020, www.theguardian.com/commentisfree/2020/jul/17/duda-victory-poland-europe-putin-orban-polish-lgbt (accessed July 31, 2020).
8 Brit Dawson, "How the UK and US are Rolling Back Vital Trans Rights," *Dazedigital*, June 2020, www.dazeddigital.com/politics/article/49531/1/how-the-uk-and-us-are-rolling-back-vital-trans-rights-donald-trump-boris-johnson (accessed August 28, 2020).

9 See Jasbir K. Puar, *The Right to Maim: Debility, Capacity, Disability* (Durham, NC: Duke University Press, 2017), p. x.
10 See Alexandru Lăzescu, "Gender Studies and the Thought Police" ("StudiiledeGenșipolițiaGândirii"),*Contributors.ro*,www.contributors. ro/studiile-de-gen-și-poliția-gindirii/ (accessed June 30, 2020).
11 Vic Parsons, "It Will Soon Be Illegal to Even Discuss Being Trans in Romanian Schools," *Pinknews*, www.pinknews.co.uk/2020/06/ 26/romania-trans-promotion-gender-identity-banned-schools-klausiohannis/ (accessed July 27, 2020).
12 Florin Buhuceanu, "Homoconspiracy," *Dilema veche*, December 14 2019, https://dilemaveche.ro/sectiune/dileme-on-line/articol/ homoconspiratia (accessed August 28, 2020).

Bibliography

Films

Czechoslovakia

Sun in the Net (*Slnko v sieti*, Uher, 1963)

Hungary

Angi Vera (Gábor, 1979)
Another Way (*Egymásra nézve*, Makk, 1982)

Romania

The Cruise (*Croaziera*, Danieliuc, 1980)
The District of Gaiety (Marcus, *Cartierul veseliei*, 1964)
Impossible Love (*Imposibila iubire*, Vaeni, 1983)
Love and Revolution (*Dragostea și Revoluția*, Vitanidis, 1982)
The Man Next to You (*Omul de lângă tine*, Popescu, 1961)
Postcards with Wild Flowers (*Ilustrate cu flori de câmp*, Blaier, 1975)
The Snowstorm (*Vifornița*, Moldovan, 1973)
The Valley Resounds (*Răsună Valea*, Călinescu, 1949)
Virgo (*Zodia Fecioarei*, Marcus, 1966)

United States

Bolshevism on Trial (Knowles, 1919)
Rebel without a Cause (Ray, 1955)
The Right to Happiness (Holubar, 1919)
Strangers on a Train (Hitchcock, 1951)
Tangerine (Baker, 2015)

Bibliography 227

USSR

Alone (*Odna*, Kozintsev and Trauber, 1931)
Battleship Potemkin (*Bronenosets Potyomkin*, Eisenstein, 1925)
Bed and Sofa (*The Third Meschanskaya*, Room, 1927)
Chapaev (Furmanov, 1934)
Dream (*Mechta*, Romm, 1943)
The Fiddlers (*Lăutarii*, Loteanu, 1972)
New Babylon (Kozintsev and Trauberg, 1929)
The Parisian Cobbler (*Parizhskii sapozhnik*, Ermler, 1929)

Books and articles

Ahuja, Neel. *Bioinsecurities: Disease Interventions, Empire, and the Government of Species* (Durham, NC: Duke University Press, 2016).
Amadae, S. M. *Rationalizing Capitalist Democracy: The Cold War Origins of Rational Choice Liberalism* (Chicago: University of Chicago Press, 2003).
Anderson, Warwick, Deborah Jenson and Richard Keller (eds), *Unconscious Dominions: Psychoanalysis, Colonial Trauma, and Global Sovereignties* (Durham, NC: Duke University Press, 2011).
Arvatov, Boris. *Art and Production*. Ed. John Roberts and Alexei Penzin, trans. Shushan Avagyan (London: Pluto Press, 2017).
Asavei, Alina. "Rewriting the Canon of Communist Visual Art." M.A. dissertation (Budapest: Central European University, 2007), www.etd.ceu.edu/2007/asavei_maria.pdf (accessed June 10, 2019).
Ashtor, Gila. "The Ideology of Transference: Laplanche and Affect Theory," *Studies in Gender and Sexuality*, 19:2 (2018), 89–105.
Atanasoski, Neda and Erin McElroy. "Postsocialism and the Afterlives of Revolution: Impossible Spaces of Dissent." In N. Pireddu (ed.), *Reframing Critical, Literary, and Cultural Theories* (London: Palgrave Macmillan, 2018), 273–297.
Atanasoski, Neda and Kalindi Vora. "Postsocialist Politics and the Ends of Revolution," *Social Identities*, 24:2 (2017), 139–154.
Badiou, Alain. *The Communist Hypothesis* (London: Verso, 2010).
Bahun, Sanja and John Haynes. *Cinema, State Socialism and Society in the Soviet Union and Eastern Europe, 1917–1989* (London: Routledge, 2014).
Baker, Catherine. *Race and the Yugoslav Region: Postsocialist, Post-Conflict, Postcolonial?* (Manchester: Manchester University Press, 2018).
Baker, Catherine. "Wild Dances and Dying Wolves: Simulation, Essentialization, and National Identity at the Eurovision Song Contest," *Popular Communication*, 6:3 (2008), 173–189.
Bao, Hongwei. *Gay Identity and Tongzhi Activism in Postsocialist China* (Copenhagen: NIAS Press, 2018).

Barad, Karen. "Troubling Time/s and Ecologies of Nothingness: Re-Turning, Re-Membering, and Facing the Incalculable," *New Formations*, 92 (2017), 56–86.
Baraitser, Lisa. *Enduring Time* (London: Bloomsbury, 2017).
Barr, Murray and Michael Bertram. "A Morphological Distinction between Neurones of the Male and Female and the Behavior of the Nuclear Satellite during Accelerated Nucleoprotein Synthesis." *Nature*, 163 (1949), 676–677.
Beck, John and Ryan Bishop. "Introduction: The Long Cold War," in John Beck and Ryan Bishop (eds), *Cold War Legacies* (Edinburgh: Edinburgh University Press, 2016), 1–32.
Beckert, Sven. *Empire of Cotton: A Global History* (New York: Knopf, 2014).
Belich, James. *Replenishing the Earth. The Settler Revolution and the Rise of the Anglo World, 1783–1939* (Oxford: Oxford University Press, 2009).
Benjamin, Walter. *Illuminations: Essays and Reflections* (New York: Schocken, 2007).
Berdhal, Daphne. "'(N)Ostalgie' for the Present: Memory, Longing, and East German Things," *Ethnos*, 64:2 (1999), 192–211.
Berger, Peter and Thomas Luckmann. *The Social Construction of Reality: A Treatise in the Sociology of Knowledge* (London: Penguin, 1966).
Bersani, Leo. *"Is the Rectum a Grave?" and Other Essays* (Chicago: Chicago University Press, 2009).
Bhambra, Gurminder K. *Rethinking Modernity: Postcolonialism and the Sociological Imagination* (New York: Palgrave Macmillan, 2007).
Bogdanov, Alexander. "What Is Organization Science?" ("Ocherki organizatsionnoi nauki"), *Proletarskaya kul'tura*, 7/8 (April–May 1919), https://en.wikipedia.org/wiki/Alexander_Bogdanov (accessed April 2, 2020).
Brooks, Daphne. *Bodies in Dissent: Spectacular Performances of Race and Freedom 1850–1910* (Durham, NC: Duke University Press, 2006).
Brown, Wendy and Janet E. Halley. *Left Legalism/Left Critique* (Durham, NC: Duke University Press, 2002).
Buden, Boris. "Children of Postcommunism," *Radical Philosophy*, January–February 2021, www.radicalphilosophy.com/article/children-of-postcommunism (accessed February 24, 2021).
Buden, Boris. *Zonă de trecere: Despre sfârșitul post-communismului*. Trans. Maria-Magdalena Anghelescu, preface by Costi Rogozanu (Cluj: Tact, 2012).
Buhuceanu, Florin. "Homoconspiracy," *Dilema veche*, December 14 2019, https://dilemaveche.ro/sectiune/dileme-on-line/articol/homoconspiratia (accessed August 28, 2020).
Butler, Judith. "Critically Queer," *GLQ*, 1:1 (1993), 17–32.
Butler, Judith. *Gender Trouble: Feminism and the Subversion of Identity* (London: Routledge, 1999).
Butler, Judith. *Giving an Account of Oneself* (New York: Fordham University Press, 2005).

Bibliography

Butler, Judith. "Merely Cultural," *New Left Review*, 1:227 (January–February 1998), 33–45.

Campbell, Russell. "Radical Cinema in the 1930s: The Film and Photo League," *Jump-Cut*, 14 (1985), 123–133.

Carleton, Gregory. *Sexual Revolution in Bolshevik Russia* (Pittsburgh, PA: University of Pittsburgh Press, 2005).

Chambers, Samuel. *The Lesson of Rancière* (London: Oxford University Press, 2013).

Chelcea, Liviu and Oana Druţă. "Zombie Socialism and the Rise of Neoliberalism in Post-Socialist Central and Eastern Europe," *Eurasian Geography and Economics*, 57:4–5 (2016), 521–544.

Chirot, Daniel. "Social Change in Communist Romania," *Social Forces*, 57:2 (1978), 457–499.

Chukhrov, Keti. *Practicing the Good: Desire and Boredom in Soviet Socialism* (Minneapolis: University of Minnesota Press, 2020).

Chukhrov, Keti, Alexei Penzin, and Valeri Podoroga, "Marx against Marxism, Marxism against Marx," *Stasis*, 5:2 (2017), 268–288.

Cistelecan, Alex and Andrei State. *Plante exotice: Teoria şi practica marxiştilor români* (Cluj-Napoca: Tact, 2015).

Connolly, Brian and Marisa Fuentes. "Introduction: From Archives of Slavery to Liberated Futures?," *History of the Present: A Journal of Critical History*, 6:2 (2016), 105–116.

Corber, Robert J. *In the Name of National Security: Hitchcock, Homophobia, and the Political Construction of Gender in Postwar America* (Durham, NC: Duke University Press, 1993).

Crawford, Lucas Cassidy. "Transgender without Organs? Mobilizing a Geoaffective Theory of Gender Modification, in Susan Stryker and Aren Aizura (eds), *The Transgender Studies Reader 2* (London: Routledge, 2013), pp. 473–482.

Dawson, Brit. "How the UK and US are Rolling Back Vital Trans Rights," *Dazedigital*, June 2020, www.dazeddigital.com/politics/article/49531/1/how-the-uk-and-us-are-rolling-back-vital-trans-rights-donald-trump-boris-johnson (acessed August 28, 2020).

Dayan, Joan. *Haiti, History and the Gods* (Berkeley: University of California Press, 1998).

De Lauretis, Teresa. "Queer Theory. Lesbian and Gay Sexualities: An Introduction," *Differences: A Journal of Feminist Cultural Studies*, special issue, 3:2 (1991), iii–xviii.

Dean, Robert D. *Imperial Brotherhood: Gender and the Making of Cold War Foreign Policy* (Amherst: University of Massachusetts Press, 2002).

Dean, Tim. "Uses of Perversity: Commentary on Saketopoulou's 'To Suffer Pleasure,'" *Studies in Gender and Sexuality*, 15:4 (2014), 269–277.

Debord, Guy. "Report on the Construction of Situations and on the International Situationist Tendency's Conditions of Organization and Action." *Situationist International Online* (1957), www.cddc.vt.edu/sionline/si/report.html (accessed April 18, 2020).

Debord, Guy and Gil Wolman. "A User's Guide to Détournement." *Les lèvres nues*, 8 (1956), www.cddc.vt.edu/sionline/presitu/usersguide.html (accessed August 14, 2020).

Delton, Jennifer. *Rethinking the 1950s: How Anticommunism and the Cold War Made America Liberal* (Cambridge: Cambridge University Press, 2013).

Derrida, Jacques. *Specters of Marx: The State of the Debt, the Work of Mourning, and the New International* (New York: Routledge, 2011).

Dinshaw, Carolyn. *Queer/Early/Modern* (Durham, NC: Duke Univesity Press, 2006).

Dobrenko, Evgeny. *Stalinist Cinema and the Production of History: Museum of the Revolution* (Edinburgh: Edinburgh University Press, 2008).

Dumančić, Marko. "Hidden in Plain Sight: The Histories of Gender and Sexuality during the Cold War." in Philip E. Muehlenbeck (ed.), *Gender, Sexuality and the Cold War: A Global Perspective* (Nashville: Vanderbilt University Press, 2017).

Dumančić, Marko. "Spectrums of Oppression: Gender and Sexuality during the Cold War," *Journal of Cold War Studies*, 16:3 (2014), 190–204.

Dzenovska, Dace and Larisa Kurtović. "Introduction: Lessons for Liberalism from the 'Illiberal East,'" *Cultural Anthropology*, April 25 2018, https://culanth.org/fieldsights/1421-introduction-lessons-for-liberalism-from-the-illiberal-east (accessed April 4, 2020).

Editors of *Encyclopaedia Briannica*, 'Imprimatur.'" *Britannica* (2020), www.britannica.com/topic/imprimatur (accessed April 11, 2020).

El Tayeb, Fatima. *European Other: Queening Ethnicity in Postnational Europe* (Minneapolis: University of Minnesota Press, 2011).

Eng, David, José Muñoz and Jack Halberstam. "What Is Queer about Queer Studies Now?," *Social Text*, 23:3–4 (2005), 1–17.

Eng, David L. and Jasbir K. Puar, "Introduction: Left of Queer," *Social Text*, 38:4 (December 2020), 1–23.

Engebretsen, Elisabeth L. *Queer Women in Urban China: An Ethnography* (London: Routledge, 2013).

Ferguson, Roderick. *Aberrations in Black: Toward a Queer Critique of Color* (Minneapolis: University of Minnesota Press, 2003).

Ferguson, Roderick. *The Reordering of Things: The University and Its Pedagogy of Minority Differences* (Minneapolis: University of Minnesota Press, 2012).

Fischel, Joseph. *Sex and Harm in the Age of Consent* (Minneapolis: University of Minnesota Press, 2016).

Floyd, Kevin. *The Reification of Desire: Toward a Queer Marxism* (Minneapolis: University of Minnesota Press, 2009).

Foucault, Michel. *The History of Sexuality*, Vol. I, *An Introduction*. Trans. Robert Hurley (New York: Pantheon, 1978).

Foucault, Michel. "Preface." In Gilles Deleuze and Felix Guattari, *Anti-Oedipus: Capitalism and Schizophrenia* (Minneapolis: University of Minnesota Press, 1983), xi–xiv.

Gare, Arran. "Aleksandr Bogdanov: Proletkult and Conservation." *Capitalism, Nature, Socialism*, 5:2 (1994), 65–94.
Gevisser, Mark. "Duda's Victory in Poland Helps Draw a 'Pink Line' through Europe," *Guardian*, July 17, 2020, www.theguardian.com/commentisfree/2020/jul/17/duda-victory-poland-europe-putin-orban-polish-lgbt (accessed July 31, 2020).
Gilroy, Paul. *There Ain't No Black in the Union Jack: The Cultural Politics of Race and Nation* (London: Hutchinson, 1987).
Goldiş, Alex. "The Ideology of Semiosis in Romanian Prose under Communism," *Primerjalna književnost*, 39:2 (2016), 89–100.
Green, Richard. "Robert Stoller's Sex and Gender: 40 Years On," *Archives of Sexual Behaviour*, 39 (2010), 1457–1465.
Groys, Boris. *Art Power* (Cambridge, MA: MIT Press, 2008).
Groys, Boris. "The Cold War between the Medium and the Message: Western Modernism vs. Socialist Realism," *eflux*, 104 (2019), www.e-flux.com/journal/104/297103/the-cold-war-between-the-medium-and-the-message-western-modernism-vs-socialist-realism/ (accessed April 18, 2020).
Groys, Boris. *The Communist Hypothesis*. Trans. Thomas H. Ford (London: Verso, 2009).
Groys, Boris. *In the Flow* (London: Verso, 2016).
Groys, Boris. "A Style and a Half: Socialist Realism between Modernism and Post-Modernism," in Thomas Lahusen and Evgeny Dobrenko (eds), *Socialist Realism without Shores* (Durham, NC: Duke University Press, 1995), 76–91.
Groys, Boris. *The Total Art of Stalinism: Avant-Garde, Aesthetic Dictatorship, and Beyond*. Trans. Charles Rougle (Princeton: Princeton University Press, 1992).
Gržinić, Marina. *Fiction Reconstructed: Eastern Europe, Post-Socialism, and the Retro-Avant-Garde* (Vienna: Edition Selene, 2000).
Halberstam, Jack. *Trans*: A Quick and Quirky Account of Gender Variability* (Berkeley: University of California Press, 2017).
Hartmann, Saidiya. *Scenes of Subjection: Terror, Slavery and Self-Making in Nineteenth-Century America* (Oxford: Oxford University Press, 1997).
Hartmann, Saidiya. "Venus in Two Acts," *Small Axe*, 12:2 (2008), 1–14.
Hayles, Katherine. *How We Became Posthuman: Virtual Bodies in Cybernetics, Literature and Informatics* (Chicago: University of Chicago Press, 1999).
Heller, Agnes, *The Theory of Need in Marx* (London: Allison and Busby, 1973).
Healey, Dan. *Sexual and Gender Dissent: Homosexuality as Resistance in Stalin's Russia* (Ithaca: Cornell University Press, 2002).
Henderson, Kevin. "Becoming Lesbian: Monique Wittig's Queer-Trans-Feminism," *Journal of Lesbian Studies*, 22:2 (2018), 185–203.
Hennessey, Rosemary. *Profit and Pleasure: Sexual Identities in Late Capitalism* (New York: Routledge, 2000).

Herzog, Dagmar. *Cold War Freud: Psychoanalysis in the Age of Catastrophes* (Cambridge: Cambridge University Press, 2017).
Herzog, Dagmar. *Sex after Fascism: Memory and Morality in Twentieth-Century Germany* (Princeton: Princeton University Press, 2005).
Herzog, Dagmar. *Sexuality in Europe: A Twentieth-Century History* (Cambridge: Cambridge University Press, 2011).
Herzog, Dagmar. *Unlearning Eugenics: Sexuality, Reproduction, and Disability in Post-Nazi Europe* (Madison: University of Wisconsin Press, 2018).
Hoffman, David L. *Stalinist Values: The Cultural Norms of Soviet Modernity, 1917–1941* (Ithaca: Cornell University Press, 2018).
Horne, Gerald. *The Apocalypse of Settler Colonialism* (New York: Monthly Review Press, 2018).
Imre, Anikó. *A Companion to Eastern European Cinemas* (London: Wiley-Blackwell, 2012).
Iriye, Akira and Pierre-Yves Saunier. "Introduction: The Professor and the Madman," in Akira Iriye and Pierre-Yves Saunier (eds), *The Palgrave Dictionary of Transnational History* (London: Palgrave Macmillan, 2009), xvii–xx.
Isaac, Joel and Duncan Bell. "Introduction," in Joel Isaac and Duncan Bell (eds), *Uncertain Empire: American History and the Idea of Cold War* (Oxford: Oxford University Press, 2012).
Jakovljevic, Branislav. *Alienation Effects: Performance and Self-Management in Yugoslavia, 1945–91* (Ann Arbor: University of Michigan Press, 2016).
James, C. Vaughan. *Soviet Socialist Realism: Origins and Theory* (London: Palgrave Macmillan, 1973).
Karkov, Nicolay R. and Zhivka Valiavicharska. "Rethinking East-European Socialism: Notes toward an Anti-Capitalist Decolonial Methodology," *Interventions*, 20 (2018), 785–813.
Kellner, Douglas. *Herbert Marcuse and the Crisis of Marxism* (London: Macmillan, 1984).
Kepley, Vance, Jr. "*Intolerance* and the Soviets: A Historical Investigation," in Richard Taylor and Ian Christie (eds), *Inside the Film Factory: New Approaches to Russian and Soviet Cinema* (London: Routledge, 1991), 51–61.
Kiaer, Christina. *Imagine No Possessions: The Socialist Objects of Russian Constructivism* (Cambridge, MA: MIT Press, 2008).
Kirn, Gal. "Between Socialist Modernization and Cinematic Modernism: The Revolutionary Politics of Aesthetics of Medvedkin's Cinema-Train," in Ewa Mazierska and Lars Kristensen (eds), *Marxism and Film Activism: Screening Alternative Worlds* (New York: Berghahn, 2018), 29–57.
Klein, Christina. *Cold War Orientalism: Asia in the Middlebrow Imagination* (Berkeley: University of California Press, 2003).
Kligman, Gail. *Politica duplicității: Controlul reproducerii in România lui Ceaușescu* (Bucharest: Humanitas, 2000).

Kligman, Gail and Susan Gal (eds). *The Politics of Gender after Socialism: A Comparative-Historical Essay* (Princeton: Princeton University Press, 2000).
Kuhar, Roman and David Paternotte (eds). *Anti-Gender Campaigns in Europe: Mobilizing against Equality* (London: Rowman & Littlefield, 2017).
Kulpa, Robert. "Western Leveraged Pedagogy of Central and Eastern Europe: Discourses of Homophobia, Tolerance and Nationhood," *Gender, Place and Culture: A Journal of Feminist Geography*, 21:4 (2014), 431–448.
Kulpa, Robert and Joanna Mizielińska. *De-Centering Western Sexualities* (Farnham: Ashgate, 2011).
Kuznick, Peter J. and James Gilbert. "US Culture and the Cold War," in Peter J. Kuznick and James Gilbert (eds), *Rethinking Cold War Culture* (Washington, DC: Smithsonian, 2010), 1–13.
Laplanche, Jean. *Essays on Otherness* (London: Routledge, 1999).
Laplanche, Jean. "Gender, Sex, and the Sexual," trans. Susan Fairfield, *Studies in Gender and Sexuality*, 8:2 (2007), 201–219.
Lăzescu, Alexandru. "Gender Studies and the Thought Police" ("Studiile de Gen și poliția Gândirii"), *Contributors.ro*, www.contributors.ro/studiile-de-gen-și-poliția-gindirii (accessed June 30, 2020).
Lenin, Vladimir Ilyich. *The Development of Capitalism in Russia*, Marxists Internet Archive (1964), www.marxists.org/archive/lenin/works/1899/devel/index.htm#Chapter7 (accessed April 4, 2020).
Liu, Petrus. *Queer Marxism in Two Chinas* (Durham, NC: Duke University Press, 2015).
Liu, Petrus. "Queer Theory and the Specter of Materialism," *Social Text*, 38:4 (2020), 25–47.
Lott, Eric. *Black Mirror: The Cultural Contradictions of American Racism* (Cambridge, MA: Harvard University Press, 2017).
Lugones, Maria. "Heterosexualism and the Colonial/Modern Gender System." *Hypatia*, 22:1 (2007), 186–209.
Lugones, Maria. "Toward a Decolonial Feminism." *Hypatia*, 25:4 (2010), 742–759.
Lukács, Mihai. "Roma Slave Jesters: The Origins of Theater in Wallachia and Moldavia." *Romarchive* (2018), www.romarchive.eu/en/theatre-and-drama/roma-slave-jesters/ (accessed August 6, 2020).
Mai, Joseph. *Jean-Pierre and Luc Dardenne* (Urbana: University of Illinois Press, 2010).
Marcuse, Herbert. *Eros and Civilization: A Philosophical Inquiry into Freud* (Boston, MA: Beacon Press, 1955).
Marx, Karl. *Economic and Philosophic Manuscripts of 1844*, www.marxists.org/archive/marx/works/1844/manuscripts/comm.htm (accessed April 18, 2020).
Marx, Karl. "Preface," in *A Contribution to the Critique of Political Economy*, trans S. W. Ryazanskaya (Moscow: Progress, 1993),

www.marxists.org/archive/marx/works/1859/critique-pol-economy/preface.htm (accessed February 22, 2021).

Marx, Karl and Friedrich Engels. *The German Ideology*, www.marxists.org/archive/marx/works/1845/german-ideology/ch01a.htm (accessed April 18, 2020).

Masco, Joseph. "Engineering the Future as Nuclear Ruin," in Ann Laura Stoler (ed.), *Imperial Debris: On Ruins and Ruination* (Durham, NC: Duke University Press, 2013), 252–287.

Mateescu, Oana. "The Romanian Family Referendum; or, How I Became a Sexo-Marxist," *Focaalblog*, October 23, 2018, www.focaalblog.com/2018/10/23/oana-mateescu-the-romanian-family-referendum-or-how-i-became-a-sexo-marxist/ (accessed February 24, 2020).

Mbembe, Achille. "Necropolitics," In Timothy Campbell and Adam Sitze (eds), *Biopolitics: A Reader* (Durham, NC: Duke University Press, 2013).

McCumber, John. *Time in the Ditch: American Philosophy and the McCarthy Era* (Evanston: Northwestern University Press, 2001).

McLellan, Josie. *Love in the Time of Communism: Love and Intimacy in the GDR* (Cambridge: Cambridge University Press, 2011).

Medevoi, Leerom. "The Race War Within: The Biopolitics of the Long Cold War," in Steven Belletto and Daniel Grausam (eds), *American Literature and Culture in an Age of Cold War: A Critical Reassessment* (Iowa City: University of Iowa Press, 2012), 163–186.

Medevoi, Leerom. *Rebels: Youth and the Cold War Origins of Identity* (Durham, NC: Duke University Press, 2005).

Meyerowitz, Joanne. *How Sex Changed: A History of Transsexuality in the United States*. (Cambridge, MA: Harvard University Press, 2002).

Middleton, John. "'Bolshevism in Art': Dada and Politics." *Texas Studies in Literature and Language*, 4:3 (1962), 408–430.

Mieli, Marco. *Homosexuality and Liberation: Elements of a Gay Critique*. Trans. David Fernbach (London: Gay Men's Press, 1980).

Miller, Martin. "Freudian Theory under Bolshevik Rule: The Theoretical Controversy during the 1920s," *Slavic Review*, 44:4 (Winter 1985), 625–646.

Mitchell, Juliet. *Siblings* (Cambridge: Polity Press, 2003).

Mitchell, Timothy. *Carbon Democracy: Political Power in the Age of Oil* (London: Verso, 2011).

Money, John. "Dyslexia: A Postconference Review," in John Money (ed.), *Reading Disability: Progress and Research Needs in Dyslexia* (Baltimore: Johns Hopkins University Press, 1962), 9–35.

Money, John. *Love and Love Sickness: The Science of Sex, Gender Difference, and Pair-Bonding* (Baltimore: Johns Hopkins University Press, 1980).

Money, John and Anke A. Ehrhardt. *Man & Woman, Boy & Girl: Gender Identity from Conception to Maturity* (Baltimore: Johns Hopkins University Press, 1972).

Bibliography

Money, John and J. L. Hampson. "Imprinting and the Establishment of Gender Role," *AMA Archives of Neurology and Psychiatry*, 77 (1957), 333–336.
Moten, Fred. *Black and Blur* (Durham, NC: Duke University Press, 2017).
Moten, Fred. *In the Break: The Aesthetic of the Black Radical Tradition* (Minneapolis: University of Minnesota Press, 2003).
Muñoz, José Esteban. *Cruising Utopia: The Then and There of Queer Futurity* (New York: New York University Press, 2009).
Muñoz, José Esteban. *Disidentifications: Queers of Colors and the Performance of Politics* (Minneapolis: University of Minnesota Press, 1999).
Naiman, Eric. *Sex in Public: The Incarnation of Early Soviet Ideology* (Princeton: Princeton University Press, 1997).
"National Security Council Report, NSC 68, 'United States Objectives and Programs for National Security,'" Wilson Center Digital Archive, https://digitalarchive.wilsoncenter.org/document/116191.pdf?v=2699956db534c1821edefa61b8c13ffe (accessed May 8, 2020).
O'Donnell, Victoria. "Science Fiction Films and Cold War Anxiety" (1990), *History of the American Cinema*, www.encyclopedia.com/arts/culture-magazines/science-fiction-films-and-cold-war-anxiety (accessed March 1, 2021).
Olssen, Mark. "Foucault and Marxism: Rewriting the Theory of Historical Materialism," *Policy Futures in Education*, 2:3–4 (2004), 454–482.
Olusoga, David. *Black and British: A Forgotten History* (London: Macmillan, 2016).
Oushakine, Serguei Alex. "'Against the Cult of Things': On Soviet Productivism, Storage Economy, and Commodities with No Destination," *Russian Review*, 73 (April 2014), 198–236.
Oushakine, Serguei Alex. *The Patriotism of Despair: Nation, War and Loss in Russia* (Ithaca: Cornell University Press, 2009).
Parsons, Vic. "It Will Soon Be Illegal to Even Discuss Being Trans in Romanian Schools," *Pinknews*, www.pinknews.co.uk/2020/06/26/romania-trans-promotion-gender-identity-banned-schools-klaus-iohannis/ (accessed July 27, 2020).
Parvulescu, Anca and Manuela Boatcă. "The *Longue Durée* of Enslavement: Extracting Labor from Romani Music in Liviu Rebreanu's *Ion*," *Literature Compass*, 17:1–2 (2020), https://doi.org/10.1111/lic3.12559 (accessed July 11, 2021).
Pârvulescu, Constantin. *Orphans of the East: Postwar Eastern European Cinema and the Revolutionary Subject* (Bloomington: Indiana University Press, 2015).
Pavlidis, Periklis. "Socialism, Labour and Education: From Marx to Makarenko," *International Journal of Educational Policies*, 11:1 (2017), 3–16.

Popa, Bogdan. "Shame and Cognitive Strikes: What Would It 'Really' Mean for Queer Psychoanalysis to Enter the Perverse?," *Studies in Gender and Sexuality*, 19:2 (2017), 145–156.
Preciado, Paul. *Pornotopia: Arquitectura y sexualidad en "Playboy" durante la Guerra Fria* (Barcelona: Anagrama, 2010).
Prisching, Manfred. "Why Are Peter L. Berger and Thomas Luckmann Austrians?," in Michaela Pfadenhaue and Hubert Knoblauch (eds), *Social Constructivism as Paradigm? The Legacy of the Social Construction of Reality* (London: Routledge, 2018).
Puar, Jasbir K. "'I would rather be a cyborg than a goddess': Intersectionality, Assemblage, and Affective Politics," *transversal texts* (2011), https://transversal.at/transversal/0811/puar/en (accessed August 28, 2020).
Puar, Jasbir K. "Rethinking Homonationalism," *International Journal of Middle East Studies*, 45:2 (2013), 336–339.
Puar, Jasbir K. *The Right to Maim: Debility, Capacity, Disability* (Durham, NC: Duke University Press, 2017).
Raha, Nat. "The Limits of Trans Liberalism," *Verso Books* (2015), www.versobooks.com/blogs/2245-the-limits-of-trans-liberalism-by-nat-raha, (accessed April 5, 2020).
Rancière, Jacques. *Disagreement: Politics and Philosophy*. Trans. Julie Rose (Minnesota: University of Minnesota Press, 2010).
Rancière, Jacques. "L'image fraternelle: Entretien avec Jacques Rancière," *Cahiers du cinéma*, 268–269 (1976), 7–19.
Rancière, Jacques. *The Method of Equality*. Trans. Julie Rose (Cambridge: Polity Press, 2016).
Repo, Jemima. *The Biopolitics of Gender* (Oxford: Oxford University Press, 2015).
Rifkin, Mark. *When Did Indians Become Straight? Kinship, the History of Sexuality, and Native Sovereignty* (Oxford: Oxford University Press, 2011).
Robinson, Cedric J. *Black Marxism: The Formation of the Black Radical Tradition* (Chapel Hill: North Carolina University Press, 2000).
Rosenberg, Jordana and Amy Villarejo, "Queerness, Norms, Utopia," *GLQ*, 18:1 (2011), 1–18.
Ross, Marlon. "Beyond the Closet as Raceless Paradigm," in E. P. Johnson and M. G. Henderson (eds), *Black Queer Studies: A Critical Anthology* (Durham, NC: Duke University Press, 2005), 161–189.
Rubin, David A. "'An unnamed blank that craved a name': A Genealogy of Intersex as Gender," *Signs: Journal of Women in Culture and Society*, 37:4 (2012), 883–908.
Rubin, Gayle. *Deviations: A Gayle Rubin Reader* (Durham, NC: Duke University Press, 2011).
Saketopoulou, Avgi. "To Suffer Pleasure: The Shattering of the Ego as the Psychic Labor of Perverse Sexuality," *Studies in Gender and Sexuality*, 15:4 (2014), 254–268.
Schuller, Kyla. *The Biopolitics of Feeling: Race, Sex, and Science in the Nineteenth Century* (Durham, NC: Duke University Press, 2018).

Schuster, Alice. "Women's Role in the Soviet Union: Ideology and Reality," *Russian Review*, 30:3 (1971), 260–267.
Scott, Joan W. "Gender: A Useful Category of Historical Analysis," *American Historical Review*, 91:5 (1986), 1053–1075.
Sedgwick, Eve Kosofsky. *Epistemology of the Closet* (Berkeley: University of California Press, 1990).
Sedgwick, Eve Kosofsky. *Touching Feeling: Affect, Performativity and Pedagogy* (Durham, NC: Duke University Press, 2003).
Selvage, Douglas. "Operation 'Denver': The East German Ministry of State Security and the KGB's AIDS Disinformation Campaign, 1985–1986 (Part 1)," *Journal of Cold War Studies*, 21:4 (Fall 2019), 71–123.
Sharpe, Cristina. *In the Wake: On Blackness and Being* (Durham, NC: Duke University Press, 2016).
Shaw, Tony. *Hollywood's Cold War* (Edinburgh: Edinburgh University Press, 2007).
Shepard, Tom. *The Invention of Decolonization: The Algerian War and the Remaking of France* (Ithaca: Cornell University Press, 2006).
Silva, Denise Ferreira da. *Toward a Global Idea of Race* (Minneapolis: University of Minnesota Press, 2007).
Smith, Michael G. *Language and Power in the Creation of the USSR, 1917–1953* (Berlin: De Gruyter, 1998).
Sochor, Zenovia. *Revolution and Culture: The Bogdanov–Lenin Controversy* (Ithaca: Cornell University Press, 2018).
Somerville, Siobhan. *Queering the Color Line: Race and the Invention of Homosexuality in American Culture* (Durham, NC: Duke University Press, 2000).
Spade, Dean. *Normal Life: Administrative Violence, Critical Trans Politics, and the Limits of Law* (New York: South End Press, 2011).
Spillers, Hortense. "Mama's Baby, Papa's Maybe: An American Grammar Book," *Diacritics*, 17:2 (Summer 1987), 64–81.
Stanciu, Cezar. "The End of Liberalizaton in Communist Romania." *Historical Journal*, 56:4 (December 2013), 1063–1085.
Stanley, Eric A. and Nat Smith (eds). *Captive Genders: Trans Embodiment and the Prison Industrial Complex* (Edinburgh: AK Press, 2011).
Stephanson, Anders. "The Cold War Considered as a US project," in Silvio Pons and Federico Romero (eds), *Reinterpreting the End of the Cold War: Issues, Interpretations, Periodizations* (London: Routledge, 2004), 52–68.
Stephanson, Anders. "Cold War Degree Zero," in Joel Isaac and Duncan Bell (eds), *Uncertain Empire: American History and the Idea of Cold War* (Oxford: Oxford University Press, 2012), 19–51.
Stoler, Ann Laura. *Duress: Imperial Durabilities in Our Time* (Durham, NC: Duke University Press, 2016).
Stoler, Ann Laura. *Race and the Education of Desire: Foucault's History of Sexuality and the Colonial Order of Things* (Durham, NC: Duke University Press, 1995).

Stoller, Robert J. "Gender-Role Change in Intersex Patients." *JAMA*, 188:7 (1964), 684–685.
Stryker, Susan. "My Words to Victor Frankenstein above the Village of Chamounix: Performing Transgender Rage." *GLQ*, 1:3 (1994), 237–254.
Stryker, Susan. "Stray Thoughts on Transgender Feminism and the Barnard Conference on Women," *Communication Review*, 11:3 (2008), 217–218.
Stryker, Susan. "Transgender Feminism: Queering the Woman Question," in Stacy Gillis, Gillian Howie and Rebecca Munford (eds), *Third Wave Feminism: A Critical Exploration*, 2nd edn. (Basingstoke: Palgrave Macmillan, 2007), 59–70.
Stryker, Susan. "Transgender Studies: Queer Theory's Evil Twin." *GLQ*, 10:2 (2004), 212–215.
Stryker, Susan. "*We Who Are Sexy*: Christine Jorgensen's Transsexual Whiteness in the Postcolonial Philippines," *Social Semiotics*, 19:1 (March 2009), 79–91.
Stryker, Susan and Aren Aizura, "Introduction: Transgender Studies 2.0," in Susan Stryker and Aren Aizura (eds), *The Transgender Studies Reader 2* (London: Routledge, 2013), 1–12.
Taylor, Richard and Derek Spring. *Stalinism and Soviet Cinema* (London: Routledge, 1993).
Tessier, Hélène. "The Sexual Unconscious and Sexuality in Psychoanalysis: Laplanche's Theory of Generalized Seduction," *Psychoanalytic Quarterly*, 83:1 (2014), 169–183.
Thoburn, Nicholas. *Deleuze, Marx and Politics* (London: Routledge, 2003).
Tlostanova, Madina. *What Does It Mean to Be Post-Soviet? Decolonial Art on the Ruins of the Soviet Empire* (Durham, NC: Duke University Press, 2018).
Tobin, Robert D. *Peripheral Desires: The German Discovery of Sex* (Philadelphia: University of Pennsylvania Press, 2015).
Tudor, Alyosxa. "Dimensions of Trans-Nationalism." *Feminist Review*, 117:1 (2017), 20–40.
Turai, Ráhel Katalin. "Sexual Transitions: Biographical Bisexuality in Post-Socialist Hungary," Ph.D. dissertation (Central European University Budapest, 2017), www.etd.ceu.edu/2018/turai_rahel.pdf (accessed April 11, 2020).
Turing, Alan M. "Computing Machinery and Intelligence." *Mind*, 49 (1950), 433–460.
Turner, William. *A Genealogy of Queer Theory* (Philadelphia: Temple University Press, 2000).
Van der Linden, Marcel. *Western Marxism and the Soviet Union: A Survey of Critical Theories and Debates since 1917* (Leiden: Brill, 2007).
Vasile, Aurelia. "Le cinéma roumain pendant la période communiste: Représentations de l'histoire nationale," Ph.D. thesis (Université de Bourgogne and Universitatea București, 2011).

Verdery, Katherine. "An Anthropologist in Communist Romania," *Problems of Post-Communism*, 60:4 (July–August 2013), 35–42.
Verdery, Katherine. *The Political Lives of Dead Bodies: Reburial and Postsocialist Change* (New York: Columbia University Press, 1999).
Verdery, Katherine. *What Was Socialism and What Comes Next?* (Princeton: Princeton University Press, 1996).
Verdery, Katherine and Sharad Chari. "Thinking between the Posts: Postcolonialism, Postsocialism, and Ethnography after the Cold War," *Comparative Studies in Society and History*, 51:1 (2009), 6–34.
Westad, Arne. *The Cold War: A World History* (London: Basic, 2017).
Wiegman, Robyn. *Object Lessons* (Durham, NC: Duke University Press, 2012).
Widdis, Emma. *Socialist Senses: Film, Feeling and the Soviet Subject, 1917–1939* (Bloomington: Indiana University Press, 2017).
Willey, Angela. "Monogamy's Nature: Global Sexual Science and the Secularization of Christian Marriage," in Veronika Fuechtner, Douglas E. Haynes and Ryan M. Jones (eds), *A Global History of Sexual Science 1880–1960* (Berkeley: University of California Press, 2018), 97–117.
Woll, Josephine. *Real Images: Soviet Cinema and the Thaw* (London: I.B. Tauris, 2000).
Woodcock, Shannon. "Gender, Sexuality and Ethnicity in the Stereotypical Construction of Ț. Slaves in the Romanian Lands, 1385–1848," in Jan Selling, Markus End, Hristo Kyuchokov, Pia Laskar and Bill Templar (eds), *Antiziganism: What's in a Word?* (Cambridge: Cambridge Scholars, 2015), 176–186.
Ye, Shana. "Red Father, Pink Son: Queer Socialism and Post-Socialist Queer Critiques." PhD. dissertation (University of Minnesota, Minneapolis, 2017), https://conservancy.umn.edu/handle/11299/206412 (accessed July 11, 2021).
Yurchak, Alexei. *Everything Was Forever, until It Was No More: The Last Soviet Generation* (Princeton: Princeton University Press, 2005).
Zhuk, Sergei. "Hollywood's Insidious Charms: The Impact of American Cinema and Television on the Soviet Union during the Cold War." *Cold War History*, 14 (2014), 593–617.

Index

abolition theory 220
abortion 11, 23, 39, 41, 45, 57, 59, 60, 61, 62, 63, 64, 69, 221
Alone 50, 51
analytic 6, 7, 11, 13, 14, 17, 18, 20, 23, 24, 33, 37, 43, 53, 63, 64, 70, 71, 76, 98, 110, 111, 113, 114, 115, 116, 118, 120, 123, 124, 131, 137, 139, 156, 158, 171, 174, 175, 181, 183, 194, 200, 202, 204, 220, 222
Angi Vera 100, 105, 106
Another Way 100, 102, 104, 105
anti-communism 4, 5, 7, 8, 11, 12, 20, 23, 25, 33, 34, 44, 63, 70, 71, 73, 74, 80, 81, 84, 85, 89, 97, 98, 99, 100, 101, 107, 133, 134, 159, 171, 174, 175, 180, 200, 201, 214
anti-racism 18, 33, 158, 201
Arvatov, B. 6, 19, 27, 46, 47, 49, 54, 65, 67, 68, 109, 146, 159, 176
Aviance, K. 147, 152, 164

Baker, S. 25, 214
Baraitser, L. 183, 194, 195, 197, 198, 199
Basquiat, J.M. 147
Bed and Sofa 62

Berger, P. 26, 44, 64, 65, 78, 79, 80, 94
Bersani, L. 182, 197
binary 19, 34, 56, 64, 81, 87, 91, 111, 132, 178, 200
biopolitics 18, 71
blackness 70, 81, 84, 86, 89, 147, 183, 185, 190, 195
  black abolitionism 18, 185
  black culture 85, 87, 89
Bloch, E. 142, 161, 176
Bogdanov, A. 6, 19, 27, 31, 32, 46, 47, 65
Bolshevism 29, 46, 66, 84, 155, 196, 229, 234
Buden, B. 21, 28, 140, 154
Butler, J. 5, 19, 23, 24, 98, 99, 107, 110, 111, 114, 115, 116, 117, 118, 119, 121, 122, 123, 124, 125, 128, 129, 179, 180, 182, 196, 197

Camera Buff 169, 177
capitalism vii, 4, 5, 8, 9, 12, 15, 16, 17, 21, 24, 25, 26, 37, 39, 40, 43, 44, 46, 48, 50, 52, 53, 55, 57, 58, 60, 64, 66, 73, 74, 84, 89, 99, 107, 109, 115, 116, 117, 120, 123, 124, 125, 131, 132, 133, 137, 139, 140, 142, 143, 144, 145, 146, 147,

Index

148, 149, 152, 154, 157, 158, 159, 160, 161, 162, 163, 164, 165, 175, 179, 180, 181, 185, 187, 190, 193, 195, 200, 201, 202, 203, 204, 206, 208, 210, 212, 214, 215, 216, 220, 221, 222, 224, 231
Ceaușescu, N. 29, 41, 53, 57, 126, 156
Chirot, D. 39, 41
Chukhrov, K. 5, 14, 21, 27, 30, 31, 123, 129, 158, 176
civil rights movement 33, 86
class struggle 20, 22, 114, 143, 214
Cold War 1, 3, 4, 5, 6, 7, 8, 9, 10, 11, 12, 13, 16, 17, 19, 21, 23, 25, 27, 28, 29, 30, 31, 32, 33, 34, 35, 36, 37, 39, 40, 43, 44, 47, 49, 57, 62, 63, 64, 66, 67, 68, 70, 71, 72, 73, 74, 76, 77, 78, 80, 81, 83, 84, 85, 89, 90, 92, 95, 97, 98, 99, 100, 101, 108, 110, 111, 112, 114, 117, 121, 123, 124, 125, 134, 140, 151, 158, 172, 175, 178, 179, 180, 181, 196, 200, 201, 203, 205, 206, 207, 208, 214, 216, 217, 234
   anti-communism 17
   gender 4, 7, 16, 23, 43, 49, 70, 76, 90, 97, 121
   colonialism 15, 72, 76, 79, 119, 124, 162, 179
   commodity 14, 21, 47, 49, 50, 51, 52, 66, 67, 134, 144, 157, 158, 159, 160, 161, 162, 163, 164, 165, 166, 168, 171, 172, 174, 176, 204, 219, 221
   communism 1, 3, 4, 5, 8, 10, 11, 12, 14, 16, 17, 18, 20, 23, 25, 26, 27, 28, 31, 33, 35,

36, 38, 40, 44, 45, 47, 48, 49, 51, 54, 55, 56, 57, 58, 60, 63, 64, 70, 73, 74, 75, 77, 79, 80, 81, 83, 84, 90, 95, 99, 100, 101, 103, 104, 105, 106, 107, 108, 109, 116, 121, 123, 126, 131, 137, 140, 142, 143, 148, 154, 161, 162, 166, 167, 174, 175, 179, 180, 200, 201, 202, 203, 204, 205, 206, 214, 219, 221, 222, 223, 224
   communist sexuality 1, 4, 5, 6, 7, 17, 48, 144
conservative feminism 110, 113
counterfeit 185, 188, 189, 190, 191, 194, 195
counterfetishes 14, 21, 24, 134, 146, 157, 158, 159, 162, 164, 165, 168, 171, 175, 221
critical race theory 26, 165
Cruise, The 169, 170, 171, 173, 174, 175, 221169, 170, 171, 173, 174, 175, 221
cultural studies 5, 7, 8, 26, 28, 98, 122, 158, 179
curse 189, 190, 192, 194, 195
Czechoslovakian cinema 106

Danieliuc, M. 159, 166, 167, 168, 169, 170, 171, 172, 173, 175, 177
Debord, G. 20, 22, 35, 36, 131
decolonial 76, 93, 202, 216
de-contextualization 6, 22, 137, 138, 141
defamiliarization 156, 190
Deleuze, G. 20, 35, 107, 116, 128, 178, 180, 181, 196
deviancy 80, 81, 82, 83
dialectics 4, 54, 78, 80, 82, 90, 214
District of Gaiety, The 23, 45, 57, 59, 60, 61, 62, 221

Dobrenko, E. 27, 43, 64, 65, 66, 67, 142, 153, 155
Dumančić, M. 11
dyslexia 88, 89

eastern European Marxism 6
End of the Night, The 170
Eng, D. 3, 4, 26, 34, 123, 125, 129, 134, 219, 224
enigmatic messages 184, 185, 190, 195, 222
enslavement 33, 72, 73, 119, 120, 163, 185, 187, 188, 189, 190, 191, 192, 193, 194, 195
exchange value 50, 66, 163, 172, 175, 204, 221

feminism 71, 90, 98, 110, 112, 113, 115, 116, 127, 128
Fiddlers, The 15, 25, 134, 181, 185, 187, 190, 191, 192, 193, 194, 195
Floyd, K. 5, 26, 27, 125, 132, 219, 221, 224
freedom 4, 9, 10, 12, 17, 23, 33, 37, 38, 39, 40, 43, 47, 49, 53, 63, 64, 70, 74, 75, 77, 78, 89, 90, 94, 99, 100, 101, 102, 106, 107, 108, 110, 123, 126, 161, 177, 204, 209, 223
fugitives 185, 187

Gábor, P. 100
gay communism 99, 108, 121
gay identity 125
gay liberation 99, 161, 162, 176, 221
gender
   identity 23, 37, 43, 54, 62, 64, 80, 89, 106, 112, 117, 127
   ideology 8, 28, 122, 223
   presentation 16, 72, 152
   queer 8

   roles 8, 9, 57, 60, 77, 80, 83, 85, 87, 91, 93, 96, 107, 111, 127, 201, 235
   trouble 110, 116, 179, 204
Grigorescu, I. vi, 101, 102, 167, 171
Groys, B. 21, 22, 24, 31, 35, 36, 44, 64, 133, 135, 137, 139, 140, 141, 142, 145, 152, 153, 154, 155, 156
Guattari, F. 107, 116, 128, 178, 180, 181

Heller, A. 19, 157, 165, 175, 177
Hennessey, R. 5, 7, 26, 28, 98, 125, 221, 224
Herzog, D. 30, 35, 36, 41, 58, 59, 68, 69, 180, 196
heteronormativity 14, 18, 19, 72, 89, 100, 107, 110, 117, 152, 160, 161, 165, 202
heterosexuality 72, 81, 83, 84, 95, 205, 212
historical materialism 1, 3, 6, 7, 11, 22, 98, 115, 122, 124, 178, 194, 200, 215, 219
Hitchcock, A. 82, 83, 92
Hobsbawm, E. 10, 29
homosexuality 13, 82, 83
human emancipation 3, 11, 25, 40, 43, 54, 57, 114, 122, 124, 131, 133, 158, 174, 193, 201, 204, 214, 215, 219, 220, 222
humanity 8, 44, 48, 49, 81, 85, 110, 112, 143
Hungarian cinema 100, 105, 106

identity 4, 11, 12, 16, 47, 49, 55, 73, 75, 76, 79, 80, 82, 84, 87, 90, 93, 95, 97, 101, 105, 110, 117, 170
   construction 74, 79
Impossible Love 51, 106, 170
imprimatur 23, 77, 81, 93, 94
indigeneity 51, 72, 88, 89

Index

individualism 48, 50, 64, 67, 76, 100, 109
intersex 73, 76, 77, 78, 87, 90, 93, 127, 236
It Came from Outer Space 25, 200, 201, 205, 206, 214

James, C.L.R. 65, 67, 106, 142, 143, 155
jazz 160, 163, 190
Jorgensen, C. 71, 72, 75, 91, 125, 207, 218

Kiaer, C. 146, 154
Kieślowski, K. 169, 177
Klein, C. 12
Kollontai, A. 48, 60, 66

Laplanche, J. 15, 25, 26, 178, 180, 181, 182, 183, 184, 185, 187, 188, 194, 195, 196, 197, 198, 199, 222
Lenin, V. 16, 17, 19, 31, 32, 46, 47, 49, 65, 67, 78, 154
LGBT 8, 16, 28, 223
liberalism 7, 19, 21, 25, 34, 35, 63, 73, 74, 92, 124, 178, 201, 203, 207
  liberal capitalism 5, 64, 89, 116, 131
Liu, P. 5, 7, 19, 27, 28, 34, 123, 124, 129, 221, 233
Love and Revolution 51
Luckmann, T. 26, 44, 64, 65, 78, 79, 80, 94

Man Next to You, The 51, 55
Makk, K. 100, 167, 171
Marr, N. 15, 178, 194, 195
Marx, K. 3, 14, 19, 26, 29, 31, 35, 36, 47, 66, 78, 115, 129, 134, 135, 157, 162, 163, 164, 165, 175, 176, 220
Marxism 3, 4, 5, 6, 7, 8, 9, 10, 11, 12, 14, 15, 16, 17, 19, 20, 21, 22, 23, 25, 26, 27, 28, 29, 31, 34, 35, 37, 38, 39, 40, 41, 43, 44, 46, 53, 62, 63, 66, 70, 73, 74, 78, 80, 81, 91, 97, 98, 100, 101, 102, 106, 107, 108, 109, 110, 111, 113, 114, 115, 116, 117, 118, 121, 122, 123, 124, 125, 126, 128, 129, 131, 132, 133, 137, 138, 139, 140, 141, 142, 143, 151, 152, 154, 155, 157, 158, 159, 161, 162, 165, 166, 167, 169, 171, 173, 174, 175, 178, 180, 194, 198, 200, 201, 214, 219, 220, 222, 223, 224
Marxism-Leninism 5, 9, 16, 19, 38, 98, 133, 151, 219
Marxist art 149, 151
Marxist epistemology 9, 12, 14, 22, 24, 37, 44, 47, 98, 121, 131, 134, 137, 219
materiality 4, 8, 14, 21, 24, 47, 50, 51, 55, 79, 98, 132, 134, 139, 145, 153, 157, 158, 164, 166, 174, 175, 220, 221
Medevoi, L. 27, 28, 32, 68, 76, 84, 92, 93, 95, 105, 125, 126
Mieli, M. 14, 99, 100, 106, 107, 108, 109, 121, 122, 126, 127
Mirror for a Hero 170
Mitchell, J. 108, 127
Mitchell, T. 204
Money, J. 23, 26, 64, 70, 71, 76, 77, 78, 80, 81, 84, 85, 86, 87, 88, 89, 90, 93, 94, 95, 96, 97, 101, 107, 122, 127
Moten, F. 14, 24, 158, 160, 162, 163, 164, 165, 174, 177, 187, 190, 191, 192, 198, 199

Muñoz, J.S. 9, 14, 24, 26, 34, 36, 132, 134, 137, 139, 141, 142, 143, 146, 147, 148, 149, 153, 154, 155, 156, 158, 160, 161, 162, 163, 164, 165, 166, 176, 177, 215, 218

Nazism 10, 58, 59, 60, 61, 69
necropolitics 40, 42
needs 1, 3, 8, 9, 14, 17, 49, 55, 56, 61, 64, 66, 78, 79, 83, 86, 98, 109, 112, 117, 132, 133, 134, 139, 141, 153, 157, 158, 159, 163, 165, 166, 171, 172, 174, 175, 183, 196, 201, 206, 207, 209, 212, 214, 215, 220, 221, 222
New Left 180
noise 184, 186, 187, 188, 191, 194, 195

Oushakine, S. 21, 27, 35, 47, 49, 65, 67, 157, 158, 159, 165, 166, 168, 176, 177

Panaitescu, I. vi, 101, 102
Parisian Cobbler, The 55, 169
performativity 14, 53, 196
personal identity 4, 73, 74, 78, 82, 97, 121
Plekhanov, G. 46
post-identity epistemology 121
poststructuralism 7
productive bodies 4, 6, 43, 45, 55, 57, 62
productivism 27, 40, 46, 47, 54, 57, 63, 67, 159, 165, 167, 221
proletariat 46, 47, 138, 167, 181
Proletkult 6, 16, 46, 47, 65
psychoanalysis 25, 29, 99, 107, 128, 179, 180, 183, 194, 196, 221

Puar, J. 3, 4, 26, 42, 123, 125, 129, 134, 178, 196, 219, 223, 224, 225

queer anti-racism 6, 7, 17, 131, 175
queer of color 9, 14, 24, 124, 125, 131, 137, 156, 158, 159, 174, 175, 220
queer communism 6, 25, 224
queer feminism 111, 121
queer identity 16
queer liberalism 223
queer Marxism 5, 123, 158, 219
queer postsocialism 201
queer studies 1, 3, 4, 5, 7, 18, 19, 21, 24, 25, 34, 63, 90, 98, 99, 121, 131, 132, 140, 154, 166, 175, 199, 216, 219, 221, 222, 224, 236
queer theory 1, 3, 4, 5, 6, 7, 8, 9, 10, 13, 14, 15, 18, 22, 23, 24, 25, 26, 37, 62, 71, 90, 97, 98, 99, 110, 111, 113, 115, 121, 122, 123, 124, 125, 127, 131, 133, 137, 139, 140, 141, 143, 151, 152, 157, 158, 159, 160, 164, 165, 166, 174, 175, 178, 179, 181, 182, 196, 202, 219, 220, 221, 224

racial capitalism 72, 73, 89, 131, 158, 184, 185, 191, 194, 198, 200, 208, 214
racialization 13, 23, 31, 33, 72, 84, 87, 101, 124, 174, 190, 191
racism 18, 85, 132, 175, 189, 193, 195
radical needs 157
rage 202, 203, 216
Rancière, J. 25, 201, 203, 204, 212, 214, 217
Repo, J. 23, 71, 72, 73, 91, 93, 94, 95, 125

Index 245

revolutionary politics ii, 107, 114, 200, 203
Rifkin, M. 72, 91, 96
Robinson, C. 73, 125
Roma people 15, 25, 133, 134, 172, 174, 181, 185, 186, 187, 188, 189, 190, 191, 192, 193, 194, 195, 198, 222
Romanian cinema 57, 106, 153
Romanian film 15, 23, 45, 57, 106, 159, 169, 174
Romanian socialism 23, 38, 53, 57, 61, 62, 67, 126, 143, 166, 221
Rosenberg J. 3, 26, 125, 132, 134
Rubin, D.A. 77, 85
Rubin, G. 7, 14, 93, 94, 95, 96, 98, 99, 107, 110, 111, 112, 113, 114, 115, 116, 117, 118, 119, 120, 122, 125, 126, 127, 128

scenes of seduction 184, 185, 194, 197
science fiction 200, 206
Scott, J. 23, 115, 118, 119, 121, 122, 129
Sedgwick, E. 14, 19, 31, 99, 115, 133, 135
sensuousness 24, 51, 134, 158, 166, 170, 188
sexual identity 109, 110, 115
sexuality iii, vii, viii, 1, 3, 5, 6, 7, 8, 9, 10, 11, 12, 13, 14, 15, 16, 17, 18, 19, 23, 24, 25, 28, 29, 31, 34, 37, 39, 40, 41, 44, 45, 54, 57, 58, 60, 61, 62, 63, 64, 68, 70, 72, 82, 85, 86, 87, 90, 91, 97, 98, 99, 100, 105, 106, 107, 108, 110, 111, 112, 113, 114, 115, 116, 117, 118, 119, 121, 122, 123, 124, 127, 128, 134, 137, 138, 140, 144, 147, 148, 151, 152, 156, 161, 162, 167, 174, 175, 178, 179, 180, 182, 185, 198, 207, 215, 221, 222, 224
sex worker 207, 209, 212, 213
Sharpe, C. 183, 197
Situationism 5, 6, 22
slavery 15, 33, 39, 86, 89, 115, 119, 133, 134, 163, 181, 183, 184, 185, 186, 187, 188, 189, 190, 191, 193, 194, 195, 222
social constructionism 122
socialism 8, 9, 10, 11, 12, 17, 19, 20, 21, 23, 24, 27, 30, 31, 32, 34, 35, 37, 38, 39, 40, 41, 43, 45, 47, 48, 50, 52, 53, 55, 56, 57, 58, 62, 63, 64, 65, 66, 67, 68, 69, 84, 92, 97, 101, 103, 104, 105, 106, 109, 115, 123, 131, 132, 138, 140, 141, 142, 144, 148, 149, 151, 153, 156, 158, 159, 162, 166, 167, 168, 172, 173, 174, 175, 177, 180, 197, 201, 208, 216, 219, 220, 221, 223
socialist realism 20, 22, 38, 43, 47, 50, 51, 54, 64, 65, 66, 101, 126, 131, 133, 137, 139, 140, 141, 145, 151, 153, 154, 155, 169
solidarity 116, 117, 192, 200, 208, 209, 210, 213, 214, 215
Somerville, S. 84, 85, 95
Soviet Marxism 6, 8, 9, 10, 12, 13, 14, 15, 16, 19, 20, 21, 22, 24, 29, 39, 40, 44, 45, 46, 47, 63, 70, 74, 78, 89, 98, 100, 109, 121, 124, 140, 152, 154, 157, 158, 159, 162, 166, 169, 178, 179, 180, 181, 194, 201
specters 25, 36, 123, 189

Spillers, H. 23, 72, 91, 115, 119, 120, 121, 122, 124, 129
Stalinism 10, 12, 13, 14, 24, 104, 105, 133, 153, 155
  Stalinist art 20, 24, 137, 140, 144, 145, 146, 152
Stalin, J. 31, 32, 36, 47, 65, 142, 155, 195
Stryker, S. 23, 25, 34, 71, 72, 91, 125, 196, 200, 201, 202, 203, 204, 207, 210, 214, 215, 216, 218
subjectless critique 5, 98

Tangerine 15, 25, 200, 202, 208, 209, 214, 215
theory of identity 89
Tlostanova, M. 39, 40, 41
trans 4, 8, 13, 15, 16, 18, 24, 25, 34, 73, 87, 98, 100, 107, 108, 109, 122, 123, 126, 132, 134, 153, 154, 200, 201, 202, 203, 204, 207, 208, 210, 211, 212, 213, 214, 215, 216, 217, 222, 223, 224, 225, 229, 231, 235, 236
  of color 214
  theory 132, 200, 201, 202, 214, 215
  transgender 8, 15, 16, 18, 32, 71, 75, 76, 122, 142, 178, 200, 201, 202, 216, 222

transgender identity 75, 202
transgender studies 4, 132, 200, 215
trauma 188, 190
true identity 80, 90
Turing, A. 81, 94

unconscious 4, 8, 15, 24, 108, 134, 178, 179, 180, 181, 182, 183, 184, 185, 187, 188, 194, 195, 196, 197, 199, 221, 222
US cinema 38, 105, 217
US Cold War 11, 33, 70, 83, 205

Vaeni, C. 106, 170
Valley Resounds, The 24, 51, 52, 53, 54, 55, 57, 58, 60, 134, 138, 143, 147, 149, 151, 153, 154, 221
Verdery, K. 16, 31, 38, 39, 41, 52, 53, 63, 64, 66, 67, 68, 69
Veroiu, M. 170
Villarejo, A. 3, 26, 125, 132, 134

whiteness 84, 85, 87, 88, 89, 91, 95, 125, 187, 212, 218
white masculinity 73, 82, 83, 85
white working class 206
Widdis, E. 6, 27, 30, 36, 50, 51, 66, 67, 68, 145, 146, 155, 156

EU authorised representative for GPSR:
Easy Access System Europe, Mustamäe tee 50,
10621 Tallinn, Estonia
gpsr.requests@easproject.com